D1548269

Joyce and the Victorians

The Florida James Joyce Series

Florida A&M University, Tallahassee
Florida Atlantic University, Boca Raton
Florida Gulf Coast University, Ft. Myers
Florida International University, Miami
Florida State University, Tallahassee
University of Central Florida, Orlando
University of Florida, Gainesville
University of North Florida, Jacksonville
University of South Florida, Tampa
University of West Florida, Pensacola

Joyce and the Victorians

Tracey Teets Schwarze

University Press of Florida
Gainesville · Tallahassee · Tampa · Boca Raton
Pensacola · Orlando · Miami · Jacksonville · Ft. Myers

Copyright 2002 by Tracey Teets Schwarze
Printed in the United States of America on acid-free paper
All rights reserved

07 06 05 04 03 02   6 5 4 3 2 1

Library of Congress Cataloging-in-Publication Data
Schwarze, Tracey Teets, 1961–
Joyce and the Victorians / Tracey Teets Schwarze.
p. cm.—(The Florida James Joyce series)
Includes bibliographical references and index.
ISBN 0-8130-2437-4 (acid-free paper)
1. Joyce, James, 1882–1941—Political and social views. 2. Great
Britain—Social conditions—19th century. 3. Joyce, James 1882–1941
—Views on sex role. 4. National characteristics, Irish, in literature.
5. Ireland—Social conditions—19th century. 6. Sex role in literature.
I. Title. II. Series.
PR6019.O9 Z79443 2002
823'.912—dc21   2001043727

The University Press of Florida is the scholarly publishing agency
for the State University System of Florida, comprising Florida A&M
University, Florida Atlantic University, Florida Gulf Coast University,
Florida International University, Florida State University, University of
Central Florida, University of Florida, University of North Florida,
University of South Florida, and University of West Florida.

University Press of Florida
15 Northwest 15th Street
Gainesville, FL 32611–2079

To Bob,
with love and gratitude

Contents

Foreword by Zack Bowen   ix

Acknowledgments   xi

Abbreviations   xiii

Introduction: Dilemmas of Discourse   1

"Not a Strong Swimmer": Submersions of Dedalus

1. Colonial Pathology and the Ideology of Irishness in Victorian and Edwardian Dublin   17

2. "Religions of Unbelief": Spiritual Orthodoxies and Romantic Dissent   43

Caught in the Currents: Victorian Manliness, Public Morality, and Leopold Bloom

3. "Do you call that a man?": The Discourse of Anxious Masculinity in *Ulysses*   71

4. Urban Spectatorship, Victorian Vice, and the Discourse of Social Reform   93

Fracturing the Discursive Feminine: Joyce and the "Woman Question"

5. Deconstructing the Discourse of Domesticity   117

6. Female Complaints: "Mad"women, Malady, and Resistance in Joyce's Dublin   142

7. New Women, Male Pests, and Gender in the Public Eye   161

Afterword: Lost in the Labyrinth   193

Notes   197

Bibliography   221

Index   237

Foreword

Tracey Schwarze's book examines Joyce's works within the context of contemporary cultural studies theory. Written with full cognizance of previous cultural studies on Joyce, her work builds on the major criticism in the field in new and interesting ways. There are new documents and sources for Joyce's depiction of turn-of-the-century Ireland and the cultural influences on his characters, yielding new insightful explanations of both Joyce's intent and construction of his characters' motivations.

Schwarze's principal interests lie in gender criticism and how it affects the interpretation of Joyce's works. She builds on the discoveries and arguments of pioneering feminist scholars, regarding the contribution of medicine as well as popular science and literature to the formation of patriarchal imperialist rationales for the systematic abuse of Victorian women, as she examines the literature of "anxious masculinity" through the Lacanian notions of the gaze and voyeurism, the discourses of social reform and utopianism, the valorization of women as sufferers, their denigration as hysterics, and their emergence as the "New Women" who make incursions on traditionally male provinces.

Zack Bowen
Series Editor

Acknowledgments

It is hard to know where to begin my thanks for the support I have received in this project from family, friends, and colleagues. I count myself extraordinarily fortunate to have met and studied under Kimberly Devlin when I was a graduate student at the University of California, Riverside; Kim's generous encouragement of me and of this book—in all of our respective incarnations—has been invaluable to me, both as a student of Joyce and as a teacher of his work. I am also deeply indebted to Zack Bowen, Michael Gillespie, and Brandy Kershner for their careful readings of this manuscript, their helpful suggestions for its improvement, and their collective faith in its worth. Amy Gorelick and Gillian Hillis at the University Press of Florida have patiently answered all of my questions and guided me through the publishing process; the timely assistance of Amy Boykin and Leslie Condra at Christopher Newport University's Smith Library has also been essential in the final stages of manuscript preparation and source checking.

As *Joyce and the Victorians* evolved into its present form over the last five years, many other people have generously perused its various sections. Along with Kim Devlin, Steve Axelrod and Parama Roy read it as a dissertation and provided valuable assistance at that stage. The Junior Faculty Writing Group at the University of Nevada read and commented on early drafts of book chapters and provided intellectual sustenance: I benefited from reading the work of Jane Hafen, Linda Lang-Peralta, Beth Rosenberg, Susan Taylor, and Susan Wood and profited immensely from their insights. The enthusiasm for both teaching and scholarship among my new colleagues at Christopher Newport University—Jean Filetti, Douglas Gordon, Kara Keeling, Ashby Kinch, Terry Lee, the late Al Millar, Roark Mulligan, John Nichols, Jay Paul, Scott Pollard, Roberta Rosenberg, and Rebecca Wheeler—has deepened and encouraged my own.

Friends and family have buoyed me throughout the writing and revision processes. I am grateful to Lynda Self, Shari Krause, Holly Kress, Chuck Culpepper, and Sheryl Stolberg for either listening to or reading countless emails about my latest enthusiasms or complaints. The support of my family has similarly been unflagging: my parents, Ken and Encie Teets, and my in-laws, Bob and Lucille Schwarze, have shared in my excitement over this project. My parents, especially, have always believed in me and pushed me to be and do anything I could imagine; for this faith in possibility that has been their legacy to me, I will always be grateful.

This book is dedicated to my husband, Bob, whose confidence in me never wavered and whose love and support made it possible.

Permissions

Portions of this manuscript have appeared elsewhere, in earlier incarnations, and are used here with permission: Chapter 2, "Colonial Pathology and the Ideology of 'Irishness' in Victorian and Edwardian Dublin," appeared as "Silencing Stephen: Colonial Pathologies in Victorian Dublin" in *Twentieth Century Literature* 43.3 (fall 1997): 23–63. Chapter 5, "Urban Spectatorship, Victorian Vice, and the Discourse of Social Reform," appeared in *Joyce Studies Annual 1997*, pp. 39–59, as "Voyeuristic Utopias and Lascivious Cities: Leopold Bloom, Urban Spectatorship, and Social Reform"; copyright 1997 by the University of Texas Press; all rights reserved. An early version of chapter 3, "'Do you call that a man?' The Discourse of Anxious Masculinity in *Ulysses*," appeared in *Masculinities in Joyce: Postcolonial Constructions* (European Joyce Studies 10), ed. Christine van Boheemen-Saaf and Colleen Lamos (Amsterdam and Atlanta: Rodopi, 2001).

Abbreviations

References to James Joyce's works are cited parenthetically within the text, using the following abbreviations and editions:

CW   *The Critical Writings of James Joyce.* Ed. Ellsworth
            Mason and Richard Ellmann. New York: Viking Press,
            1959. Foreword by Guy Davenport. Reprint. Ithaca,
            N.Y.: Cornell University Press, 1989, 1993.

D   *Dubliners.* Ed. Robert Scholes in consultation with
            Richard Ellmann. New York: Viking Press, 1967.

FW   *Finnegans Wake.* New York: Viking Press, 1939.

Letters I   *Letters of James Joyce.* Ed. Stuart Gilbert. Vol. 1. New
            York: Viking Press, 1957.

Letters II, III   *Letters of James Joyce.* Ed. Richard Ellmann. Vols. 2
            and 3. New York: Viking Press, 1966.

P   *A Portrait of the Artist as a Young Man. Text, Criticism
            and Notes.* Ed. Chester G. Anderson. New York: Viking
            Press, 1968.

SH   *Stephen Hero.* Ed. John J. Slocum and Herbert Cahoon.
            New York: New Directions: 1944, 1963.

U   *Ulysses.* Ed. Hans Walter Gabler. New York: Vintage
            Random House, 1986.

Introduction

Dilemmas of Discourse

In book 1, chapter 5, of James Joyce's densest, most allusive and elusive novel, *Finnegans Wake,* a professorial voice discussing the discovery of Anna Livia Plurabelle's previously buried letter warns us that "to concentrate solely on the literal sense . . . of any document to the sore neglect of the enveloping facts . . . circumstantiating it is just as hurtful to sound sense" as imagining naked ("in her natural altogether") a clothed woman to whom one has just been introduced (*FW* 109.12–20). Part diversion from the letter's allegations against ALP's sleeping husband, Humphrey Chimpden Earwicker, and part an attempt to discredit the writer herself, this curious pronouncement regarding "feminine fiction" posits—in its punning references that link the envelope enfolding the letter to the garments enveloping the imaginary woman's body—an intriguing connection between texts, identities, and the external forces that enclose them. Both envelopes and clothing are "full of local colour and personal perfume," the narrator observes (*FW* 109.25–26); to ignore such wrappers by immediately seeking some underlying essence—here, the unadorned "meaning" of the text or the unclad body—is also to delimit, quite unnecessarily, the richness and variety of self-constructions made available by costume as well as by written (ad)dress. More important, neglecting such frames also ensures that our understanding of that which they enfold will be always incomplete, for the "facts" of context necessarily shape the shifting "fictions" of self. In the infinite possibilities they present for the shaping of subjectivity, textiles and texts converge in this passage; as the professorial voice observes, the written word, like clothing, can be "suggestive, too, of so very much more . . . capable of being stretched, filled out, if need or wish were" (*FW* 109.26–27). Subjectivity, then, is revealed here to be both constructed and vicissitudinal, a text created by contexts rather than an essence to be uncovered. The analogy also may be extended to suggest a critical approach to Joyce's texts in the aggregate: to demand essence of his fiction without examining the contexts Joyce proffers is not only to forfeit multiplicity, to surrender the richness inherent in both his texts and his characterizations, it is also to deny what critics such as Margot Norris and Garry Leonard ably have demonstrated—that in Joyce's work, such centers do not hold.[1]

Certainly Joyce's methods of writing—his compulsion for Irish news-papers, magazines, and books sent to him by his aunt Josephine Murray, his requests for topographic detail,[2] and his painstaking use of sources such as the 1904 edition of *Thom's Official Directory* for names and ad-dresses of local Dubliners and their business establishments—alert us to the importance that context plays in his work.[3] But Joyce's obsession with minute, realistic detail also reflects his concern with the broader ideologi-cal conditions that shaped subjectivity in Victorian and Edwardian Ire-land. His short stories and novels not only reflect the surfaces of daily life in turn-of-the-century Dublin, they also expose and engage the larger cul-tural contexts of colonial politics, religiosity, and gender that both envel-oped and colonized modern subjectivity.

Louis Montrose has argued that the self, like language, is created *"within* history, culture, society, politics, institutions, class and gender conditions" (16–17); Montrose, like Fredric Jameson before him, owes a debt to Ferdinand de Saussure's notion of the synchronicity of language, poststructuralist reformulations of Saussure's conclusions, and Lacanian psychoanalytic theory.[4] Such presumptions—that language is constituted within shifting cultural paradigms and that the self is constructed through language—posit an indeterminacy within subjectivity itself: engulfed in a vast sea of cultural discourse, the self absorbs influence and is accordingly altered; like language, subjectivity exists in a state of continual flux. Joyce's conception of the shifting currents of language and culture—and their impact on identity—is made clear in a 1907 essay, "Ireland, Island of Saints and Sages." Here Joyce argues—rebutting attempts by various cul-tural revival movements to define and purify Irish culture and purge it of non-Gaelic influence—that "Irish" civilization is actually a cultural ad-mixture of "nordic aggressiveness and Roman law, new bourgeois con-ventions and the remnant of a Syriac religion"; he characterizes national identity not as an essence but as a "convenient fiction" based on mutabili-ties—of race and language, of "blood and the human word" (CW 166). Joyce's description evokes not only the instability of identity and its cul-tural signifiers, it also alludes to their fictive constructedness and estab-lishes a metaphorical link between culture, identity, and textuality similar to the one theorized by Yuri M. Lotman. In his essay "The Text Within the Text," Lotman argues that "culture in its entirety may be considered a text—a complexly structured text, divided into a hierarchy of intricately interconnected texts within texts. To the extent that the word 'text' is etymologically linked to weaving, the term's original sense has been re-stored" (384). In Joyce's estimation, too, the cultural "text" is a tightly constructed tapestry of innumerable fibers, each discursive thread, when loomed, becoming inseparable from the others. In his novels, Joyce transforms Irish-Victorian and Irish-Edwardian culture into a multifaceted, discursive narrative composed of a variety of rhetorics—political, religious, gendered—and gives us characters whose subjectivities are surrounded and shaped by the force this discourse exerts. In *A Portrait of the Artist as a Young Man,* for instance, Stephen Dedalus recognizes and attempts to resist the cacophony of "hollowsounding voices" of nationalism, Catholicism, and masculinism that echoes through his consciousness. He perceives culture as polylogue, a convergence of multiple discourses urging him simultaneously to be "a gentleman" and a "good catholic above all things," to be "strong and manly and healthy" and "true to his country": Stephen is happy only when he imagines himself removed from the influence of such voices, when he is "beyond their call, alone" (*P* 83–84). *Ulysses'* Leopold Bloom is less disturbed than Stephen Dedalus by the daily discursive assaults that he experiences; nonetheless, Bloom succinctly describes (in the metaphorical terms of *Ulysses'* "Lestrygonians" episode) the intellectual *ragout* produced by the confluence of cultural pronouncements and their effect on the stew of subjectivity: "Never know whose thoughts you're chewing," Bloom thinks to himself (*U* 8.717–18). Such rhetorical bombardments constitute the texture and fabric of modern consciousness in Joyce's fiction; in spite of Stephen's ringing disavowal in *Portrait*—"I will not serve" (*P* 239)—the pervasive and invidious nature of societal influence in Joyce's work renders his characters nearly powerless to overcome the strictures that bind their thought.

Joyce's presentation of identity as a social construct rather than as a personal or archetypal essence goes beyond its seeming anticipation of Jameson's pronouncement that "human consciousness . . . [is] not timeless and everywhere essentially the same, but rather situation-specific and historically produced" (152); Joyce not only exposes the social forces at work on subjectivity, he also grapples with the weighty question of whether modern consciousness can effectively resist the ideological force of the culture that produces it. Cultural materialists since Althusser and Jameson have interrogated the ramifications of their predecessors' assertions that subjectivity is constituted always within ideology, but Alan Sinfield frames the question most succinctly: "If we come to consciousness within a language that is continuous with the power structures that sustain the social order, how can we conceive, let alone organize, resistance?" (*Faultlines* 35). Joyce's fiction resonates with Sinfield's answer to this important query, that "dissidence" derives not from "essential qualities in individuals"—for instance, the desire or ability to think independently of the structures that enclose them—but from contradictions contained within and among dominant ideological structures themselves (*Faultlines* 41). Sinfield names these vulnerabilities "faultlines" and argues that the fissures they open create spaces in which the self may dissociate from the ascendant social order; thus the potential for dissidence is realized. In contrast to the view of modernism in which the individual mind is believed to transcend the traditional Victorian authorities of Nation, Church, Manliness, Morality, and Womanliness, I argue that Joyce's characters never fully manage to supplant these powerful arbiters of conscious and subconscious thought. Instead, Joyce's narratives create only the potential for such supercession; they expose the pervasive influence of ideological structures on subjectivity and illuminate the fissures contained within the social discourse itself. While it is not my intention to argue for Joyce as "the last Victorian"—that would be a contrarian absurdity—it is my aim to acknowledge and excavate the heretofore largely unexplored late-Victorian and Edwardian ethos that undergirds Joyce's fiction and to suggest that Joyce himself, much like his characters, was simultaneously bound by, as well as critical of, the ideologies of his age.

Joyce's early letters and essays, written during and shortly after a brief sojourn in Paris as a medical student in 1902–3, reveal an acute awareness of Edwardian Irish culture as an oppressive, assimilating force. Born in 1882, Joyce came of age in late-Victorian Dublin, a city suffused not only by the steady tides of Catholicism and British rule but also—as I will show in later chapters—by the rising currents of nationalist politics, spiritualism, masculinism, public purity crusades, and women's rights agitations. In his personal writings, Joyce repeatedly marks gender constructs, colonial politics, and religiosity as the dominant ideological forces of his time and reiterates the difficulties of existing and creating outside their sphere as well as his determination to do so. He wrote to Nora Barnacle in 1904 that he repudiated conventional mores and believed himself to be "fighting a battle with every religious and social force in Ireland" (*Letters II* 53); in other missives, Joyce is more specific about the components of this force: "My mind rejects the whole present social order and Christianity— home, the recognized virtues, classes of life, and religious doctrines . . . . I cannot enter the social order except as a vagabond" (*Letters II* 48). Though he treated with disdain the notion of women's equality advanced by his friend Francis Sheehy-Skeffington ("it is only Skeffington, and fellows like him, who think that woman is man's equal" [*Letters II* 96]), Joyce nonetheless framed his personal refusal to marry Nora Barnacle in terms of an attempt to free their relationship from the gender strictures that "home" implied as well as the religion that it propagated. In May 1905 Joyce explained to his brother Stanislaus his "attempt to live a more civilised life than my contemporaries": "But why should I have brought Nora to a priest or a lawyer to make her swear away her life to me? And why should I superimpose on my child the very troublesome burden of belief which my father and mother superimposed on me?" (*Letters II* 89). Such seeming contradictions—perhaps worthy of Molly Bloom herself— are found also in Joyce's political statements and, to a lesser extent, in his remarks about the Catholic Church; taken together, such pronouncements reveal not only the author's desire to stand against the subordinating force of social discourse but also its insidious ability to infuse his own thought. Like Stephen Dedalus and the rest of Joyce's characters, Joyce himself was a product of Victorian Ireland, of "this country and this life" (*P* 203); his writing showcases both the insurgencies of modernist thought and the indoctrinations that characterized fin de siècle subjectivity.

Joyce perceived Ireland's politics to be as dangerously stifling as its gender structures. In spite of his evident rejection of British imperial control of the island, he refused to align himself fully with nationalist ideologies, believing them guilty of replicating the destructive chauvinism of the colonizer. In November 1906 Joyce predicted that either Sinn Fein or British imperialism would supplant the Catholic Church as the dominant social force in Ireland, and though he was wrong about the Church's imminent demise, Joyce's reflection reveals his sense of the intense power wielded by burgeoning political rhetoric within his society. The Triestine essays of 1907–12 reflect his preoccupation with nationalism and imperialism and further assert the mesmerizing influence of nationalist rhetoric over the Irish populace: Fenianism had repeatedly "remodelled the character of the Irish people," Joyce notes, and Charles Stewart Parnell, leader of the Irish Parliamentary Party between 1880 and 1890, had exercised a hold over them not easily explained (*CW* 191, 225). This recognition of the growing power of political suasion notwithstanding, Joyce never fully relinquished his belief that the Catholic Church was the most insidious oppressor of the Irish people and tried hard to shake its influence on his own life, refusing to baptize his children and declaring himself apostate. But Joyce continued in these early years to recognize the immense control the Catholic Church wielded over not only Ireland but also over his own thinking. Though he proclaimed himself "incapable of belief of any kind," Joyce also reported to Stanislaus that others were not so convinced of his dissent, given his habit of frequenting Greek Orthodox Mass in Trieste:

"[A fellow Berlitz instructor] says I will die a Catholic because I am always moping in and out of the Greek Churches and am a believer at heart," Joyce confessed to his brother (*Letters II* 89). In 1906 Joyce wrote again, "I think my policy of subtracting oneself and one's progeny from the church is too slow. I don't believe the church has suffered vitally from the number of her apostates" (*Letters II* 165–66). The dissonance in such remarks betrays a nagging suspicion on Joyce's part that forces as powerful as the Church ultimately may be insurmountable by lone dissenters; certainly his professional life is bracketed by facts that demonstrate the inevitable acquiescence that social strictures can demand. The youthful idealism implicit in Joyce's self-styled "escape" with Nora Barnacle from Church and State is ironically dashed by a sequence of events that begins in 1906 with an English printer's moralistic objections to—and refusal to publish—*Dubliners* and culminates in Joyce's ultimate marriage to Nora in 1931, in London and under English law, in order to secure the rights of his literary estate to his progeny.

While Joyce's earliest fiction, the *Dubliners* stories, purports to represent a relentless cultural and individual stolidity, his subsequent writing struggles with means to free both the artist and modern consciousness itself from all forms of ideological constraint. In *Dubliners,* Joyce presents us with a city whose inhabitants' minds are constituted within the tangled nets of discourse and who remain largely unaware of the circumscription of their thought. The vision of both children and adults is stymied within this text; not even epiphanies assure their liberation. The narrator of the collection's first story, "The Sisters," never does discover what had "gone wrong" with old Father Flynn, nor does he understand why he himself feels "freed" by the fact of the priest's death; the young narrator of "Araby" never realizes, in spite of his final epiphany, how his image of Mangan's sister is shaped by his culture's vision of the Ideal Feminine; Mrs. Kearney, the bested heroine of "A Mother," never fully comprehends the patriarchal nature of the nationalist power structure that she defies. In a series of now-famous exchanges with publisher Grant Richards in 1906, Joyce wrote that his intent in representing Ireland's "paralysis" in the volume was to counter this ideological blindness by providing the Irish people with "one good look at themselves in my nicely polished looking-glass" (*Letters I* 64); he viewed such exposure and the possibility of self-recognition by his Irish readers as the "first step towards the spiritual liberation of my country" (*Letters I* 63). Joyce's subsequent work renders the confining ideologies of his era progressively more visible, but though his characters become increasingly aware of their enclosure within such structures, they are no more able to escape them than are the priests, children, parents, and lovers of *Dubliners.*

Joyce evidently intended his first novel, *Stephen Hero* (begun slightly before *Dubliners* in 1904), to provide a protagonist who breaks free from the chains of politics, Catholicism and morality; he wrote to Stanislaus on February 28, 1905, that shorter novels might be easier to write, but "what I want to wear away in this novel cannot be worn away except by constant dropping" (*Letters II* 83). It is common practice in Joyce criticism to conflate the protagonists of *Stephen Hero* and *Portrait,* but Joyce's revision of his early draft in fact reveals an altered sense of the ability of modern consciousness to exist and create independent of cultural influence. In *Stephen Hero,* Joyce fashions a protagonist able to rise above "those big words . . . which make us so unhappy" (*U* 2.264) and devises a budding writer largely able to hold himself aloof from all ideologies save those of his own creation; Joyce takes great pains to present this Stephen Daedalus not as one who indiscriminately or unconsciously absorbs social discourse but as an original and deliberate thinker. Stephen studies Skeat's *Etymological Dictionary* and peruses the prose of Freeman and Morris "as one would read a thesaurus"; he first devises a theory and then begins "to explore the language *for himself* and to choose, and thereby rescue . . . the words and phrases most amenable to his theory" (*SH* 26, my emphasis). Indeed, this Stephen determines whether to immerse himself in style, syntax, or substance; the *Portrait* Stephen, however, is awash in all three simultaneously, his perspectives and perceptions filtered through his culture. Whereas the Daedalus of *Stephen Hero* insists to his mother that "art is not an escape from life" (*SH* 86), his *Portrait* counterpart uses the novels of Dumas and Bulwer-Lytton in just this way, imagining a new life for himself as the heroic Edmond Dantes or the victorious Claude Melnotte. The Stephen of the first novel also does a far more convincing job of holding himself apart from both the politics and the beliefs of his age: he remains calmly detached from McCann's pleas to sign the petition for universal brotherhood (*SH* 114), but in *Portrait* he reacts with "scorn and anger" toward MacCann's petitioners (*P* 194). In *Stephen Hero,* he dismisses with relative surety Irish Catholicism's Christ as someone who "makes general remarks on life" with which he disagrees (*SH* 141); in *Portrait,* he is "not at all sure" of the falsity of Catholicism (*P* 243).

In contrast to the protagonist of *Stephen Hero,* the Stephen of *Portrait* is irretrievably immersed in the discourse of politics, language, and religion from the novel's opening pages; he is revealed as contained within narrative and, by extension, ideology, from his first conscious moment: in the bedtime tale Stephen's father tells, the young Dedalus "*was* baby tuckoo" (*P* 7, my emphasis).[5] Although he arrives at an awareness of its force, Stephen never entirely frees himself from the power of political or religious dogma; the Baby Tuckoo story gives way to steadily more complex systems of containment that Stephen must decode: among them, tales of Irish colonial factionalism, the fall of Parnell (signified by Dante's red and green brushes), and the litany of the Blessed Virgin. Joyce replaces the radical, independent Ibsen as the principal arbiter of Stephen's thought with Byron, Shelley, and Newman and presents a Stephen who—despite his overwhelming desire to cast himself as an independent thinker—is deeply and inextricably mired not in modern skepticism but in nineteenth-century romanticism. This Stephen is denied the ability to opt out of the cultural narrative accorded to his predecessor, who anticipates his "escape" with excitement and surety (*SH* 141); by contrast, the Stephen of *Portrait* vows only to "*try* to fly by those nets" of "nationality, language, [and] religion" (*P* 203, my emphasis). His friend Cranly notes the difficulty of achieving such independence: Stephen's mind is "supersaturated" with the very doctrines he would disbelieve; he has absorbed their messages too thoroughly to ever fully reject them (*P* 240). The first Stephen's declaration—"I am a product of Catholicism; I was sold to Rome before my birth. Now I have broken my slavery but I cannot in a moment destroy every feeling in my nature. *That takes time*"—implies a confidence in the ultimate purgation of cultural influence that the *Portrait* Stephen does not entirely share (*SH* 139, my emphasis). Each text presents the story of a mind awakening to the consciousness of ideological influence, but the emphasis in *Stephen Hero* is on the protagonist's dispassionate resolve and absolute rejection of such hegemony; by contrast, the Stephen of *Portrait* is besieged by the discourses he would reject and wages a difficult battle against their authority, one whose outcome is not at all certain. Each time the *Portrait* Stephen actively attempts to resist the forces that bind him, he is brought violently to heel: Wells shoulders him into a cesspool at Clongowes for refusing to swap his snuffbox and defying the schoolyard hierarchy; Heron and Boland pound him with cabbage stumps for the heresy of championing Byron over Tennyson and for resisting conventional mores; the Catholic Church browbeats him into penance with threats of hellfire and damnation (in *Stephen Hero,* a liberated Stephen later marvels at the self that allowed itself to be terrorized by such rhetoric [*SH* 56–57]). *Portrait,* unlike *Stephen Hero,* is finally the story of culture's intractable power to influence subjectivity and the complex struggle, rather than the easy insouciance, required to resist its influence.

Stephen's departure for Paris at the end of *Portrait* posits, to his conscious mind, a strong chance for independence, but his diary also betrays an intense anxiety over the possibility of never achieving this freedom: before he can conjure a kinship with peoples of distant nations, Stephen imagines a death contest with an old Irishman: "It is with him I must struggle all through this night till day come, till he or I lie dead, gripping him by the sinewy throat till . . . Till what? Till he yield to me? No. I mean him no harm" (*P* 252). Stephen should have slain the old man when he had the chance, for another alternative in fact exists—"till I yield to him"—one that Stephen does not consciously acknowledge until it is too late. *Portrait*'s hopeful flight is cut short by the opening of *Ulysses*, as D(a)edalus-become-Icarus falls back to earth with a thud: in this context of clipped flight, of foiled escape, Haines's remark in the "Telemachus" episode—"I should think you are able to free yourself"—stings painfully. Stephen's heated rejoinder attests that the ideological nets have been tightly woven and well cast; he has found himself unable to escape them. *Portrait*'s ringing declaration, "I will not serve" (*P* 246), is now rendered, "I am the servant of two masters, . . . an English and an Italian. . . . And a third . . . there is who wants me for odd jobs" (*U* 1.638–41). Something more, though, is implied within this exchange, especially if we recall that Daedalus, the artificer of Greek myth, not only found himself imprisoned within the labyrinth and fashioned wings of escape for himself and his son but also, as builder of it, was the architect of his own confinement. As the exchange between Stephen and Haines invokes the mythological image, it also suggests another way in which consciousness and culture are intertwined for Joyce: individuals, their subjectivities shaped by cultural discourse, also become the agents of its perpetuation; like D(a)edalus, they unknowingly help to forge the ties that bind them.

Stephen's transformation between *Stephen Hero* and *Portrait* has its roots in Joyce's own experiences between February 1906—when, a thousand pages into *Stephen Hero*, he suspended its writing (*Letters I* 60)—and September 1907, when he decided to revise the massive draft (twenty-six chapters with thirty-seven still to go) into the five-episode *Portrait*. The period was tumultuous personally as well as financially; after leaving his teaching job at the Berlitz School in Trieste, Joyce moved his family to Rome in 1906, where he worked unhappily as a bank clerk for six months before returning to Trieste in 1907. More important to his artistic vision than the personal upheaval of this period, however, was Joyce's contentious correspondence with Grant Richards over the publication of *Dubliners*. Rooted in the offense taken by Richards's printer at "Two Gallants" as well as Joyce's liberal use of the word "bloody," the dispute resulted in the publisher's final rejection of the manuscript in October 1906 (*Letters I* 60–61). Ellmann reports that Joyce's reading during this period included Hardy, Wilde, Moore, Kipling, Gissing, and Hauptmann; Joyce praised Kipling for his use of detail and Hauptmann for his frankness—the rest he tellingly panned for "beating around the bush" (*James Joyce* 233). It is the frankness and independence of *Dubliners* that Joyce tried to preserve from the editor's pen, but even at such a distance from London and Dublin, the author fell victim to the implacable, censorial sensibilities of those cities. The manuscript was again rejected in February 1907 (this time by John Long), and it would not be until 1914 and several more rebuffs that any printer would "endanger his immortal soul" to publish the book (*Letters I* 61). In the wake of this tempest, Joyce composed "The Dead," which, as Margot Norris has brilliantly argued in *Joyce's Web,* concerns itself with offering "back answers" to various structures of patriarchal authority represented within and by the text; he also attempted to destroy *Stephen Hero* and its free-thinking protagonist (97). In 1920 Joyce would write to Harriet Shaw Weaver about *Portrait:* "the 'original' original I tore up and threw in to the stove about eight years ago in a fit of rage on account of the trouble over *Dubliners.* The charred remains of the MS were rescued by a family fire brigade and tied up in an old sheet where they remained for some months. I . . . sorted them out and pieced them together as best I could and the present MS is the result" (*Selected Letters* 247). The consequent *Portrait* is one of a young man who no longer functions independently of his culture, but who is instead thoroughly bound by its discourses.

Though by shifting its narrative attention to other characters *Ulysses* appears to lose interest in Stephen Dedalus and his failed attempts to loosen the political and religious fetters that bind both his art and his mind, it is in this novel that Joyce expands his exploration of the impact of Victorian and Edwardian cultural discourse on subjectivity, through new characters who often exhibit much less awareness than Stephen of the influences that act upon them.[6] The sensibilities of Leopold and Molly Bloom, as well as those of other characters, are shaped by the social forces of gender, politics, and religion. But as these ideas begin to collide within the swirl of individual consciousness, they formulate a new possibility for dissidence according to Sinfield's model, one that destabilizes ideological authority by exposing the fissures and contradictions that exist within authority itself. Joyce's most powerful method of achieving this deconstruction is the conflation of apparently dissimilar discourses into unsettling synthesis. For example, as Bloom ruminates in All Hallow's Church, he subconsciously associates the confession/penance ritual emblematic of ecclesiastical power with the cruelty of the dominatrix and the punishment fixation of the flagellant he has read about in the fiction of Sacher-Masoch: "Confession. Everyone wants to. Then I will tell you all. Penance. Punish me, please. Great weapon in their hands. More than doctor or solicitor" (U 5.425–27). Such reflections subvert the dominant ecclesiastical discourse by demystifying and denaturalizing it: according to Bloom's associative logic, priests are not chaste, humble servants of a compassionate God, chosen to dispense God's mercy to the faithful; instead they morph into sexual sadists who employ the "weapon" of confession to inflict pain upon their all-too-willing victims. Similarly seditious conflations and demystifications occur in the musings of Gerty MacDowell, whose consciousness, like Bloom's, is formulated within a confluence of religious dogma, popular melodrama, and contemporary advertising;[7] filtered through Gerty's subjectivity, the icon of the Blessed Virgin is suspiciously subtended by the image of the "fallen" woman, and the home presided over by the "angel of the house" turns out to be physically and emotionally abusive. Critics have long noted that Molly Bloom contradicts herself throughout the "Penelope" episode,[8] but so, too, do the social standards that would dictate her behavior. In her important essay, "Pretending in 'Penelope': Masquerade, Mimicry, and Molly Bloom," Kimberly Devlin contends that Molly performs not one role but several subversive ones, "doing and undoing ideological gender acts" (81); I would further suggest that as Molly attempts to make and remake herself in her final speech, its most disruptive trait is its exposure of the contradictions and double standards that exist within and between the models offered for her emulation. In the books that Molly reads, the fate of the "angel of the house" is often indistinguishable from that of the fallen woman: the adulteress of Mrs. Henry Wood's East Lynne is punished for her sexual infidelity, but the chaste and faithful women of The Shadow of Ashlydyat die similarly painful and untimely deaths, while neither text chastises its philandering men. Molly discerns the operation of a sexual double standard within her society, and in this newly opened space of recognition, she speculates freely on what late Victorian and Edwardian society referred to as "the Woman Question": as Bonnie Scott has observed, beneath Molly's final remarks runs a "questioning refrain," "Who made life the way it is for women?" (Joyce and Feminism 169). The discordant eruptions of Molly Bloom fracture what Jameson has termed the "collective unconscious," that realm in which certain choices and behaviors, specifically those that would fly in the face of culturally determined norms, are repressed and eliminated by ideological force. Molly's speech helps to denaturalize and to make visible those power structures whose control is rooted in their very imperceptibility. Although she may not be able to exact change for herself, Molly's ruminations perhaps create new spaces where such transformations might take place. This predilection of Joyce's characters not only to absorb cultural systems of belief but also to transform these systems is vital to his ironic exposure and critique of the multiple ideologies that shaped late-Victorian and Edwardian thought.

My study is indebted to the work of earlier contextual critics such as Cheryl Herr (*Joyce's Anatomy of Culture*) and R. B. Kershner (*Joyce, Bakhtin, and Popular Literature*), as well as to recent historiographic studies by Robert Spoo (*James Joyce and the Language of History*) and James Fairhall (*James Joyce and the Question of History*). While Herr examines the pervasive, censorial influence of the press, the stage, and the pulpit on Joyce's Dublin, Kershner demonstrates the ideological function of the popular texts that appear in Joyce's work, presenting their effects on the characters of *Dubliners, Portrait,* and *Exiles.* Spoo and Fairhall have analyzed Joyce's treatment of the repressive hegemony of historical narrative; Spoo argues that Joyce, ultimately, recognizes that there is no freedom from the self's confinement within history; Fairhall takes perhaps a too-optimistic view, seeing in the linguistic play of *Ulysses* and *Finnegans Wake* a wish to evade the "authority of the word" (10). My sense is that what Joyce achieves by perforating the ideological mesh of nationalism, religion, and gender is not so much the dismantling of a belief system as it is an important awareness of its existence, and while some characters— Stephen and Molly, for instance—are more cognizant of ideology than others, they are no more able to escape its influence than are Gerty Mac-Dowell or Leopold Bloom. In other words, Joyce effects for his characters the possibility of what Sinfield refers to as "dissidence" rather than revolution, the potential for refusing an "aspect of the dominant" rather than its complete dismantling (*Faultlines* 49).

My method has been to foreground the cultural "voices" that Stephen Dedalus and others hear in fin de siècle Dublin and to reconstruct the discursive contexts that envelop Joyce's characters by examining documents contemporaneous to the period. My artifacts range more widely than those of my predecessors—I review letters, diaries, newspapers, journals, poems, novels, laws, and medical texts, as well as various cultural studies of the period—in order to reconstruct salient voices wherever they emerged. Additionally, I examine Joyce's personal writings, his letters and essays, as further examples of cultural documents that reflect dominant currents of his milieu. My point of departure in each case has been allusions to contemporary mores made by Joyce's characters themselves; after locating and reconstructing the broader cultural contexts of these references, I have constructed a close reading of Joyce's text in order to discern its relationship to the discourse in question. My focus is necessarily broader than that of previous studies; my goal has been to sketch a vista of Victorian and Edwardian Dublin that identifies and engages its most significant cultural discourses in terms of Joyce's work—specifically, those currents of colonial politics, spiritualism, masculinism, public morality, and the changing status of women.

This book is organized into three sections: parts one and two focus on Stephen Dedalus and Leopold Bloom, respectively. Specifically, section one, "'Not a Strong Swimmer': Submersions of Dedalus," examines the political and religious discourses that circulated throughout Victorian and Edwardian Ireland and analyzes their impact on the subjectivity of Stephen, who seems entirely unable to "fly by th[e]se nets" in either *Portrait* or *Ulysses*. The section includes two chapters: one that analyzes Stephen's subject position in relation to both colonial politics and the ideology of Irishness that it propagated and another that looks at Stephen's connections to the popular religious philosophies that vied with the authority of contemporary Catholicism within the context of what is often referred to as the nineteenth century's "crisis of faith." Section two of the book, "Caught in the Currents: Victorian Manliness, Public Morality, and Leopold Bloom," deals with the constructs of masculinity and public morality as they migrated to Ireland from England in the late Victorian era and explores the ways in which Bloom's subjectivity is constituted according to specific models that are available to him in popular discourse, especially that of the "Muscular Christian" and the social reformer. Bloom's manifestation of these discourses not only reveals their pervasive impact on the social fabric of Edwardian Ireland, it also exposes the ironic fissures and contradictions located within the discourses themselves. The first chapter in this section examines the influence of Anglican minister Charles Kingsley and his rhetoric of "Christian manliness" on both Bloom and Irish colonial culture at-large as well as the discourse of aestheticism that undermined it; the second analyzes Joyce's gleeful subversion of the moralistic discourse of social reform by exposing, through his own prurient reformer, the ironic link that exists between vice and vigilance.

Molly Bloom provided the initial focus for the book's third section, but as I began to examine her discursive contexts, it became clear that while Molly is indeed a unique creation and not merely a female archetype (as

Robert Boyle pointed out so many years ago), she also functions as a Joycean evolution, a character who manifests the progression of conflicting cultural messages regarding womanhood in late Victorian and Edwardian Ireland. Because other constructed femininities in Joyce's work also appeared to owe a great deal to this cultural context, it seemed important to trace Joyce's exploration of this discourse through multiple figures, including women from *Dubliners, Stephen Hero, Portrait, Ulysses,* and *Finnegans Wake.* Therefore, section three, "Fracturing the Discursive Feminine: Joyce and the 'Woman Question,'" examines the popular textual discourse that purported to represent the feminine experience in the late nineteenth and early twentieth centuries and analyzes the ways Joyce engages the cultural constructions of womanhood in Victorian and Edwardian Ireland. I argue for Joyce's awareness of such diverse figures as the domestic angel, the hysteric, and the New Woman and assert his attempts to write into his texts real women whose lives were circumscribed by the all-too-real boundaries of gendered discourse. A brief introduction establishes the ubiquitous role that the angel, the "mad"woman, and the New Woman each played in Victorian/Edwardian Dublin, then separate chapters discuss the influence of each figure in Joyce's work, as I argue that Joyce's women, from *Dubliners* to *Finnegans Wake,* warp the feminine icon beamed at them through the prism of popular culture, often beyond recognition.

Ultimately, Joyce's work does not liberate modern consciousness from the authoritarian structures of nation, religion, morality, and gender; instead, Joyce explores the potential for personal release by denaturalizing dogma and exposing it, not as a foundation but as a quicksand that submerges and assimilates the tide of individual thought. Though he wanted his readers to perceive the forces of influence, Joyce realized that recognition alone was not, finally, enough to achieve the "spiritual liberation" that he had hoped to foment with *Dubliners.* This is the lesson of Stephen D(a)edalus, who knows what ideologies suffuse his thought and constrain his art, but who cannot, after all, free himself; it is also the lesson of Leopold and Molly Bloom, who have internalized both the divergent discourses of their culture and its perpetuating mechanisms of constraint and control. The possibility of intellectual and spiritual freedom both fascinated and eluded James Joyce throughout his life; his fiction works to uncover the illusion of the self and its liberation from ideology even as it showcases the fissures within the discourses that confine us.

"Not a Strong Swimmer": Submersions of Dedalus

Colonial Pathology and the Ideology of Irishness in Victorian and Edwardian Dublin

James Joyce's Stephen Dedalus is an insatiable reader of the political discourses that comprise turn-of-the-century Dublin. Critics such as R. B. Kershner rightly have noted the ways in which the Stephen of *Portrait* romantically reenacts Alexandre Dumas's *Count of Monte Cristo* and Edward Bulwer-Lytton's *Lady of Lyons* in order to escape the ever-downward spiral of life in the Dedalus household, but the themes of these latter two works have even broader implications in the political development of the young artist.[1] They also reflect and solidify the sense of betrayal that Stephen comes to recognize as a pivotal motif in Irish colonial politics. Both works depict lovers estranged by treachery, but this important theme is also encoded with the signifiers of self-betrayal: the protagonists of these stories are deceived not from without but from within; Edmond Dantes and Claude Melnotte are betrayed first by ill-chosen friends and then, to a lesser degree, by the women they love. This triangulated motif of male-male infidelity and female inconstancy is reenacted in both *Stephen Hero* and *Portrait*, as Stephen suspects his confidants Davin and Cranly of usurping his own romantic interest in Emma Clery; such disloyalties among men, Joyce broadly insinuates in a 1904 letter, were endemic to Irish character itself. Joyce wrote to Nora Barnacle of one of his own estranged companions (whom Ellmann identifies as J. F. Byrne, a model for Cranly) as if this friend, too, had been a faithless lover: "When I was younger I had a friend to whom I gave myself freely—in a way more than I give to you and in a way less. He was Irish, that is to say, he was false to me" (*Letters II* 50). In *Portrait*, Stephen associates the trope of the betrayed lover with his country's ill-fated aspirations to political independence; he likens Davin's nationalist fervor to the inconstant passions of the fickle paramour and to the treachery of a trusted third party. Asked by Davin to join the nationalist cause, Stephen offers to assist the next rebellion's inevitable betrayal of itself by locating its "indispensable informer" and rails at his associate: "No honorable and sincere man . . . has given up to you his life and his youth and his affections from the days of

Tone to those of Parnell but you sold him to the enemy or . . . left him for another. And you invite me to be one of you. I'd see you damned first" (*P* 203). Stephen's sentiment, I will argue, is also Joyce's; in both *Portrait* and *Ulysses,* Joyce relentlessly depicts a country whose shifting internal allegiances continually betray its leaders, artists, and aspirations—and doom its political romance with colonial independence.

In spite of, or perhaps because of, the clearly nationalist sympathies recorded in his Triestine lectures and essays of 1907–12, Joyce heartily rebukes within these same documents Ireland's historical predilection to play false to its republican aspirations.[2] In "Ireland, Island of Saints and Sages," Joyce contends that his country repeatedly acquiesced in its own political subordination, noting the island was first invaded by the English at the behest of an Irish king, Dermot MacMurrough, and observing that the 1800 Act of Union that dissolved the Irish Parliament "was not legislated at Westminster but at Dublin, by a parliament elected by the vote of the people of Ireland, a parliament corrupted and undermined . . . by the agents of the English prime minister, but an Irish parliament nevertheless" (*CW* 162).[3] This pattern of political self-betrayal continued into the late nineteenth century, Joyce argues, with the failure of the Irish Parliamentary Party to stand by its leader, Home Rule proponent Charles Stewart Parnell, amid the adultery scandal that toppled him from power late in 1890. Although the party initially did reelect Parnell to the chair on November 25, 1890—just days after the divorce court delivered its verdict against him—it shortly repudiated this decision in response to English political pressure. Parnell had kept secret British Prime Minister William Gladstone's demand that Parnell resign his position as party leader; he had also suppressed Gladstone's threats to resign his own position or veto the Irish Parliamentary Party's decision and hold Home Rule hostage if it affirmed Parnell's position as chair. Once Gladstone's threats were revealed, however, the party reconsidered its stand. In a manifesto titled "To the People of Ireland," Parnell noted the loss of political independence that would necessarily result should the Irish Parliamentarians "consent to throw me to the English wolves now howling for my destruction" (312); nevertheless, forty-five of the Irish delegation's seventy-two members bowed to British pressure and walked out of Committee Room 15 at Westminster, declaring Parnell's leadership terminated. Certainly Parnell's attempts to quell debate and his refusal to allow a vote on whether he should be chair fueled the party split, but it is significant that Joyce derides nationalist duplicity, not English perfidy or Parnell's intransigence, when he recalls the ways in which an Irish clergy, press, and citizenry "entered the lists to finish him [Parnell] off" (*CW* 227). In his 1912 essay "The Shade of Parnell," Joyce's prose ironically echoes Parnell's own plea and squarely levies the blame for the politician's demise: "They [the Irish] did not throw him [Parnell] to the English wolves; they tore him to pieces themselves" (*CW* 228). The implications of this internal treachery for both Stephen Dedalus and colonial Ireland become clear as we follow Stephen's reading of Irish political discourse and note his inescapable conclusion: it is not England who is Ireland's chief betrayer, it is Ireland itself.

Enda Duffy, Emer Nolan, and Vincent J. Cheng have rescued Joyce's fiction from the apolitical aestheticism ascribed to it by the New Critics and have argued forcefully for Joyce's position as a subaltern writer concerned with representing the divisive and devastating effects of colonial oppression in Ireland. Duffy and Nolan claim for Joyce an ardently nationalistic stance: Duffy, for instance, sees *Ulysses* as "*the* book of Irish postcolonial independence," exposing the oppressive mechanisms of the colonial regime and the insular nationalism that was its legacy (3); Nolan wants to rescue Joyce's work from generations of critics who, she claims, willfully submerged his politics beneath a tide of modernist aestheticism. Cheng emphasizes Joyce's nationalist sympathies but stresses the author's distrust of the self-defeating binary that he perceived in Celticism as it pursued its exclusivist doctrine of racial purity.[4] My position is somewhat more conservative than most: I, too, view Joyce as a highly politicized, colonial figure writing against canonical and political hegemony, and while I agree that Joyce sees British imperialism as a fundamental cause of Irish political chaos in the late Victorian and Edwardian periods ("Can the back of a slave forget the rod?" Joyce asks [*CW* 168]), I would also insist that his purpose in depicting this discordant factionalism is not so much to condemn Irish mistreatment at British hands as it is to expose and deride Ireland's oppression of its own sons and daughters as it continually betrayed its own aspirations to political unity and attempted the impossible, and in Joyce's view, undesirable, task of "purifying" or "de-Anglicizing" Irish culture. Early critics may have mistaken Joyce's simultaneous critique of British imperialism and chauvinistic nationalisms for an apolitical aesthetic, but we must not attempt to correct this oversight with another selective elision. We must recall that in *Critical Writings,* Joyce outlines not only the various tyrannies Ireland suffered under centuries of British rule—including the plunder of its economy and the "reign of terror" perpetrated against Catholic citizens—he also rejects as futile continued "invectives against the English despoiler" and calls for Ireland to take responsibility for halting its continuing self-dissolution (*CW* 168, 173).

Various cultural nationalisms gained ground in Ireland after Parnell's fall. As the son of a Protestant landowner, Parnell's greatest ability had been to forge unlikely but effective alliances between Michael Davitt's insurrectionist Land League and the anti-Fenian Catholic Church in support of parliamentary agitation for Home Rule.[5] But in the wake of Parnell's political destruction and subsequent death in 1891, the political unity of the 1880s disintegrated; Joyce's most pointed description of the political movement's decade-long impotence occurs in the *Dubliners* story "Ivy Day in the Committee Room," where national party operatives canvass for a candidate they do not trust and suspect one another of spying for the opposition, uniting only in their desire for stout and a sentimentalized, conveniently elliptical remembrance of their "Uncrowned King" (*D* 134). In his 1904 account, *The Fall of Feudalism in Ireland,* Davitt described the ensuing chaos that divided the country: "The Irish party was split in two. . . . Friends were driven asunder. Families even became divided. Some town or village in a county would be found practically of one way of thinking, while another hamlet or town, a few miles away, would hold to the opposite side. This was what happened in Ireland" (642–43).[6] In this climate of political disarray, the era's cultural revival movements and their attempts to reconstruct an Irish culture apart from Saxon influence were reinvigorated. Organizations such as the Society for the Preservation of the Irish Language (1876), the Gaelic Athletic Association (1884), the National Literary Society (1892), the Gaelic League (1893), the Irish Literary Theatre (1899), and the Irish National Theatre Society (1902) looked toward language, sport, and art to reconstruct the shards of national unity.

Both the Gaelic Revival and the Literary Revival sought to refresh and reorganize the nationalist agenda by redefining a center that stood apart from political agitation: instead of campaigning for parliamentary home rule or republican separatism, such groups focused on locating and purifying an Irish "essence" apart from a British culture they viewed as degraded and oppressive, valorizing the Irish peasant and the pastoral, and attempting to reinvent an Irish mythology for the modern world. Led by Douglas Hyde, the Gaelic League latched onto a linguistic solution to Ireland's internal divisiveness; Hyde, a Protestant, chose the Gaelic language rather than Catholicism as a signifier of Irishness in hopes of attracting Protestants and Catholics to his movement. In a lecture delivered before the National Literary Society in 1892, "The Necessity for De-Anglicising Ireland," Hyde depicts an Ireland that for centuries had in fact assimilated its invaders—Danes, Normans, Saxons—in a form of inverse colonization until they became, in Hyde's words, "more Hibernian than the Hibernians themselves" (529). By the end of the nineteenth century, however, Hyde, along with D. P. Moran, foresaw an Irish culture whose Celtic origins had been obliterated by Englishness.[7] Hyde and Moran faulted Ireland's mimicry of English culture, along with a neglect of Gaelic language and traditions, for this troubling reverse-assimilation. In Hyde's view,

> What the battleaxe of the Dane, the sword of the Norman, the wile of the Saxon were unable to perform, we have accomplished ourselves. We have at last broken the continuity of Irish life, and just at the moment when the Celtic race is presumably about to largely recover possession of its own country, it finds itself deprived . . . of its Celtic characteristics, cut off from the past, yet scarcely in touch with the present. . . . Just when we should be starting to build up anew the Irish race and the Gaelic nation . . . we find ourselves despoiled of the bricks of nationality. The old bricks that lasted eighteen hundred years are destroyed; we must now set to, to bake new ones, if we can, on other ground and of other clay. (530)

To reestablish its claim to racial and political authenticity, the Irish race must purify itself, Hyde argued: it must counter the menacing penetration of Englishness by uniting behind a linguistic barrier—the Gaelic language.

A similar desire to purge Irish culture of Saxon influence and establish a new cultural and spiritual essence underwrote the Irish Literary Revival. William Butler Yeats and George W. Russell (who would part ways themselves for reasons I will detail later in this chapter) looked to create their "Irish Ireland" through a distinctive Irish literature—written in English. The literary movement took issue with Hyde's contention that reviving Gaelic was the only way to "de-Anglicise" Ireland, though it did not disdain the resurrection of the old language. Yeats replied to Hyde in an 1892 letter to *United Ireland:* "Can we not build up a national tradition, a national literature, which shall be none the less Irish in spirit from being English in language? Can we not keep the continuity of the nation's life . . . by translating or retelling in English, which shall have an indefinable Irish quality of rythm [sic] and style, all that is best of the ancient literature?" (*Uncollected Prose* 1.255). In spite of Yeats's contrarian attempt to cultivate a linguistic hybridity (English with "an indefinable Irish quality") as well as an openness of theme, the Literary Revival, like the Gaelic Revival, aimed ultimately to foment homogeneity in Ireland—and determined to do so through art. The founders of the Irish Literary Theatre

(Yeats, Augusta Gregory, and Edward Martyn) announced at its 1899 inception that they intended their plays to reveal a cohesive Irish identity grounded in "an ancient idealism" and a character that stood apart from "all the political questions that divide us" (Gregory, "Our Irish Theatre" 378–79).

Thus a new ideological discourse on Irishness emerged, one that aimed to construct a unified national character out of an "authenticity" that could be located within culture and race. Although such nationalisms can function to critique the imperial state and subvert the colonizing power, postcolonial critics like Frantz Fanon and Edward Said have shown that these movements also tend to replicate the oppressive, exclusionary rhetoric of the colonizer as they pursue their goal of cultural homogenization. In his book *Anomalous States: Irish Writing and the Post-Colonial Moment*, David Lloyd takes a different view, defending this monologism as an essential precursor to Ireland's subsequent political and military struggles against imperialism; in *Inventing Ireland: The Literature of the Modern Nation*, Declan Kiberd goes even further, asserting that cultural nationalists in Ireland "committed themselves in no spirit of chauvinism" (3). But Joyce evidently viewed such movements less charitably; he objected to the homogeneity these groups fomented, and he interrogated throughout his own narratives the discourse of Irishness that they propagated—not because he opposed the ultimate nationalist objective of political separation from England but because he believed this discourse of cultural apartheid to constitute yet another narrative of national self-betrayal.[8] Joyce wrote in 1907:

> To tell the truth, to exclude from the present nation all who are descended from foreign families would be impossible, and to deny the name of patriot to all those who are not of Irish stock would be to deny it to almost all the heroes of the modern movement—Lord Edward Fitzgerald, Robert Emmet, Theobald Wolfe Tone and Napper Tandy, leaders of the uprising of 1798, Thomas Davis and John Mitchel, leaders of the Young Ireland movement, Isaac Butt, Joseph Biggar, the inventor of parliamentary obstructionism, many of the anticlerical Fenians, and, finally, Charles Stewart Parnell, who was perhaps the most formidable man that ever led the Irish, but in whose veins there was not even a drop of Celtic blood. (*CW* 161–62)

Kiberd has suggested that Joyce's critique of contemporary Ireland aligns him both with and against the cultural Revivalists—like them, Kiberd argues, Joyce opposed colonial occupation and usurpation, but unlike the

Revivalists, Joyce also "proceeds to indict the native culture for not living up to expectations of it, for not being an authentic *elsewhere*" (336). While I find this notion of doubleness regarding Joyce's politics to be useful, I do not believe that Joyce impeaches cultural nationalisms because they failed to create an "authentic elsewhere";[9] rather, Joyce objects to these movements because they failed to recognize that "Irishness," in all its assimilative and assimilated hybridity, already was evolving into a new place—or in Joyce's words, "a new entity." "Do we not see that in Ireland the Danes, the Firbolgs, the Milesians from Spain, the Norman invaders, and the Anglo-Saxon settlers have united to form a new entity, one might say under the influence of a local deity?" Joyce asks (*CW* 166). The author's fascination with the cultural hybridity of modern Ireland is evident throughout his fiction; his texts are populated with amalgamous Irish characters who create fissures within the signifiers of racial and linguistic identity posited by the Revivalists and who repeatedly—and ironically—call into question the cultural nationalists' notion of Irishness. The query posed first in *Portrait* to the politically disaffected Stephen by his nationalist friend, Davin—"What with your name and your ideas . . . Are you Irish at all?" (*P* 202)—reverberates through *Ulysses*. The old milkwoman of "Telemachus" neither speaks nor understands Gaelic; she simultaneously represents the cultural decay that Hyde decried and defies the romantic, Revivalist representations of the "folk" as the locus of Irish "essence." The ambiguous ethnicity of Leopold Bloom also signifies a similar destabilization of "authenticity" and essence with regard to Revivalist constructions of Irishness; the concepts of "Jewishness" and "Irishness" are problematized in the Irish-born Bloom, whose father was a Jew but whose mother was a Protestant and who, for his own part, has been baptized a Catholic. In spite of this racial and religious mixing, Bloom's political attitudes—that is, his nationalist politics—are beyond reproach: Bloom is rumored, for instance, to have provided the idea for Sinn Fein to Arthur Griffith—but even this is not enough to vindicate him in the eyes of the Cyclopian nationalists of chapter 12, who demand to know, "What is your nation . . . ?" (*U* 12.1430). In these terms, then, the continued pursuit by cultural nationalists of an essential Gaelicness becomes, for Joyce, yet another self-betrayal of the nation, a failure to recognize its own.

Joyce perhaps agreed with Revivalist assertions on one important point: the vital role of the artist to the success of the nationalist project. Joyce believed that it was indeed the artist who might rouse the conscience of the nation, but not by creating a purified cultural essence or a new racial authenticity. Instead, Joyce gives us, in *Portrait* and *Ulysses*, a poet who

tries to combat these ideologies of Irishness as well as a country determined to reject his message—and with it, its own hopes for intellectual
and colonial independence. As Stephen Dedalus moves through the politically charged narratives of *Portrait* and *Ulysses,* his encounters with the
evolving Irish nation—as well as his exclusion at every turn from its emer-
gent discourses on Irishness and authenticity—reveal Joyce's implicit con-
demnation of his compatriots who not only re-create the very political and
cultural constructs that they would overthrow but who also silence the
artist who might reveal the "nation-ness" that they so fervently seek.[10]

It is a repetitiously bloody and complex colonial heritage that the young
Stephen Dedalus must decode, a national experience characterized by
more than six centuries of British occupation and Irish revolt. Beginning in
1171 with the arrival of Henry II's forces on Irish soil and continuing until
the 1922 partition of the island into Northern Ireland and the Irish Free
State, Irish history records the gamut of colonial oppression aimed at ex-
pediting the absorption of the "foreign" culture and reaping the economic
harvests of colonization. The impact of colonization on the subaltern
identity—as well as the extraordinarily problematic task of resurrecting
and/or re-creating the subsumed culture—has been observed by a host of
postcolonial critics, most notably Frantz Fanon and Gayatri Spivak. Both
Fanon and Spivak have marked the inherent impossibility that underlies
cultural revival movements that would return "national" culture to a
precolonized state. Fanon explains the inseparability of colonial history
from the rest of a nation's heritage: "At the very moment when the native
intellectual is anxiously trying to create a cultural work he fails to realise
that he is utilising techniques and language which are borrowed from the
stranger in his country. . . . The artist who has decided to illustrate the
truths of the nation turns paradoxically towards the past and away from
actual events. . . . But the native intellectual who wishes to create an authentic work of art must realize that the truths of a nation are in the first
place its realities" (180–81). Joyce similarly observed that appeals to the
past that neglect present realities are invalid (*CW* 173); he also believed
the modern nation's history to be inextricable from centuries of assimilation, invasion, and conquest. As he put it: "Our civilization is a vast fabric,
in which the most diverse elements are mingled. . . . In such a fabric, it is
useless to look for a thread that may have remained pure and virgin without having undergone the influence of a neighbouring thread. What race,
or what language . . . can boast of being pure today?" (*CW* 165–66).
Spivak problematizes the nationalist project from an additional perspec-

tive; she notes that the subaltern culture of the present moment never can be accurately recorded because neither the peasants themselves nor those who are most likely to transcribe their stories—members of the "counter-insurgency" or the nationalist "elite"—are immune from the influence of the Anglo-Saxon Other (203). Early in *Ulysses,* Joyce will demonstrate just this difficulty as Haines, Mulligan, and Stephen greet the old Irish woman who delivers their morning milk. Vincent Cheng has noted Haines's problematic pose as an Englishman engaged in Irish ethnography (and suggests his work will undoubtedly perpetuate the racial/racist stereotypes of the islanders pervasive at the turn of the century) as well as Mulligan's hopeful pimping of Irishness for the project. The Buck's first offering is an impressive one: colorful tales of the countryside, an "authentic" peasant woman, and Dedalus, the morose Irish poet (Cheng 156). Enda Duffy has also proposed that the old woman may not be as dispossessed from her language as most readers of Joyce initially assume; Duffy suggests she may be feigning ignorance in order to dupe—and resist—those who would collect her as some sort of national specimen (50). What becomes most clear in this scene, however, is Joyce's insistence on the impossibility of representing/recovering/purifying subalternity outside Anglicized space. Multiple possibilities for transcribing subaltern identity are rendered here but all are irretrievably tainted by British influence: Haines, the only character actively engaged in the project, is an Englishman; Mulligan, a mercenary version of Spivak's nationalist "elite," pursues English sovereigns as he trades on Irishness. Neither Stephen Dedalus nor the milkwoman are any less contaminated: Stephen's embittered, anti-imperialist eruptions later in the episode reveal the extent to which he believes himself to have been adversely affected by the imperial presence; the milkwoman, whether or not she speaks Gaelic, certainly does speak English and, as Stephen notes, seems infatuated with both Haines and Mulligan, "her conqueror and her gay betrayer" (*U* 1.405).

As Mulligan makes his offerings to the Englishman, Joyce manages to impeach not only the impracticability and the motives of the cultural Revivalist program but also the verisimilitude and originality of its representations—for a second point of this scene is to expose the speciousness that characterized Revivalist renditions of Irishness as well as the pervasiveness of this discourse. In his useful article, "The Imaginary Irish Peasant," Edward Hirsch has argued that the Irish Literary Revival "fundamentally 'created' and characterized [the peasant] for posterity" during an era in which rural life had been so dramatically changed by emigration and urbanization that the "single undifferentiated entity called 'the folk'" no longer existed

(1116–18). Hirsch suggests that the Revival imbued its peasant figure with a transcendent, spiritual nature intended to counter the image of the drunken, simianized "Paddy" so familiar in the English press; the peasant's connection to the soil functioned to assert not only the peasant's purity but also deep-rooted Irish property rights against colonial misappropriations. Yeats linked the figure of the peasant with the speaking of Gaelic in his postscript to *Ideals in Ireland,* a 1901 collection of essays by prominent Revivalists edited by Augusta Gregory; together the peasant and his or her dialect signified "a tradition of life that existed before commercialism, and the vulgarity founded upon it," Yeats wrote ("Postscript" 105). That Joyce felt compelled to engage and critique the pastoral figure in an urban-centered novel like *Ulysses* attests to its wholesale invasion of the popular culture; Joyce's "realistic" peasant is not only linguistically deficient but also economically savvy— probably "vulgarly" so, in Yeats's view: the milkwoman sells her milk to the young men and precisely calculates the amount they owe her with blurring rapidity. "Well, it's seven mornings a pint at twopence is seven twos is a shilling and twopence over and these three mornings a quart at fourpence is three quarts is a shilling. That's a shilling and one and two is two and two, sir" (*U* 1.442–45). In spite of the way in which her words belie the pastoral stereotype, it is also clear that both the milkwoman and Haines buy into the ideal for which Mulligan shills: the old woman wishes that she spoke Gaelic, a language she romanticizes, and it is perhaps Haines's disappointment in her ironically insufficient Irishness that drives him to the National Library in search of better material. Once there, of course, Haines will discover Douglas Hyde's *Love Songs of Connacht* (1893), a slender volume filled with the romantic, pastoral images (rendered in Gaelic and in an English translation) that the Revival propagated.[11] Even Stephen, who rejects the old woman's symbolic role, is fully aware of that which she signifies in the Revivalist usurpation of the popular imagination: "Silk of the kine and poor old woman, names given her in old times. A wandering crone, lowly form of an immortal . . . a messenger from the secret morning. To serve or to upbraid, whether he could not tell: but scorned to beg her favour" (*U* 1.403–7). In Stephen's reading, the woman becomes Yeats's Cathleen ni Houlihan, the disguised goddess who pleads for young men to defend her house against the strangers who have entered there. Stephen's scorn signifies both his defiance of her creators and his resistance to the figure's constructed innocence: this scene further functions to indict the susceptibility of the Irish populace to following false prophets—not as unwitting dupes but with full cognizance of the choices arrayed before them. "She bows her old head to a voice that speaks to her loudly, her bonesetter, her medicineman: me she slights," Stephen chafes (*U* 1.418–20). As the old woman thralls not to Stephen but to Mulligan, who attempts to betray them both, the motif of male-male infidelity and female inconstancy plays itself out once more: the popular imagination allows itself to be usurped by false enthusiasts while it disregards the man who might be its true prophet.

Certainly the signifiers of political self-betrayal—especially the inability to recognize and remain loyal to the right leader—intrude upon the consciousness of *Portrait*'s Stephen from the novel's first page, which records his earliest memories—hearing the Baby Tuckoo story, wetting the bed, and dancing the sailor's hornpipe. Stephen here also observes that "Dante had two brushes in her press. The brush with the maroon velvet back was for Michael Davitt and the brush with the green velvet back was for Parnell" (*P* 7). It is the earliest text of colonial impact that Stephen tries to read; it records the temporary unity of nationalist factions—including Davitt's Fenian Irish National Land League and the Catholic Church—under Parnell's leadership. With Parnell's political demise in 1890 and his death in 1891, however, came the renewal of virulent factionalism. A few pages later, Dante has "ripped the green velvet back off the brush that was for Parnell . . . and . . . told him that Parnell was a bad man" (*P* 16), and Stephen wonders "which was right, to be for the green or for the maroon" (*P* 16). Before his terror-stricken eyes, Christmas dinner is transformed into a metaphoric civil war, each side accusing the other of deception, treachery, and betrayal: John Casey and Simon Dedalus violently deride the Catholic priests and the "priests' pawns" who denounced Parnell because of his liaison with Kitty O'Shea; just as vehemently, Dante Riordan defends the priests' action as a vindication of "God and morality and religion" (*P* 38). Stephen momentarily recalls happier days when both sides united against British imperialism: "He was for Ireland and Parnell and so was father; and so was Dante too for one night at the band on the esplanade she had hit a gentleman on the head with her umbrella because he had taken off his hat when the band played 'God Save the Queen' at the end" (*P* 37). But with Parnell's fall, the union he had forged fractured; in the Dedalus dining room, faces darken in anger, voices quiver with rage, and fists crash onto the table. That this is Christmas dinner, that time of year when "goodwill among men" mythically pervades, intensifies the violence and causes the scene to reverberate with irony. Stephen's confusion over the argument—"Who was right then?" (*P* 35)—underscores the prismatic nature of an increasingly factionalized nationalist discourse.

The fragmented discourse that Stephen endeavors to decode is often underwritten by gendered and sexualized subtexts that further confuse him. As the evolving dogmas of Irishness became increasingly obsessed with cultural purification, such notions spilled over (not surprisingly) into the realm of sexuality: Englishness came to be associated with immorality, while Irishness began to signify a transcendent sexual purity—a characterization that "nauseated" Joyce and one that he vowed to undermine in his novels (*Letters II* 191).[12] In *Stephen Hero,* Madden articulates the sexual-spiritual quality that his nationalist movement claimed as integral to Irish character, telling Stephen, "The Irish are noted for at least one virtue all the world over . . . they are chaste" (*SH* 55). Thus hard-line, conservative Catholic outrage over Parnell's adultery has its basis not only in the Ten Commandments but also in the perceived betrayal of Irish national character. Tellingly, the Christmas dinner scene also seems to be as much about O'Shea and her tainted English sexuality as it is about Parnell; the story Casey relates about the old woman who taunted him with Parnellite slurs turns on her final vilification of O'Shea in sexualized terms: "I let her bawl away, to her heart's content, *Kitty O'Shea* and the rest of it till at last she called that lady a name that I won't sully this Christmas board nor your ears . . . nor my own lips by repeating" (*P* 36).

Only vaguely perceiving the gendered subtext of the political argument, Stephen unwittingly makes the connection that remains unspoken at this table between sexual scandal and Parnell's Protestantism. Casey defends himself against Mrs. Riordan's accusations that he is a "renegade catholic," for, although he apparently rejects chastity as a signifier of Irishness, he does not (initially) seem to abjure the movement of religion into the same domain. When Dante intimates that Casey is among "the blackest protestant[s] in the land" (*P* 35), Casey retaliates, his face flushing: "I am no protestant, I tell you again" (*P* 35).[13] Stephen's immediate evocation of his Protestant friend, Eileen, is clearly connected to Dante's accusation and Casey's denial: "She [Dante] did not like him to play with Eileen because Eileen was a protestant and when she was young she knew children that used to play with protestants and the protestants used to make fun of the litany of the Blessed Virgin. *Tower of Ivory,* they used to say, *House of Gold*! How could a woman be a tower of ivory or a house of gold?" (*P* 35). The Protestant skepticism registered in this passage disputes the metaphorical descriptions of purity and value attached to the figure of the Irish Virgin. It seems that Protestantism, along with Englishness, has begun to signify a sexual suspiciousness; the notion that Protestants were sexually "loose" was a proposition perhaps demonstrated for many Irish Catholics by the Parnell-O'Shea scandal.

Certainly a complex interconnectedness exists among Irish nationalism, Irish Catholicism, and the figure of the female virgin: both ideologies desire to sheath this icon in an impenetrable purity. The sexually untouched nature of Catholicism's Virgin comes to signify, in the discourse of Irish nationalism, a nonexistent space in which land remains uninvaded and history uncolonized.[14] But Irish Catholicism—as well as Madden's definition of Irish character—also inscribes the presence of a male virgin: Catholicism reveres as chaste both its Christ and its priests. Again, the two ideologies—Catholicism and nationalism—collapse onto one another. Parnell in the *Portrait* dinner scene is characterized by both sides as a Christ-like figure: in Dante's assessment, Parnell was suited to lead so long as he remained—like Christ—sexually pure and without sin. Once he became a "public sinner," however, Parnell could no longer enact the role of Ireland's savior. Casey and Simon Dedalus see in Parnell the martyred Christ, hated by the Pharisees of his own day; they interpret the priests' denunciation of the Irish leader as Judas-like treachery (In *Ulysses*, Mr. Power will even suggest that, like Christ, Parnell will be resurrected, "that one day he will come again" [*U* 6.923–24]). Parnell betrays not only Ireland's vision of itself as "virgin" and "pure," but he also blasphemes its ideal of an immaculate God. His adultery, in the eyes of Dante and her priests, thus fuses treason with desecration, an unforgivable combination of sins that fans the heat of the quarrel at the Dedalus table.

Like his family relationships, Stephen's early school experiences are also encoded with signifiers of colonial self-deception and destruction. Partha Chatterjee has noted that the aim of nationalist movements is not to reject the principles of modern government expounded by their colonizers but to require the just application of these principles (74). Following Fanon, Edward Said takes a more problematic view of native mimicry of colonial hierarchical structures. In *Culture and Imperialism*, Said argues: "Nationalism was often led by lawyers, doctors, and writers who were partly formed and to some degree produced by the colonial power. The national bourgeoises . . . in effect tended to replace the colonial force with a new class-based and ultimately exploitative one, which replicated the old colonial structures in new terms" (223). The young Stephen first treads the halls of academia at the prestigious Clongowes Wood College, a school in which academic teams are dubbed "Lancaster" and "York" and in which Catholic Ireland's mimicry of British forms seems already well established. While the class-consciousness evident among the Irish Catholic elite may not have been representative of attitudes at the less fashionable Belvedere College (which Stephen attends after his withdrawal from

Clongowes, a move precipitated by his father's financial "trouble" [P 64]), the influence of his first alma mater on his evolving sense of Ireland's oppressive political structures is undeniable. Class hierarchies are in play among even the schoolyard boys at Clongowes; as soon as he arrives, Stephen's schoolmates try to discern his proper place in their order. His last name, neither Saxon nor Gaelic, defies classification, but Nasty Roche presses undaunted for some indication of Stephen's social status: "*What* is your father?" Roche wants to know. When Stephen replies, evasively, "A gentleman," Roche pushes further: "Is he a magistrate?" (*P* 9, my emphasis). This discussion of profession is encoded with the signifiers of Ireland's colonial status; magistrates, of course, were Irish civil servants who administered British law in the colony. Appointed by the lord lieutenant, resident magistrates decided legal questions and oversaw local police forces; they were also paid a handsome salary of up to £500 that enabled them to live a land-owning and affluent life ("Resident and Stipendiary Magistrates" 483). Drawing their power from this association with the British Crown, these young practitioners of playground politics evince Said's point that native populations frequently model exploitative class structures on those they have observed from their conquerors. Stephen feels acutely his lack of position in this order; his father has already apologized that "he was not a magistrate like the other boys' fathers" (*P* 26), but Stephen fantasizes that he might yet outrank the magistrates' sons. A promotion for Simon figures prominently in his son's dreams of the perfect Christmas vacation: "Welcome home, Stephen! Noises of welcome. . . . His father was a marshal now; higher than a magistrate" (*P* 20).

Stephen's need for an exalted place in the schoolyard hierarchy is a direct result of the oppression he experiences there. In a native appropriation of the colonial scene in which colonizers subdue indigenous populations by imposing behavioral patterns for the natives to emulate, the Irish Catholic Wells establishes himself as Stephen's superior. This enactment of nativistic self-oppression becomes unmistakable as the episode progresses. Already outranking Stephen as a magistrate's son, Wells is also positioned in the elevated "third of grammar" and owns a "seasoned hacking chestnut," significantly described by Stephen (and presumably by Wells) as "the conqueror of forty" (*P* 14). The question Wells poses to Stephen— "Tell us Dedalus, do you kiss your mother before you go to bed?"—both heralds the sexual guilt and confusion that will hound Stephen until he discovers the open sensuality of the bird girl at the end of chapter 4 and unmasks Stephen's failure to assimilate into this schoolyard hierarchy. Stephen's blushing confusion as he attempts to discover the "right" answer to the question marks the imminent failure of colonial mimesis that Homi Bhabha has argued for in "Of Mimicry and Man." Stephen tries in this scene to imitate the response he believes his tormentors require to prove he is one of them but instead produces what Bhabha calls "a difference that is almost the same, but not quite" (126); Stephen's response reveals nothing so much as his own estrangement from his countrymen's discourse and solidifies their positions over him.

As it did in the Christmas dinner episode, the gendering of this scene further contributes to its political implications. If the female figure in Irish ballad and literature is often an encoded representation of the struggles against colonial oppressions, then the power of Wells's question may derive from its appropriation of that figure. Later in *Portrait* Stephen will refuse his mother's request that he make his Easter duty, and she becomes a progressively clearer representation of Ireland and its staunch Catholicism.[15] For now, however, Stephen faces for the first time a question for which there is no "right" answer; the ambiguity of right and wrong among political texts is, of course, repeated at Christmas dinner.

These scenes, then, signify more than just schoolyard bullying; they also become miniaturized, nativistic appropriations of the conquest narrative, where British domination is replaced by an Irish Catholic rule that employs the forms of colonial subjugation as it subdues the Irish people themselves. As he grows older, Stephen becomes an increasingly more sophisticated reader of the self-oppression inherent in Victorian Dublin's colonial discourses. He not only condemns Davin's Gaelic Leaguers as turncoats and betrayers, he just as passionately despises the "patricians of Ireland," who sell their country's aspirations to line their own pockets. He wonders how he "could hit their conscience or how cast his shadow over the imaginations of their daughters, before their squires begat upon them, that they might breed a race less ignoble than their own?" (P 238). Stephen's decision to chart a course between these betrayers of Ireland is the force behind the determined quest with which he ends *Portrait,* to "forge in the smithy of my soul the uncreated conscience of my race" (P 253). But Stephen's is not the nationalist project that would create a unified Irish character. He realizes, along with Joyce, that nation-ness is no blank space awaiting the imposition of homogeneous language, literature, and custom; it is, rather, as Bhabha has argued, a contentious, heterogeneous mixture of ideas and cultures ("DissemiNation" 307). Stephen's vow is to create a "conscience" for the Irish people, a sense of moral responsibility, a capacity to divine the damage their insular political agendas have inflicted on their country. Connected to this conscience is "consciousness"—a newly awakened awareness of the multiple variations of an Irish character that has touched other cultures and has been touched by them. Stephen's project, then, parallels Joyce's own, to hold up to Irish political factionalism a "nicely polished looking-glass" that would reveal its own short-sightedness.

Just as it is impossible for a colonized nation to "purify" itself, to re-create, recover, or return to a culture unaffected by colonization, so also it is impossible for language to remain isolated and unaffected by cross-culturization. While it is true, as Bhabha contends in "The Other Question," that "the imposition of a foreign tongue" displaces native speech and becomes a means of ideological control that "differentiates the gentleman from the native, culture from civilization" (152), it is also true that the colonizer's language is likewise affected by its contact with other cultures. In the later scenes of *Portrait*, Joyce represents the two-edged impact of colonization on language and culture as well as the impossibility of asserting either cultural or linguistic "purity" in the modern nation.

As a young university student conversing with his British dean of studies, Stephen perceives the striking dissonance in their respective relationships to the same tongue: "The language in which we are speaking is his before it is mine. How different are the words *home, Christ, ale, master,* on his lips and on mine! I cannot speak or write these words without unrest of spirit. His language, so familiar and so foreign, will always be for me an acquired speech. I have not made or accepted its words. My voice holds them at bay. My soul frets in the shadow of his language" (P 189). Unlike his confusing encounter with Wells, in this dialogue Stephen begins to be a perceptive reader of the ulterior narrative of empire. Later, the young man realizes he has acquiesced once again to what Said has called the "absolute hierarchical distinction . . . between the ruler and the ruled" (228) and records his anger in his journal: "That tundish has been on my mind for a long time. I looked it up and find it English and good old blunt English too. Damn the dean of studies and his funnel! What did he come here for to teach us his own language or to learn it from us? Damn him one way or the other!" (P 251). Stephen's disaffection in this scene functions not merely to represent the colonial subject's dispossession from the colonizer's language; Joyce also problematizes and inverts this scene to convey the impact of cultural assimilation on the colonizer. When one culture endeavors to absorb another, the native does not disappear; instead, both cultures work subtle transformations on one another to create a new form. Both parties are thus forever and irremediably affected by mutual contact. As Said has pointed out, "Partly because of empire, all cultures are involved in one another; none is single and pure, all are hybrid, hetero-geneous, extraordinarily differentiated and unmonolithic" (xxv). On one level, Joyce represents this influence in the person of a British dean who has, in effect, "gone native." This Englishman's conversion is certainly less dramatic than Kurtz's transformation in *Heart of Darkness,* but as an English convert to Catholicism's priesthood, the dean of studies has none-theless betrayed his nation's "civilizing mission" by reverting to the native religion. Stephen perceives the resultant alienation from both Englishmen and Irishmen that "this halfbrother of the clergy" (*P* 190), this "poor Englishman in Ireland" (*P* 189) experiences, but as he fixates on the dean's linguistic snub, Stephen fails to notice that the priest shares his disassocia-tion from the Saxon tongue. Stephen's contention that "tundish" is an English word is correct as far as it goes; in fact, "tundish" is still identified in *Webster's New Universal Unabridged Dictionary* as "British Dialect." However, Stephen is not thorough enough in his reading of etymologies. The *Oxford English Dictionary (OED)* additionally recognizes "tundish" as a combination form of "tun" and "dish," words encoded with decid-edly more complex origins. Variations of "tun," meaning a cask or barrel designed to hold spirits, can be traced through a variety of languages, including Old and Middle English, but also to Middle Irish, Irish, and Gaelic. The *OED* concludes: "Origin uncertain; apparently not originally Latin or Romanic." This blurring of etymology results in the disaffection and foreignness that unsettle both Stephen and his dean in this scene and reveals multiple layers of colonial impact: the Englishman fails to recog-nize the Englishness of the word; the Irishman does not apprehend its Gaelic origins. Thus this English language, already a hybrid tongue, may not be comfortably claimed—or disowned—by either man. By revealing language's predilection for absorbing, evolving, and, finally, "returning not the same" (*U* 13.1103–4), Joyce demonstrates that the cultural text is an extraordinarily complex and dynamic phenomenon, one incapable of being harnessed by any singular political ideology.

Throughout the first few episodes of *Ulysses,* Stephen continues to read the signs of Ireland's self-betrayal and tentatively begins to challenge the discourse of cultural essentialism. Stephen's encounter with Garrett Deasy in the "Nestor" episode is clearly related to his run-in with Wells on the schoolyard at Clongowes; both scenes exhibit the "pathologies of power" Said has identified in colonized cultures that replicate self-oppressive structures (223). Spoo has carefully outlined Joyce's admitted use of his-tory as the episode's structural trope: "Nestor" opens with Stephen's list-less attempts to teach ancient history to the equally disengaged Dalkey boys and is punctuated with his Blakean meditations on the fictive nature of historical narrative and its implicit subjectivity. The lines Stephen recollects from Blake's *The Marriage of Heaven and Hell* serve as a useful epigram for framing Deasy's paradoxical rendition of history; at times parts of his tale are indeed "fabled by the daughters of memory," but at others, "it was in some way if not as memory fabled it" (*U* 2.7–8). Whereas the Catholic Wells and the other magistrates' sons appropriate an English class structure in order to subdue Stephen, Deasy, a Protestant unionist, appropriates Irish history to vindicate his British sympathies and bend Stephen to his will. Joyce juxtaposes Deasy's rewriting of Anglo-Protestant history in Ireland—with its unabashed elision of Catholic persecution—with Stephen's decidedly more bloody recollections of Catholics massacred at Irish Protestant or British hands at Armagh and Wexford and the economic pillage of Catholic landowners. Although Stephen is reluctant to contradict Deasy openly (the watchful eye of "Albert Edward, prince of Wales" [*U* 2.266–67] hangs over the mantelpiece, and his gold is in Stephen's pocket), Stephen here makes his first attempt to awaken the Irish conscience. Stephen mounts a challenge—a rather tentative, nervous challenge but a challenge nonetheless—to Deasy's sanitized appropriation of Irish colonial history, calling it "a nightmare from which I am trying to awake" (*U* 2.377).[16] In distinctly Tennysonian tones that recall the "glorious" British histories written by Thomas Babington Macaulay and other imperialists, Deasy justifies British colonial designs as manifest destiny, ordained by God; Stephen asserts the uncomfortable perspective of one positioned on the nightmarish receiving end of these conquests. That Stephen is quitting his job here is as significant as his refusal in *Portrait* to turn over his snuffbox to Wells; however, both gestures of rebellion are rendered ineffectual in the face of powerful political discourses that intend to silence all dissenting voices.

Stephen's reading of the tropes of nativistic self-oppression and his recognition of their hegemonic subtexts mature steadily throughout *Portrait* and *Ulysses,* culminating in "Scylla and Charybdis," where Stephen makes his boldest attempt to awaken the conscience of Ireland by forcing it to recognize the narrowness of its own definitions of both Irishness and art. Having experienced the despotism of Catholics at Clongowes and the sting of exploitation by a Protestant unionist in "Nestor," Stephen in this episode undergoes trial by a third representative of the "pathologies of power"—the members of the Irish Literary Revival. Predicated on the need to forge the nation's unified spiritual essence through literature, the Revival constituted, in Stephen's eyes, yet another attempt to rewrite Irish political history by exclusion and elision. As we have seen, the literary movement with Yeats at its head originally wanted to promote art that was "Irish in spirit" and "English in language"; Stephen's objection is rooted not in the movement's desire to create an Irish literature in English but instead involves the moral restrictions that the Revival had begun to levy upon the freedom of its artists under the influence of George Russell (A.E.). In spite of its initial claims to transcend factionalism, the Literary Revival's agenda became increasingly narrow and moralistic, a shift condemned by Yeats and supported by Russell, who, by June 1904, had become progressively more insistent that the principal function of Irish art should be to restore and represent the spiritual purity of the nation.[17]

When Russell, along with Maud Gonne and Douglas Hyde (all vice presidents of the Irish National Theatre Society since its establishment in 1902) took offense at the unflattering depictions of the Irish peasantry in John Millington Synge's *In the Shadow of the Glen* and resigned their offices after its production in October 1903,[18] Yeats (the society's president) publicly chastised the preference of his colleagues for rhetoric over art, writing:

> A community that is opinion-ridden, even when those opinions are in themselves noble, is likely to put its creative minds into some sort of a prison. If creative minds preoccupy themselves with incidents from the political history of Ireland, so much the better, but we must not enforce them to select those incidents. . . . Above all, we must not say that certain incidents which have been a part of literature in all other lands are forbidden to us. It may be our duty . . . to bring new kinds of subjects into the theatre, but it cannot be our duty to make the bounds of drama narrower. . . . Literature must take the responsibility of its power, and keep all its freedom. . . . ("An Irish National Theatre" 389–90)

For his pains, Yeats was accused of withdrawing into aestheticism; John Eglinton later charged him with omitting "all moral seriousness" from his faction of the Revivalist movement.[19] In an April 1904 letter to Russell, Yeats further detailed the philosophical split that had emerged between them. Russell's collection of younger poets' verse, *New Songs,* had appeared in March 1904 and drew sharp criticism from Yeats, who believed the poems to be overly sentimental and generally lacking in talent and discipline: Yeats noted that the "dominant mood [of sentimentality] in many of them is one I have faught [*sic*] in my self & put down" (*Collected Letters* 576–77). In the same missive, Yeats suggests that Russell ultimately cared less for art than for rhetoric: "I am nothing but an artist," Yeats wrote, "& my life is in written words & they get the most of my loves & hates. . . . You are the other side of the penny, for you are admirably careful in speech [*sic*], having set life before art, too much before it as I think for one who is, in spite of himself perhaps, an artist" (*Collected Letters* 576). Yeats is even more blunt in his 1922 recollection of the relationship, published in "The Trembling of the Veil"; here he accuses Russell's moral enthusiasm of rendering him a "bad literary critic" responsible for fostering the "poetical commonplace" (245, 243). In short, Yeats believed that Russell's unrelenting insistence on theosophical transcendence and spiritually pure peasants as the sole suitable subjects of Irish literature had blinded his artistic judgment: as Yeats described it, Russell "demand[ed] plays and poems where the characters must attain a stature of seven feet, and resent[ed] as something perverse and morbid all abatement from that measure" ("Trembling" 245–46).

In the "Scylla and Charybdis" episode of *Ulysses,* Russell's *New Songs* has not yet appeared; Don Gifford and Robert Seidman suggest that Joyce either could have mistaken the publication date or that he may have been trying to reveal Thomas Lyster's detachment from contemporary events, as he is the source of information regarding A.E.'s publishing plans (212). It is much more likely, however, that Joyce created the anachronism to critique both Russell and his faction's artistic judgment. Russell had left Joyce's own poetry out of the volume, even though he had access to the young poet's work: Joyce wrote to his brother Stanislaus in February 1903 (before he began the *Dubliners* stories in 1904) that he had left a manuscript in Russell's care when he departed for Paris; Joyce had also returned to Dublin in April 1903 because of his mother's illness, and would have been enough of a local presence to have been included in the collection. While Joyce's annoyance with Russell and Yeats is palpable in several letters,[20] *Ulysses* reflects the ultimate respect that Joyce bore Yeats as an artist as well as his utter disdain for Russell's moralistic usurpation of the literary movement that excluded both himself and his protagonist.[21]

While Joyce's early essay "The Day of the Rabblement" (1901) excoriates the Irish Literary Theatre for selling out to popular sentiment in producing Hyde's Irish-language play, *Casad-an-Sugan,* and Yeats's *Diarmuid and Grania* (coauthored with George Moore), it treads carefully around Yeats, praising the theater's first offering (which included the Yeats play, *The Countess Cathleen,* which inspired the near riot recorded in *Portrait* for its unfavorable depictions of the peasantry [226]). The essay also acknowledges Joyce's respect for Yeats's *The Wind among the Reeds* and *The Adoration of the Magi*: the latter work, especially, "shows what Mr. Yeats can do when he breaks with the half-gods. But an aesthete has a floating will, and Mr. Yeats's treacherous instinct of adaptability must be blamed for his recent association with a platform from which even self-respect should have urged him to refrain" (*CW* 71). Ultimately, it is this predilection for expediency and vacillation that Joyce seems to have disdained in Yeats; his respect for Yeats's artistic accomplishment rarely flagged.[22]

Significantly, Yeats is absent from the gathering in "Scylla and Charybdis"; Stephen confronts not Yeats's faction of the Literary Revival but Russell's. Joyce is clear about the distinction: Russell appears in the episode as a peasant-glorifying populist, surrounded in Stephen's imagination by the trappings of theosophical mysticism. Yeats, by contrast, is recognized as the patron of art, not ideology (we hear, for instance, that he has admired Padraic Colum's line, "*As in wild earth a Grecian vase*" [*U* 9.304–5]), and it is Yeats's position that Stephen defends: real literature must not become the servant of either proscriptive moralism or dictatorial nationalism.[23] Here Stephen makes his own most pointed attempt to accomplish *Portrait*'s mission, reaching and defining Ireland's conscience. This is the most animated Stephen we have seen—or will see—in *Ulysses*. He "rudely" (*U* 9.228) and "boldly" (*U* 9.670) challenges his listeners with "tingling energy" (*U* 9.147), cheers himself on and holds at bay the "Nestor" doubt that feared a "back kick" from history. Now he holds at bay those anxieties: "What the hell are you driving at?" asks the voice of self-doubt. "I know. Shut up. Blast you. I have reasons" (*U* 9.846–47). Stephen brings all his intellectual weapons to bear against this movement, which would create a literature that values political moralism before all else, endeavoring to make its representatives—Russell, Eglinton, Best, Lyster—acknowledge the damage caused to real art and to the nation by their exclusivity and insularity. Stephen's primary tactic is a re-vision of Shakespeare: not to reject him as a literary model but to expose the inconsistencies between Anglo-Ireland's rhetoric and its valorization of the English bard. Stephen makes three points about the playwright that are completely antithetical to the goals of Russell's Irish Revival: first, that Shakespeare glorified not the peasantry but the elite classes to which he himself belonged; second, that he represented in his art not the virtue of the English race but its corrupted chastity, which he had experienced first-hand (as both cuckold and adulterer); and third, that he promoted an agenda that propelled England's imperialist aims and encouraged the subjugation of the colonial populace. Stephen drives home his first two points:

> Twenty years he lived in London and, during part of that time, he drew a salary equal to that of the lord chancellor of Ireland. His life was rich. His art, more than the art of feudalism, . . . is the art of surfeit. . . . Twenty years he dallied there between conjugal love and its chaste delights and scortatory love and its foul pleasures. You know Manningham's story of the burgher's wife who bade Dick Burbage to her bed after she had seen him in *Richard III* and how Shakespeare, overhearing, . . . took the cow by the horns and, when Burbage came knocking the gate, answered from the capon's blankets: *William the conqueror came before Richard III*. (U 9.623–37)

Stephen illustrates his third point, the linchpin of his theory, through his historicized reading of Shakespeare as a jingoist whose work stoked the fires of British imperialism. Stephen twice connects the bard to the Boer War (1899–1902), Britain's effort most contemporary to *Ulysses* to expand its empire. Stephen accuses Shakespeare's histories of "sail[ing] fullbellied on a tide of Mafeking enthusiasm" (U 9.753–54) and equates the Norwegian conquest of the Danes in Shakespeare with the British subjugation of the Dutch Boers: "*Khaki* Hamlets don't hesitate to shoot," he tells his audience (U 9.133–35, my emphasis). Stephen's choice of metaphor is particularly inflammatory given his audience of Dublin nationalists, who generally supported the cause of the Boers against British aggression. The point of all this posturing, of course, is to make these worshippers of England's most acclaimed dramatist recognize that their own literary standards—which idolized both the peasantry and national virtue in the service of a proscriptive anticolonial ethos—would have silenced him. The parallels to Stephen's own exclusion from this Revival are clear; that he does not believe his own theory is entirely consistent with his argument. Stephen here appropriates the Revival's strictures and applies them to Shakespeare's art in order to reveal the Revival's narrowness; Stephen tries to get his audience to admit that no restrictions—moral, religious, political, or linguistic—should be placed on the artist as he attempts to record the life of the nation. Such freedom does not preclude the artist from rendering ideologically charged or even tendentious subjects, but his primary mission is to represent life as he sees it, unencumbered by any other "purpose." The unrelenting emphasis of Stephen's theory on the material facts of the artist's life suggests—in contrast to Russell's aestheticized claim that art's "formless spiritual essences" must be isolated from such facts (*U* 9.49, 185)—that all facets of life, and all ideas, can be important to the artist, that nothing should be excluded from the artist's sphere. Stephen concludes that Shakespeare's genius flourished precisely because he was not beholden to any exclusivist dogma; instead, "*[a]ll* events brought grist to his mill" (*U* 9.748, my emphasis). If Stephen disbelieves the material realism that his theory propounds, it is a sign, perhaps, that a vestige of *Portrait*'s romantic aestheticism (which I will discuss in chapter 3) remains with him still; he may be trying to convince his audience as well as himself of the need for a theory of art that is independent of all ties.

What begins as Stephen's most engaged campaign to reach the Irish conscience turns into his most crushing defeat. Russell walks out before he is half-finished; his remaining listeners begin to associate him with Oscar Wilde, the Irish-born satirist who turned his looking-glass on English society with disastrous personal consequences. Richard Best's empty-headed enthusiasm for Wilde and Stephen serves to cheapen each, and Stephen chafes: "Tame essence of Wilde" (*U* 9.531–32). What Stephen rejects here is the superficial understanding these Revivalists have for what Wilde really represents, both to him and to Ireland. As Margot Norris has pointed out, Stephen conceives of Wilde as a symbol of colonial oppression (*Joyce's Web* 63); he has refashioned Wilde's "Decay of Lying" aphorism into the "cracked lookingglass of a *servant*," emphasizing not the rebellious sarcasm of Wilde's social satires but his subjugation to the Crown, his role as "jester at the court of his master" (*U* 2.44).[24] For Stephen, Wilde becomes not only that vision of Ireland that prostitutes itself by trading allegiances and degrading its art, but the bizarre spectacle of his trial, precipitated by the treachery of an English lover, also becomes a symbol of the Irish-born writer's betrayal by the Crown he serves. Stephen, unlike Wilde, has chosen not to press his art into anyone's service but his own; Wilde's ultimate humiliation by his adoptive society, his death as a destitute man—whether precipitated by his subjugation or by his rebellion—registers for Stephen the futility of both alternatives. Wilde's fate resonates with irony for Stephen as he confronts a similar choice—to serve the Revival on its own terms and betray his art or to work against it and risk its wrath. These, then, are the high stakes of this scene: if Stephen is unable to change the attitudes of the Revival, he is left either to degrade his muse and join the movement (which he will not do) or to go his own way in obscurity. As Wilde's example demonstrates, either option is sure to exact great personal cost.

Just as Wilde ultimately was exiled by the citizenry of his adoptive country, so also is Stephen dismissed in this scene by the Anglo-Irish nationalists who evince an intellectual form of the self-defeating, political isolationism that the Citizen will display in "Cyclops." L. H. Platt notes Stephen's acute sense of ostracism in this scene: "The Shakespeare theory is the articulation of a dispossessed Catholic, ill at ease in his country's National Library, addressing the luminaries of the Anglo-Irish intelligentsia who are shaping Ireland's literary resurgence. Most are polite enough to listen; all seem determined to exclude him from their charmed circle" (265). Stephen is never invited to join the evening's gathering of Irish literati at Moore's, nor is he a contender to author the national epic—consensus has determined "Moore is the man for it" (U 9.309–10). As Stephen rises to depart the library chamber with Mulligan, his failure to raise the conscience of the Revival and secure its acknowledgment of himself as an Irish artist is reiterated by Eglinton's benediction: "We shall see you tonight. . . . Notre ami Moore says *Malachi Mulligan* must be there" (U 9.1098–99, my emphasis). Stephen wonders, "What have I learned? Of them? Of me?" (U 9.1113). "Cease to strive" (U 9.1221) is Stephen's acknowledgment of his defeat at the hands of his tormentors and marks his weary surrender of his *Portrait* pledge to create an independent Irish conscience.

Of course, Joyce did not hold England blameless for Irish political chaos, yet even when he presents the British presence, he refuses to allow Ireland to forfeit responsibility for its plight. In "Circe," a drunken and despairing Stephen broods over his own fate and his country's as he confronts the fourth and final contender for ascendancy in colonial Ireland: the British Crown. Face to face with two surly redcoats, Stephen echoes Yeats's Cathleen ni Houlihan, who despaired of British "strangers" in her house. A few pages later, Stephen's mind conjures Cathleen's very image in the form of "Old Gummy Granny": "You met with poor old Ireland and how does she stand?" the crone asks him (U 15.4587–88). Stephen's meetings with Ireland have convinced him, sadly, that her betrayal lies in her own intransigence. Stephen's cries resurrect images of familial deceit and self-victimization: "I know you, gammer! Hamlet, revenge! The old sow that eats her farrow!" (U 15.4582–83). When Private Carr decks Stephen because of the insult he perceives to Edward

VII, Stephen begins to mumble another of Yeats's early poems about self-betrayal as he regains consciousness. "Who Goes with Fergus?" evokes the ancient Irish king who foolishly relinquished his throne and his sovereignty to his stepson, Conchubar, and never regained them. The lines represent Joyce's unrelenting refusal to allow colonial Ireland the fruitless luxury of "fulminat[ion] against . . . English tyranny" (CW 173). Like Fergus, Ireland has betrayed itself by twice forfeiting its sovereignty, a fact Joyce is careful to point out in his Triestine lectures. Even more important, however, Ireland's own citizens continue to practice that moral and intellectual intolerance first demonstrated at *Portrait*'s Christmas dinner, which renders true nation-ness an impossibility. The latter point is made abundantly clear when Carr attacks Stephen; of the mob in attendance, only Bloom comes to Stephen's defense; the rest fight among themselves:

A Hag

What call had the redcoat to strike the gentleman and he under the influence. Let them go and fight the Boers!

The Bawd

Listen to who's talking! Hasn't the soldier a right to go with his girl? He gave him the coward's blow.

(They grab at each other's hair, claw at each other and spit.) (U 15.4758–64)

Again, the gendering of the scene helps to strengthen its theme of Ireland's self-betrayal. The principal female figure in this scene is the prostitute; the implications of the trope for Irish nation-ness are clear: defiled by their colonial oppressors, Cissy Caffrey, Biddy the Clap, and Cunty Kate nevertheless side with the British soldiers over a native Irishman; the voice of the bawd goes so far as to claim, "The red's as good as the green. And better. Up the soldiers! Up King Edward!" (U 15.4519–20). In such a setting, the true Irish artist can only loll semiconscious on the pavement, nursing a sore jaw.

In his final confrontation with the pathologies of power that vied to control colonial Ireland, then, Stephen's defeat is complete; he has been silenced by all: Irish Catholics, Protestant unionists, Protestant nationalists, and British soldiers. Unlike Joyce, Stephen will never be a successful Irish writer; Stephen recognizes the forces that would constrain his art and his thought and attempts to vanquish their influence, but he is finally unable to make his voice heard over those who would employ the discourses of Irishness and nationality to suppress it. To Stephen as well as to Joyce, each restrictive dogma, adapted from the colonizer and deployed by the Irish against their own, constitutes a betrayal of both the artist and the nation—the political discourse that presumes to dictate authenticity and "Irishness" to Stephen Dedalus ironically silences the voice of Irish nationness as violently and effectively as Private Carr's fist.

2

"Religions of Unbelief"

Spiritual Orthodoxies and Romantic Dissent

Despite strong feelings about Ireland's postcolonial fate, Joyce believed that the despotism of the Roman Catholic Church was ultimately a more diffusive, destructive force in his native country than any tyranny perpetrated by the British Empire (CW 173). Again, Stephen Dedalus becomes his model for the devastating effects of uncountered excess; regardless of his early disavowals of Church tenets, in *Portrait* and *Ulysses* Stephen continues to manifest the inexorable influence of religious indoctrination in Victorian and Edwardian Ireland. Even as he consciously determines to "fly by those nets" of nationality, language, and religion in fulfillment of his artistic calling (*P* 203), Stephen subconsciously is still deeply entangled in those dogmas that he would reject. His companion Cranly points out what critics have since confirmed:[1] "it is a curious thing, . . . how your mind is supersaturated with the religion in which you say you disbelieve" (*P* 240). Even Buck Mulligan recognizes the intensity of the indoctrination that continues to plague Stephen into *Ulysses:* "They [the priests of the Catholic Church] drove his [Stephen's] wits astray by visions of hell. He will never capture the Attic note. . . . That is his tragedy. He can never be a poet" (*U* 10.1072–74). In contrast with the cleaner and more decisive break that Stephen makes with the Church in *Stephen Hero,* in *Portrait* Joyce represents his protagonist as unsteady in his disbelief, a shift that testifies to the insidious impact of Catholicism on the artist's subjectivity. In *Stephen Hero,* Daedalus tells Cranly that he has left the Church because he refuses any longer to submit to its authority; Stephen's criticism is rooted in an essential desire to "do as I please" (*SH* 140), unrestrained by religious taboos, as well as in the hypocrisy he believes he has uncovered in the institution; the Catholics of his association "don't believe in [Jesus]; they don't observe his precepts" (*SH* 141). Such ideas give way in *Portrait* to less strident convictions clearly riddled with uncertainty; Stephen seems less sure of his own disbelief than he is of the doctrines he attempts to disavow. He confesses, when prodded by Cranly, to be "not at all sure" that "our religion is *false* and that Jesus was not the son of God" (*P* 243, my emphasis). To be unsure of a belief's falsity is quite a different matter from doubting its veracity; the first alternative implies not fundamental skepticism but essential conviction. Stephen in *Portrait* turns agnostic rather than atheistic, uncertain of the possibility of knowing God but stopping far short of absolutely denying God's existence.[2] Such interrogation of belief but unwillingness to banish it aligns Stephen with the tumultuous religious attitudes of the nineteenth century, a period marked not only by the multiple crises of faith spawned by scientific rationalism but also by intense intellectual struggles against the spiritual hegemony perpetrated by dominant faiths such as Catholicism and Anglicanism. Romantic poets such as Blake, Byron, and Shelley began the epoch questioning the ascendance of the Anglican Church and its construction of God, while Victorian society, as G. M. Young has observed, would exist on the cusp of a double paradox, avowing "practical ideals that were at odds with its religious professions, and . . . religious belief . . . at issue with its intelligence" (34). The resultant angst led to a search for other means of spiritual fulfillment: "Those Victorians whose doubts had carried them beyond the harbor of a church cried out for a *new* faith that would end their distress of mind," observes Walter Houghton (97). This "new faith" took a variety of forms; in the midcentury work of Tennyson's *In Memoriam* and the ecclesiastical writings of John Henry Newman, it simply affirmed that doubt could coexist with and even strengthen the force of original, elemental creeds. But later in the period, dispossessed intellectuals flocked in increasing numbers to other forms of romantic spiritualism that undercut Christian teleology, such as Helena Blavatsky's theosophical mysticism and Friedrich Nietzsche's humanistic apostasy. Thus Stephen's "crisis of faith," along with his subsequent failed encounters with dissidence, is an essentially Victorian experience with its genesis in romantic precursors. To read Stephen's agnosticism as a purely self-generated event—no doubt Stephen's own preference, as Kershner has noted (9)—is to ignore the impact on the young Dedalus of a century's struggle with religious hegemony and nonconformity.

In this chapter I will argue that Joyce's novels critique ever more clearly Stephen's investment in a romantic ethos as he attempts to liberate himself from the Church's discursive orthodoxy. Stephen intends his selective appropriations of the Romantic poets (Blake, Byron, Shelley), as well as his dabblings in the spiritual romanticism represented by sources as diverse as Newman's theology, Blavatsky's theosophy, and Nietzsche's prophecy, to serve as models for a personal dissent that would light the road to intellectual and artistic freedom. However, these romanticisms reveal themselves to be, at best, insufficient to the task; at worst, they are themselves exposed as enemies of heterodoxy. In this chapter I will detail the romanticisms that permeate Stephen's consciousness from *Portrait* through *Ulysses* as well as his changing responses to these discourses; I will also examine Joyce's exposure of the ultimate failure of romantic idealism as an artistic model in the modern world. Joyce once remarked to Arthur Power: "In realism you are down to facts on which the world is based: that sudden reality which smashes romanticism into a pulp. What makes most people's lives unhappy is some disappointed romanticism, some unrealizable or misconceived ideal. In fact you may say that idealism is the ruin of man, and if we lived down to fact, . . . we would be better off. . . . In *Ulysses* I tried to keep close to fact" (Power 98). As the idealism of *Portrait* gives way to the realism of *Ulysses* and Stephen Dedalus moves from one text into the next, the remnants of both an unresolved romanticism and an unvanquished Catholicism continue to envelop him and impede his progress toward intellectual and artistic independence.

The work of the Romantic poets conveys a pervasively deep distrust and ultimate rejection of the Church as an institution as they revised the neoclassical belief in God as inventor and master of a supremely ordered universe. Though subject to individual philosophical differences, these poets shared a core belief in the intuitive mind of the artist to generate a powerfully redemptive creativity in harmony with the natural environment.[3] And because the Romantics believed that the Church stifled the creative impulse they claimed to be their final redeemer, they ultimately renounced the institution. Most did not, however, completely dismiss the idea of God (Shelley would be their only avowed atheist); rather, they repudiated the Church's conception of a rigid, passionless deity whose only design was chastisement, "to impress on men the fear of death, to teach / Trembling & fear, terror, constriction, abject selfishness" (Blake, *Milton* 2.43, lines 415–16). As Stephen Dedalus endeavors to construct his own cartographies of dissent, he first looks toward the tenets of Romantic rebellion: from Blake he derives a suspicion of doctrinal order and suppression; from Byron and even from Newman, his two favorite writers (*P* 80–81), Stephen adopts the stance of the outcast hero who attempts to exile himself from the institutions that define and confine him; from Shelley (as much as from Aquinas) he acquires significant portions of the aesthetic with which he endeavors to replace his Catholicism. Yet in each case, Stephen's application of his models is subconsciously flawed in a way that subverts his wished-for sedition; such fissures highlight the power of the dogma that governs his subjectivity and anticipate his pronouncement to Haines within the context of *Ulysses:* "You behold in me . . . a horrible example of free thought" (*U* 1.625–26). The term "free thought" initially implied an intellectual liberation from Christian doctrine; in its Victorian/ Edwardian context it had evolved to include a somewhat broader skepticism directed at social as well as religious orthodoxies.[4] Stephen's remark further demarcates a shift in attitude between *Stephen Hero,* where the President accuses Stephen of "modern freethinking" in reference to his artistic theory, an assessment that this Stephen proudly accepts (*SH* 91), and *Portrait,* where the dean of studies makes the same judgment but the young artist points out the paradox of the label and hesitates to accept it: "I . . . am sure that there is no such thing as free thinking inasmuch as all thinking must be bound by its own laws" (*P* 187). The *Ulysses* exchange suggests not only that Stephen's suspicion in *Portrait* —that "free thought" might be in fact an illogical misnomer—has been borne out by his recent experience; it also underscores the implausibility of his intellectual liberation within this society.

Joyce's critical writings and conversations with contemporaries reveal his interest both in British Romanticism as a phenomenon and in Blake as a representative figure of the period's "spiritual rebellion" (*CW* 215). Blake argues that only through the imagination—and the poetry it creates—can humans be united with God; he concludes in "There Is No Natural Religion": "If it were not for the Poetic or Prophetic character the Philosophic & Experimental would soon be at the ratio of all things, & stand still, unable to do other than repeat the same dull round over again" (49). Thus human imagination is equated with regeneration and salvation; without poetic vision, we would be forever limited to the insufficient—and lifedenying, Blake claims—products of the rational mind. Repression of imagination and the stifling of desire—both sexual and poetic—are for Blake the most heinous of sins, as he reveals in his satirical treatise, *The Marriage of Heaven and Hell.* Here Blake upends conventional constructions of Good ("the passive that obeys Reason") and Evil ("the active springing from Energy") and disputes the Church's claim that "Good is Heaven. Evil is Hell" (69). On the contrary, Blake argues: "Energy [that is, passion or desire] is the only life, and is from the Body. . . . Energy is Eternal Delight" (70). Against such denials of passion, Blake unleashes his most strident criticism. In *The Marriage of Heaven and Hell,* he writes: "Those who restrain desire, do so because theirs is weak enough to be restrained. . . . And being restrain'd, it by degrees becomes passive, till it is only the shadow of desire. The history of this is written in Paradise Lost, & the Governor or Reason is call'd Messiah. . . . But in the Book of Job, Milton's Messiah is call'd Satan" (*The Marriage of Heaven and Hell* 70). The institutionalized Church, with its conception of a stern, punishing, self-denying God—and Milton's representation of Him (Blake sees Milton's energetic, passionate Satan as the real God of *Paradise Lost*)—is the subject of Blake's invective in this passage.[5] Blake believed that religion had erroneously constructed God in its own celibate and rule-bound image, thus destroying the creator's life-affirming propensities. To overcome the threats to the creative consciousness posed by oppressive religiosity, Blake offers his prophetic poet, who "Present, Past, & Future, sees; / . . . Calling the lapsed Soul, / . . . And fallen, fallen light renew!" (*Songs of Experience*, 57). The redemptive power of the bard is also evident in *Milton;* Blake's poet there liberates Milton, God, and humankind by rewriting *Paradise Lost* and continually reiterates: "Mark well my words! They are of your eternal salvation" (1.2, line 25).

Stephen's dismissal in *Stephen Hero* of a Christ "too remote and too passionless" (*SH* 111–12) echoes the miscast Messiah whom Blake mocks throughout his canon. But the Stephen of *Portrait,* anticipating the failed poet of *Ulysses,* nearly succumbs to the suppression of the creative impulse that this icon would exact; certainly the ethos of sin and punishment resonates from the earliest segment of *Portrait* ("Pull out his eyes, / Apologise" [*P* 8]). The sermon of chapter 3, replete with its vivid depictions of the "eternity of pain" (*P* 131) that awaits those who refuse to serve this punishing God, mirrors the terrible restraint mandated by the false prophet Blake warns against. The effect of this rhetoric on Stephen, of course, is tremendous; significantly, he feels he has been condemned for the physical/sexual sins he has actually committed as well as those he has only imagined (*P* 115). Repenting, Stephen tries to curb the riot of his thoughts by focusing on "the one eternal omnipresent perfect reality" (*P* 150) in order to suppress his sexual desire as well as his creative impulse. He "mortifies" his senses, stymies his imagination by devoting every waking thought to "resolute piety" (*P* 147), and tries to "merge his life in the common tide of other lives" (*P* 151), thus sacrificing not only the raw materials of artistic creation but also the artist's privileged position above the crowd that the Romantics, Joyce, and Stephen himself believed to be necessary to artistic creation.[6] Stephen's assimilation to chastity, piety, and subservience is so convincing that he is recruited to join the priesthood. Though he finds the power of the office intoxicating, Stephen rejects the vocation because he discovers that this vision of conforming "Oneness"—

with its requisite submission and its purgation of passion—will not re-deem his soul but will instead engulf it menacingly:

> It was a grave and ordered and passionless life that awaited him, a life without material cares. He wondered . . . with what dismay he would wake the first morning in the dormitory. . . . At once from every part of his being unrest began to irradiate. *A feverish quicken-ing of his pulses followed and a din of meaningless words drove his reasoned thoughts hither and thither confusedly.* His lungs dilated and sank as if he were inhaling a warm moist unsustaining air and he smelt again the warm moist air which hung in the bath in Clongowes above the sluggish turfcoloured water. *Some instinct, waking at these memories, stronger than education or piety, quickened within him at every near approach to that life, an instinct subtle and hostile, and armed him against acquiescence.* The chill and order of the life repelled him. He saw himself rising in the cold of the morning and filing down with the others to early mass and trying vainly to struggle with his prayers. . . . What had come of the pride of his spirit which had always made him conceive himself as a being apart in every order? (*P* 160–61, my emphases)

Notably, it is not Stephen's reason but the energetic, instinctive reaction of his body in collusion with his imagination—its feverish pulse, its recol-lected sensations of immersion in the ditch at Clongowes—that momen-tarily saves Stephen from forfeiting what Joyce called, in an echo of Blake, "the eternal qualities [of] . . . the imagination and the sexual instinct" to "the formal life [that] tries to suppress both" (Power 74).

Significantly, as he rejects the Order of the Jesuits, Stephen now opts instead for Blakean passion and anarchical salvation: "His destiny was to be elusive of social or religious orders. . . . He smiled to think that it was this disorder, the misrule and confusion of his father's house . . . which was to win the day in his soul" (*P* 162). Once Stephen embraces disorder, he shortly realizes his true vocation as a poet, the Christ-like redeemer of himself: "What were they now but cerements shaken from the body of death—the fear he had walked in night and day, the incertitude that had ringed him round, the shame that had abased him within and without. . . . His soul had arisen from the grave of boyhood, spurning her grave-clothes. Yes! Yes! Yes! He would create proudly out of the freedom and power of his soul, as the great artificer whose name he bore, a living thing, new and soaring and beautiful, impalpable, imperishable" (*P* 169–80).

In spite of such enthusiasm, however, Stephen's appropriations of Blake do not always suggest that the artist is victorious over suppression. Although Stephen directly acknowledges Blake only once in *Portrait* (P 249), one of his most powerful declarations—"When the soul of man is born in this country there are nets flung at it to hold it back from flight. You talk to me of nationality, language, religion. I shall try to fly by those nets"(P 203)—has an important and ironic genesis in Blake that undercuts Stephen's possibilities of successful escape. In Blake's own rendition of the fall of Man, *The Book of Urizen,* reason (Urizen) and imagination (Los) are sundered; Urizen sequesters himself, creating the measures and "dividing rule[s]" that make his race miserable. Finally,

> a Web, dark & cold, throughout all
> The tormented element stretch'd
> From the sorrows of Urizen's soul.
> . . . .
> None could break the Web, no wings of fire,
> So twisted the cords, & so knotted
> The meshes, twisted like to the human brain.
> And all call'd it *The Net of Religion.* (*Urizen* 8.462–69, my emphasis)[7]

Stephen's invocation—"I shall try to fly by those nets"—not only reflects the extent to which Blake has colored his views of the Church's censorious disposition and the importance of the circumvening imagination of the artist, it also subconsciously suggests the possibility of entrapment within this net, whose filaments manage to constrain internally as well as externally. Its imagination vanquished, the world that Urizen creates is Stephen's own, a populace that is unable to hear or to see anything but that which perpetuates its own destruction: "their children wept, & built / Tombs in the desolate places, / And form'd laws of prudence, and call'd them / The eternal laws of God" (*Urizen* 9.498–501).

The difficulty of establishing dissidence in the face of the Church's overarching authority and predilection for punishing deviance is illustrated in *Portrait*'s earliest moments but nowhere so clearly as in the persecution of Stephen for committing "heresy" in his weekly essay. His English instructor at Belvedere, Mr. Tate, levies the accusation in front of the class: "It's about the Creator and the soul . . . *without a possibility of ever approaching nearer.* That's heresy" (P 79). Unlike the unfair pandying he successfully protests at Clongowes, Stephen here recognizes the folly of attempting either to appeal or dispute the matter, which strikes at the heart of Catholic doctrine/authority, in this particular venue. Instead of arguing the point, Stephen immediately offers a modification to his statement—"I meant *without a possibility of ever reaching*"—and notes with some relief that Tate is "appeased" by the change, perceiving it as "a submission" (*P* 79). But the confrontation is far from over; outside the classroom it becomes clear that Stephen in fact has offered his listeners only superficial acquiescence. Confronted by his classmates, Stephen declares John Henry Newman to be his favorite prosist and Lord Byron his favorite poet; both choices constitute acts of defiance on Stephen's part, though his tormentors perceive just one. Byron's profligacy was well known, but Newman, the Anglican minister–turned–Catholic priest, had been made a cardinal in 1879; nonetheless, he, along with Byron, provides an ironic model for Stephen's fledgling apostasy.

Even Heron, Boland, and Nash, who, Stephen insists, have never read Byron's poetry, are familiar with the infamous misbehavior of George Gordon, Lord Byron. But even if they had perused Byron's work, their judgments of him (as "a heretic and immoral too" and "a bad man" [*P* 81]) likely would have not have changed. Works like *Don Juan* and *Manfred* fly in the face of conventional sexual and religious mores; the hapless Don Juan is continually pursued by seemingly virtuous but sexually aggressive women, and *Manfred* constitutes an undeniable assertion of human will in the face of all powers, including priests ("I shall not choose a mortal to be my mediator," Manfred swears [3.1, lines 55–56]). But it is not Byron's antinomianism to which Stephen is most indebted. It is the brooding, self-exiled rebel who exists outside moral strictures—the Byronic hero—that Stephen seeks to imitate and that his choice reflects. Byron himself provided a loose model for the protagonists of his poems; he scandalized society by his incestuous relationship with, but genuine affection for, his half-sister, Augusta Leigh, and like Don Juan, delighted in flouting propriety with numerous trysts that he reported in letters to scandalized friends.[8] Like Childe Harold, Byron traveled extensively in Spain and Portugal; he later left England to live in Switzerland and Italy before dying of fever in Greece, where he had become involved with the independence movement. He vehemently defied all attempts by friends to reform his behavior or convert him to Christian teleology, as an 1811 missive suggests: "I will have nothing to do with your immortality; we are miserable enough in this life, without the absurdity of speculating upon another. . . . Let me live, well if possible, and die without pain. The rest is with God, who assuredly, had He *come* or *sent*, would have made Himself manifest to nations, and intelligible to all" (*Letters and Journals* 2.88).

In *Portrait*, the young Dedalus attempts to take the Byronic hero's defiance of conventional morality and his exile as the texts for his own life. Certainly Byron's example has had some impact on Stephen's passion for Emma Clery; early in the novel he begins a poem to her, heading up the page "To E—C—. He knew it was right to begin so for he had seen similar titles in the collected poems of Lord Byron" (*P* 70). Stephen's later fling with sexual promiscuity might also owe something to the widely circulating knowledge of Byron's romantic escapades. In sexual impropriety, Byron sought freedom from the conventionality of moral codes; Stephen believes that his own pursuit of carnality has similarly filled him with a liberating knowledge: he reflects, "His soul had [begun to live] when he had first sinned" (*P* 222). Stephen also tries to re-create in himself an image of Byron, the self-exiled wanderer, the outcast Childe Harold, the man who ponders both his own nobility and the degradation of the human condition. "I have not loved the world, nor the world me," Childe Harold proclaims (3.113, line 1049); it is an apt epigram for the career of Stephen Dedalus, whose exchange with Cranly makes clear Stephen's own determination to be an exile:

—I do not fear to be alone or to be spurned for another or to leave whatever I have to leave. And I am not afraid to make a mistake, even a great mistake, a lifelong mistake and perhaps as long as eternity too.

Cranly, now grave again, slowed his pace and said:

—Alone, quite alone. You have no fear of that. And you know what that word means? Not only to be separate from all others but to have not even one friend.

—I will take the risk, said Stephen. (*P* 247)

For Byron and for Stephen, there is freedom in defiance: Byron's *Prometheus* and his *Manfred* bear witness to this precept; Stephen believes his refusal to "serve that in which I no longer believe" will enable him to "express myself in some mode of life or art as freely as I can" (*P* 246–47). Given his indebtedness to the Romantic poet, then, Stephen's "I don't care what he [Byron] was" (*P* 81) to Heron and his fellow bullies is not quite accurate; while Stephen may indeed believe that Byron's heresy and immoral behavior should not give cause to dismiss his art, Stephen does care very much about "what Byron was" and models his own experience accordingly.[9]

Stephen's veneration of Cardinal John Henry Newman as "the greatest writer" of prose (*P* 80) to the boys who bully him is understood by them to be a sign of Stephen's capitulation to the judgment of the schoolmaster ("Tate made you buck up the other day . . . about the heresy in your essay" [*P* 81]) and a recognition of their own ability to intimidate him into compliance.[10] When Stephen answers "Newman" to their question, Boland responds, "Is it *Cardinal* Newman?" As Stephen replies in the affirmative, "the grin broadened on Nash's freckled face," and he repeats both the question and the designator of priestly authority: "And do you like *Cardinal* Newman, Dedalus?" (*P* 80, my emphasis). Jill Muller has suggested, contra Ellmann, that there is more to Stephen's choice (and Joyce's approbation) of the cardinal than literary style;[11] Muller suggests that Stephen's championship is sourced in Newman's advocacy of a "liberal" Catholic education and a program of study in which theology would form not a centerpiece but "one of the many components" of a well-rounded curriculum (595).[12] While this is perhaps too sophisticated a reading to explain Stephen's affection for Newman at this relatively early age (his contemporaries, after all, will beat him with a cabbage stump and make him cry), this episode in which Stephen's creative issue, his essay, is condemned on grounds of moral offense certainly can be read as a formative moment in the development of his aesthetic theory, which will claim that art should not be forced to propound any specific dogma. Stephen's early choice of Newman in fact does not signify compliance with Catholicism's authority. Instead, it indicates a further attempt to embrace and enact a Romantic dissent that ultimately fails him.

John Henry Newman is the midcentury figure who best spans the divide between Romantic imagination and Victorian intellectualism; Newman's theological position, which attacks the Victorian premise that belief and intellect were necessarily at odds, argues that assent is based not on logic but on intuition. In 1841 Newman penned a letter to the *Times* that outlined his position: "The ascendancy of Faith may be impracticable, but the reign of Knowledge is incomprehensible. . . . The heart is commonly reached, not through the reason, but through the imagination. . . . After all, man is *not* a reasoning animal; he is a seeing, feeling, contemplating, acting animal. . . . [Religion] has never been a deduction from what we know: it has ever been an assertion of what we are to believe" ("Secular Knowledge" 166–69). Even though he is speaking from a position within the Church as the Romantics had always declined to do, Newman's elevation of intuition over reason as the seat of faith is certainly a Romantic (and specifically Blakean) idea; it is echoed in Stephen's thoughts as he stands on the library steps in *Portrait* and ponders "how the creatures of the air have their knowledge and know their times and seasons because they, unlike man, are in the order of their life and have not perverted that order by reason" (*P* 224–25).

Newman's teleology has suggested to Stephen that humans have "perverted that [intuitive] order [of life] by reason," but as the curious conflation of mythological figures in his thoughts indicates, Stephen is also subconsciously aware of the ways in which intuition might be manipulated by external forces to suppress the artist's creative spirit. He thinks of his Greek namesake, Daedalus, who not only escaped the confinement of the labyrinth but also was its creator, and of Thoth, "the god of writers," whose role in Egyptian mythology was to weigh the heart of the dead before the final judgment of Osiris (Gifford 267). When Stephen considers the order that circumscribes him and anticipates his moment of escape, his contemplation reveals it to be a naturalized construction, a product of dogma rather than a natural order: "he was about to leave for ever the house of prayer and prudence into which he had been born and the order of life out of which he had come" (*P* 225).

Because Newman embraces with such fervor the very Church Stephen wants to reject, one might readily assume Stephen disdains Newman's writings as well, most of which deal with theology. But Stephen's absorption of Newman has less to do with his Catholicism than it does with Newman's personal history of ostracism and dissent. *Portrait* records two specific moments of Stephen's identification with this Catholic priest: first, Stephen empathizes with the recurring theme of dispossession in Newman's work. Stephen exudes a growing sense of isolation throughout *Portrait* that continues into *Ulysses* and thinks specifically of Newman at the moment of yet another impending displacement of his family. In the news given to him by younger siblings, Stephen hears a "recurring note of weariness and pain. All seemed weary of life even before entering upon it. And he remembered that Newman had heard this note also" (*P* 164). Newman's 1848 novel, *Loss and Gain*, is the story of the sacrifice and isolation of clergyman's son Charles Reding, who converted to Roman Catholicism, and Newman's essay that recounts his own 1845 conversion, *Apologia pro vita sua*, also records painful exclusion. "Large classes of men" believed "that I was for years where I had no right to be," Newman writes in the *Apologia*. "[They believed] that I was a 'Romanist' in Protestant livery and service; that I was doing the work of a hostile Church in the bosom of the English Enlightenment, and knew it, or ought to have known it" (xxiv–xxv). This sense of fraudulence and dispossession also reverberates through the young Stephen's experience. As early as his arrival at Clongowes Stephen acutely senses his exclusion from the society of boys; having neither name nor family position to gain him admittance to their circle, Stephen fabricates connections for himself: "You told the Clongowes gentry you had an uncle a judge and an uncle a general in the army" (U 3.105–6). His pretense pays off with the boys, who take his part and encourage him to seek justice from Father Conmee after Father Dolan wrongfully accuses him of breaking his glasses to avoid schoolwork. Dolan's suspicion, epithets, and pandying are echoed in Heron's attack on him for heresy ("Admit! repeated Heron, striking him again with his cane across the calf of the leg" [P 78]); in both scenes, Stephen faces off with accusers who suspect him of shamming; in the latter he is charged—perhaps rightfully—with committing heresy in his weekly composition. He is reminded again of the ostracism his ideas and his poverty have produced; upon Tate's accusation, Stephen suddenly "was conscious of failure and of detection, of the squalor of his own mind and home, and felt against his neck the raw edge of his turned and jagged collar" (P 79). Though Stephen quietly makes the change to his paper his English master insists upon, the class is more skeptical of his pretended ignorance and "was not so soon appeased" (P 79). Neither was Newman's audience easily pacified when he shifted allegiances from the Anglican to the Catholic Church in 1848; Newman's Tractarian activities, viewed in hindsight as seditious attempts to Romanize the Church of England, continued to stir powerful sentiments even sixteen years later when Charles Kingsley published his famous attacks on Newman in *MacMillan's Magazine*. That Stephen senses the parallel of his situation to Newman's history is clear as Heron, Boland, and Nash begin to torment him on Clonliffe Road. Stephen declares Newman to be his favorite prosist, but the irony of his selection is left unremarked by his audience. Although his attackers are momentarily appeased by his choice of the cardinal, Stephen's selection in no way mitigates his own position as a fledgling nonconformist: certainly no more heretical figure than Newman could have existed for the Church of England in the late 1800s, and Stephen, like Newman, has at this early moment begun to explore the cartographies of dissent from a position within his Church. Stephen's selection of Byron as his favorite poet is simply a less subtle choice than Newman; it provides Stephen's tormentors with the evidence they need to flail him for his "heretical" opinions and exposes the difficulties of overt dissent.

In addition to Newman's history as a rebel within his Church, Stephen also admires his literary technique—his "cloistral silverveined prose" (P 176)—as well as his strategies of refutation and argumentation. Stephen's appreciation of Newman's skill in composition is not surprising; the young poet's own fixation on language is particularly close to a trait he has identified in Newman: the understanding that specific words may be variously employed—with repercussions in connotation—in distinctly different contexts. Newman's semantical gifts often generated criticism from his contemporaries, especially Kingsley. During one of their many terse exchanges in *MacMillan's* in 1864, Newman claimed that Kingsley had mistaken a phrase in one of Newman's Anglican sermons, to which Kingsley sarcastically replied: "No man knows the use of words better than Dr. Newman; no man, therefore has a better right to define what he does, or does not, mean by them" (rpt. in Svaglic 347). From *Portrait's* earliest pages Stephen obsesses over words and the mutability of meaning—"That was a belt round his pocket. And belt was also to give a fellow a belt" (*P* 9)—and so Newman's argument (which also appears in the essay "Literature" in *The Idea of a University*) that a word may be deployed differently in different contexts no doubt resonates with Stephen. Muller has argued that the conversations regarding the "liberal" and the "useful" arts that take place in *Stephen Hero* and *Portrait* between Stephen and the Jesuits (Father Butt and the dean of studies, respectively—each conveys to Stephen the "useful art" of lighting a fire), as well as his masters' misunderstanding of Stephen's allusion to the distinction Newman makes between employing words in the "literary tradition" and in the "debased" mode of the marketplace (*SH* 28, *P* 188), illustrates the Jesuits' complete incomprehension—or dismissal—of Newman's broader educational philosophies. When these men misapprehend Stephen's use of the illustrative example of the marketplace idiom, "*I hope I am not detaining you,*" they signal their betrayal of Newman's experiment in "liberal education" and their true interest not in "liberal education" but in a debased, vocational pedagogy (Muller 596–97). It is Stephen, not the Jesuits, who therefore becomes the voice of Newman's intended legacy in these scenes; however, the dilution of the cardinal's ideas and their assimilation to the discursive hierarchy—even to the point that they are scarcely recognized just forty years after they were to have been enacted at this very university—does not bode well for Stephen's own destiny as an original thinker. Because of a lack of funding, Newman left the rectorship of Dublin's Catholic University in 1858; a new charter established for the school (renamed University College) under the 1879 Universities Bill drew it under the auspices of the Royal University and required the institution to provide vocational training. The Jesuits took over in 1882, replacing Newman's Oratorians (Muller 595–96). The destruction of Newman's liberal vision of "education for its own sake" at the hands of both the State and his adoptive Church foreshadows the disintegration of Stephen's own emerging creed; the fate of Newman's vision underscores the ability of such institutions to control and manipulate a powerful ideological apparatus and to render the possibility of individual change or escape from their tenets difficult if not completely impossible.

In other confrontations, Stephen continues to employ Newman's rhetorical techniques. In the *Apologia,* Newman explains: "I was not unwilling to draw an opponent on step by step, by virtue of his own opinions, to the brink of some intellectual absurdity, and to leave him to get back as he could. . . . Also I used irony in conversation, when matter-of fact-men would not see what I meant" (46). In *Stephen Hero,* Daedalus puts Newman's devices into practice when he exposes as fraudulent the Very Reverend Dr. Dillon's objections to the work of Henrik Ibsen. The subject at hand is whether art, as the President claims, ought to manifest "a high moral aim":

—Ah, if he [Ibsen] were to examine even the basest things, said the President . . . , it would be different if he were to examine and then show men the way to purify themselves.

—That is for the Salvationists, said Stephen.

—Do you mean . . .

—I mean that Ibsen's account of modern society is as genuinely ironical as Newman's account of English Protestant morality and belief.

—That may be, said the President appeased by the conjunction.

—And as free from any missionary intention. (*SH* 92)

Here Stephen carefully leads the Jesuit to reveal not only an important affinity for the prowess of Newman's *Apologia* as it exposes the insufficiencies of Protestant doctrine but also the irony inherent in claiming it to be, against Newman's titular assertion, a proselytizing work rather than simply, as its subtitle proclaims, "a history of his religious opinions." Stephen wins the point; the President falls silent, and Stephen moves his adversary toward the brink of another "intellectual absurdity": an admission that, like the tormentors of Dedalus who have never read Byron, the President has never perused a single Ibsen drama and bases his opinions of the immorality of the playwright's work solely on what he has read "in the papers" (*SH* 93). Stephen clearly emerges as the victor in this contest of wits, according to the ethos of the early text; chagrined, the President agrees "to read some of [Ibsen's] work for myself" (*SH* 94) and commends Stephen at the end of their interview not for his position but for his skill in defending it (*SH* 98). In *Portrait,* however, though Stephen covets this same intellectual coolness, he is much less successful in achieving it. Unlike his encounter in *Stephen Hero* with the President, Stephen never gains the upper hand in his linguistic joust in *Portrait* with the dean of studies; instead, he feels disadvantaged by language and his inability to control it, becoming defensive and "disheartened" (*P* 190). Cranly becomes his sparring partner regarding religious and moral issues, and it is this young man, not Stephen, who exhibits Newman's famed powers of logic. In an exchange that clearly undercuts Stephen's attempt at spiritual rebellion, Cranly carefully leads Stephen into an admission of the belief that underlies his disavowals of Catholicism and exposes the fallacy in the claim Stephen lays to "unfettered freedom": "Freedom! Cranly repeated. But you are not free enough yet to commit a sacrilege" (*P* 246).

Shelley is the Romantic whose work encourages the fledgling poet to construct for himself a religion of art to replace the Catholicism that he attempts to reject. Shelley's writings provide Stephen with a fuller exposition of the way art and the poet might redeem, without a moralizing sensibility, not only himself but also his society. As a young man, Shelley published a pamphlet, *The Necessity of Atheism,* and got himself expelled from Oxford; throughout his life he supported a variety of political independence movements (in Spain, Greece, Mexico, South America, and Ireland).[13] In *Julian and Maddalo: A Conversation,* Shelley voices in poetry his dissatisfaction with a religion that has "made men blind" to their essential goodness; Julian, the character of the poem who most closely resembles the optimistic Shelley, insists to the skeptical Maddalo (a Byronic cynic) that there must be a "nobler" purpose for humankind than just "to live and die" but faults the Church for obscuring this hopeful teleology by teaching that humankind is innately depraved. Shelley believed that the power of beauty as expressed in poetry, not the power of Christianity, would free the world from its spiritual darkness; his "Hymn to Intellectual Beauty" presents this secularism with unmistakable religious fervor. The title of the poem itself—it is a "hymn"—points to its religiosity; its language continues the imagery: the "spirit of beauty" is the power able to "consecrate" "human thought or form" (2.13–15). As Blake did before him, Shelley conceives of the poet both as the redeemer and prophet of the new creed. In his most fully developed exposition of the poet's role, *A Defence of Poetry,* Shelley makes clear that "to be a poet is to apprehend the true and the beautiful" as well as to transform that "which is most deformed": "Poetry turns all things to loveliness; it exalts the beauty of that which is most beautiful and it adds beauty to that which is most deformed. . . . It transmutes all that it touches, and every form moving within the radiance of its presence is changed by wondrous sympathy" (1073, 1085). The poet's mind takes on a distinctly omniscient aura, containing as it does "the image of all other minds" (1075), and poems become "the mirrors in which the spectator beholds himself" and his own inner beauty (1077). Through the artistic representation of truth and beauty (which comprise their own morality, apart from any religiosity), Shelley believed that poets could change their societies; they were, he claimed, "the unacknowledged legislators of the world" (1087).

Portrait's Stephen, like Shelley, attempts to forsake the cult of Christianity to dedicate himself to the cult of beauty; in the trinity of discussions on nationalism, art, and religion that compose the last chapter of *Portrait,* Stephen proposes his aesthetic theory to Lynch with an almost religious zeal that owes as much to the influence of Shelley as to that of Aquinas, especially with regard to the role of the poet. As Gifford has observed, Stephen's definition of "claritas" denies Aquinas's pronouncement of the objective, rather than subjective, "radiance" of the beautiful object, which Aquinas believed to emanate from the object itself (253). Stephen substitutes a Shelleyan ethos instead, one that locates the object's brilliance not within itself but within the mind of the artist: "The radiance of which [Aquinas] speaks is the scholastic *quidditas,* the *whatness* of a thing. This supreme quality is felt by the artist when the esthetic image is first conceived in his imagination. The mind in that mysterious instant Shelley likened beautifully to a fading coal" (*P* 213). This transformative power of the poet is the crux of both Shelley's and Stephen's theory of art; Stephen comes to see himself, in another echo of Shelley, as a "priest of eternal imagination, transmuting the daily bread of experience into the radiant body of everliving life" (*P* 221). In the apprehension of beauty and truth, Stephen's artist becomes not just a priest but also a "God of the creation" (*P* 215), able to "express, to press out again, from the gross earth or what it brings forth, from sound and shape and colour which are the prison gates of our soul, an image of the beauty we have come to understand—that is art" (*P* 207). Stephen's conception of the poet, like Shelley's, also requires an ability to represent the universal in the personal; whereas the mind of Shelley's poet contains an "image" of all other minds,

Stephen's artist represents "the vitality which has flowed and eddied round each person" (*P* 215).

By the advent of *Ulysses,* however, Stephen's romantic energy largely has dissipated; the poetic glass that unveiled for Shelley the beauty of humankind has so far revealed to Stephen only subjugation. Instead of a "prismatic and many-sided mirror, which collects the brightest rays of human nature" (*Defence* 1078), Irish art, in Stephen's experience, more closely resembles "the cracked lookingglass of a servant" (*U* 1.146). Stephen's judgment reflects not only upon the tragic career of Oscar Wilde but also upon his own insufficiencies as an artist. His attempt at Byronic exile has failed; he has returned from Paris, critical of his attempts to enact the role of the dispossessed artist and having produced nothing of value: "You were going to do wonders, what? . . . Rich booty you brought back; *Le Tutu,* five tattered numbers of *Pantalon Blanc et Culotte Rouge;* a blue French telegram, curiosity to show: —Nother dying come home father" (*U* 3.192–99). If *Portrait* is for Stephen the book of romantic possibility, then *Ulysses* is the novel that ultimately depicts the limitations of the romantic imagination in Edwardian society; he still insists, with Shelley, on "the eternal affirmation of the spirit of man in literature" (*U* 17.29–30), but confined within himself, Stephen cannot fathom how to create such a liberating art. Stephen now employs Blake's invective, but not his faith in imaginative ascendance, to illustrate his sense of artistic entrapment by the powers of the Church and the society it has influenced.

In the "Nestor" episode, Stephen invokes Blake several times, the first only seven lines into the chapter, reflecting on his own artistic failures as he teaches a history class. The primary references in this passage are to *The Marriage of Heaven and Hell,* which has as its premise the restraints imposed on energy, passion, and imagination by both Church and State, and *A Vision of the Last Judgment,* which asserts that it is only through the exercise of imagination that we may achieve immortality. Stephen's synthesis of Blake's prophetic writing in this context suggests his sense of ideological oppression as well as his feeling about what is at stake: unable to create his art, Stephen is incapable of redeeming himself. Here is Stephen's reflection: "Fabled by the daughters of memory. And yet it was in some way if not as memory fabled it. A phrase, then, of impatience, thud of Blake's wings of excess. I hear the ruin of all space, shattered glass and toppling masonry, and time one livid final flame. What's left us then?" (*U* 2.7–10). It is history and allegory—"totally distinct & inferior kind[s] of Poetry"—that are "fabled by the daughters of memory," according to Blake in *A Vision* (161). The suggestion here is that Stephen has been able to identify only with this false muse; the true "daughters of inspiration" who surround the imagination have sequestered themselves from him. Stephen's vision of ruin is also a Blakean apocalyptic invocation; the "ruin of all space" echoes Blake's remark in a letter to William Hayley that "the ruins of Time build mansions in Eternity" (Gifford and Seidman 30). Yet while Blake seems to view the "livid final flame" as a ritual of purification, Stephen sees it as a weapon of destruction, as his final despairing question indicates: "What's left us then?" Blake ends his work proclaiming, "Every thing that lives is Holy"; for Stephen, however, all is degraded, dead, or dying. As he later sums up the human condition: "Houses of decay, mine, his and all" (U 3.105).

In "Circe," Blakean images become even more evocative of Stephen's ideological oppression, morphing now into animated menaces: "time's livid final flame" literally appears, ruining space, glass, and masonry, as Stephen smashes the chandelier with his ashplant (U 15.4244–45); Privates Carr and Compton, partial representatives of the oppressive alliance of "Priest & King" that Blake evokes throughout his poetry, physically attack Stephen for metaphorically expressing his desire to vanquish these authorities from his brain (U 15.4436–37).[14] Stephen's final invocation of Blake in this episode suggests the ultimate failure of Stephen's struggle and its implications: "The harlot's cry from street to street / Shall weave Old Ireland's windingsheet" (U 15.4641–42) is Stephen's revision of lines from Blake's "Auguries of Innocence" (Stephen has substituted "Ireland" for "England"). Blake's poem is a meditation on the prelapsarian state of human imagination and the imagination's corruption by a State that sanctions militaristic violence and exploits the underclasses by licensing prostitution and gambling. The parallels to the situation that faces Stephen in nighttown are clear; the winding-sheet called into being by the harlot's cry signifies the presence of a metaphorical death that underscores the failure of the romantic imagination in the face of too-powerful forces.

Although Stephen's romantic idealism does not entirely evaporate in *Ulysses,* his intensified sense of artistic sterility—a mark that the romantic imagination alone has failed to free him from the strong net cast by religious dogma—leads to his continued experimentation with dissidence and a more syncretic subjectivity as he attempts to find other forms of doctrinal rebellion that might accommodate his art. Just as Stephen's contestation of an insular, romantic nationalism persists into the "Scylla and Charybdis" episode, so also his exploration of irreligion continues in the early chapters of *Ulysses,* most notably with unsuccessful forays into the anthropocentric philosophies of theosophical mysticism and Nietzschean apostasy. Such varieties of unbelief have their roots in the evolving religious skepticism and anxiety that characterized the Victorian and Edwardian years; Victorians had grown accustomed to scientific rationalism by the fin de siècle, and their intellect often could no longer justify their faith. Spiritualism emerged in the mid-nineteenth century as a counterpoint to both religious dogmatism and scientific rationalism; the Theosophical Society, proclaimed by Russian-born Madame Helena Petrovna Blavatsky in 1875, endeavored to "free the public mind from 'theological superstition' and to tame subservience to the arrogance of science" (Dumbleton 36). Often its proponents accorded to theosophy a position that mediated the two extremes: one contemporary practitioner, J. S. Farmer, wrote that spiritualism, "standing midway between the opposing schools [of faith and science], . . . gives to the one a scientific basis for the divine things of old, whilst it restores to the other the much needed evidence of its expressed faith in the duality and continuity of life" (qtd. in Oppenheim 59). William Butler Yeats, another devotee, felt similarly. According to William York Tindall:

> For some years [Yeats] had held the biologists and physicists responsible for the materialism of the West and for the spiritual limitation that accompanied it. Darwin, Huxley, and Tyndall, he complained in the early 1880's, had robbed him of the religion of his youth and had given him nothing with which to replace it. Forced by his intellect and their teachings to accept materialism, he was miserable under it and longed for something to satisfy the persistent, irrational yearnings of his soul. . . . In this quandary, he discovered theosophy, which . . . offered his soul, without apparent offense to intellect, the expansion it desired. (qtd. in Cranston 465)

Theosophists devoted themselves to the formation of "a universal brotherhood of humanity, without distinction of race, creed, sex, caste, or color"; the study of "ancient and modern religions, philosophies and sciences, and the demonstration of the importance of such study"; and "the investigation of the unexplained laws of nature and the psychical powers latent in man" (Cranston xviii). Blavatsky claimed to have learned her teachings from Far Eastern "masters of wisdom," or mahatmas—"great souls"; she made several trips to India, as would Annie Besant, her most visible disciple. Blavatsky and her disciples dismissed the anthropomorphic God of theology as a "logical impossibility," asserting that Christ and Buddha were great prophets of the "universal brotherhood" but not its gods, that souls never died, they simply ascended—or transmigrated—to higher planes of consciousness (*Key* 35). A decidedly humanistic philosophy, theosophy locates within the human soul the essence of immortality and believes it to commune with a Universal Divine Principle "from which all proceeds, and within which all shall be absorbed at the end of the great cycle of Being" (*Key* 36). This universal interconnectedness, or karma, links each individual to those lives that have come before: "No one life is isolated; it is the child of all the lives before it, the parent of all the lives that follow it," writes Besant (267). Karma also was thought to unite contemporary believers: as "a member of various groups—family, national, racial"—each person also becomes party to his or her own "collective" karma; therefore, Besant continues, each individual "affects others by his thoughts" (274–77).

Turn-of-the-century Dublin was not immune to the lure of theosophy. Constantine Curran reports that "theosophy was in the air in the nineties" (32): Besant visited the First Dublin Lodge in 1890, where she addressed a lecture, "Why I Became a Theosophist," to "several hundred" Dubliners at the Antient Concert Rooms. Her impact in Belfast was limited only by the size of the meeting rooms; there she conducted three meetings of five hundred attendees each.[15] Ernest Boyd has noted in *Ireland's Literary Renaissance* that "the theosophical movement provided a literary, artistic and intellectual center . . . whose effect was felt even by those who did not belong to it" (qtd. in Cranston 463); in Joyce's *Ulysses,* theosophical premises clearly have seeped into the consciousness of everyone from barflies to intellectuals. Molly has asked about "metempsychosis," a word she has stumbled over in *Ruby: the Pride of the Ring;* Bloom has attempted to explain "transmigration of the souls"; one of the unidentified "Cyclops" narrators offers a distinctly theosophical narration of Dignam's demise (*U* 12.341–60); and Mulligan notes the soul-like properties of the wine jar in "Oxen of the Sun": "Any object, intensely regarded, may be a gate of access to the incorruptible eon of the gods" (*U* 14.1166–67). The pervasiveness of theosophy in 1904 Dublin (even Bloom's lemon soap takes on sentience in "Circe" [*U* 15.337]) reveals Joyce's sense that religion, like individual consciousness, is itself an insidious societal construction, produced and perpetuated by culture. If theosophy is able to saturate social consciousness to this degree after only twenty-nine years, how deeply ingrained must the influence of Catholicism be in Ireland after almost fifteen hundred?

Given its commitment to "universal brotherhood" without regard to race or creed, theosophy and imperialism became natural enemies; many theosophists, including Annie Besant in India and George Russell in Ireland, were also deeply involved in nationalist independence movements. Theosophy and the Irish Literary Revival were closely linked; Dublin literati such as Yeats, Russell, James Cousins, George Sigerson, and Katharine Tynan dabbled in the movement in varying degrees;[16] even Joyce once discussed its precepts with Russell but scornfully dismissed it as "a recourse for disaffected Protestants" (Ellmann, *James Joyce* 99). In spite of Joyce's own disdain for spiritualism, Stephen Dedalus is well acquainted with its precepts. Cheryl Herr has convincingly demonstrated the theosophical roots of Stephen's search in the "Proteus" episode for metaphysical knowledge and "that word known to all men" (*U* 3.435). Herr explores the connections between Blavatsky's descriptions (expounded in *The Secret Doctrine* and *Isis Unveiled*) of the indefinable logos from which everything else proceeds and Stephen's "verbal formulation of divine activity—'God becomes man becomes fish becomes barnacle goose becomes featherbed mountain'": this continuum, Herr observes, "is not only Stephen's statement of tentative belief; it is also a linguistic equation whereby all words emanate from an ineffable source-word" ("Theosophy" 50). Herr also argues that Stephen's attempts at poetic creation in this episode owe a similar debt to theosophical forms as he attempts to "tap creative Being through an esoteric vocable" ("Theosophy" 49–50);[17] in fact, some theosophist-artists like James Cousins often derived the inspiration for their work even more directly, through spirit channelings.[18] Stephen's interest in theosophical teachings is also alluded to in the "Aeolus" episode; there a story circulates that Stephen has petitioned A.E. "in the small hours of the morning" for information about "planes of consciousness" (*U* 7.786), and J. J. O'Molloy wants to know: "What do you think really of that hermetic crowd, the opal hush poets: A. E. the mastermystic?" (*U* 7.783–84).[19]

Until the meeting in "Scylla and Charybdis," then, it appears that Stephen has been impressed enough by the methods of A.E.'s group to attempt them for himself; but in this episode, Stephen's viewpoint changes dramatically, from tentative acceptance to barely concealed disdain. The fusion of theosophy to Irish nationalism in the form of the Literary Revival within an episode that focuses significantly on Stephen's artistic dispossession helps to explain his radical shift in perspective; Stephen realizes here that the group's profession of "universal brotherhood" is fraudulent, that its practice of exclusivity belies the hypocrisy of its precepts. Here it becomes painfully clear to Stephen, as perhaps it has not been before, that, while this manifestation of spiritualism may constitute an appealing type of religious nonconformity, it also has begun to dictate a political hegemony that will not tolerate artistic dissent. Russell, especially, believed that expansion of the theosophical lodges would help to create in Ireland the unified, spiritual essence that would lead not only to Ireland's independence from England but also to the establishment of Ireland as the spiritual redeemer of the world; he wrote to Yeats in 1896 that "out of Ireland will arise a light to transform many ages and peoples" ("Letter" 541). In Russell's opinion, the formation of this national soul required an Irish literature based on an idyllic Celticism to properly shape it; in spite of his initial advocacy of aestheticism in "Scylla and Charybdis"—"Art has to reveal to us ideas, formless spiritual essences" (U 9.48–49)—over the material facts of the author's life—"What is it to us how the poet lived?" (U 9.185)—Russell's project posits proscriptive requirements that belie his aesthetic. As Stephen expounds a materialist theory of art that he does not believe, he exposes the inconsistencies of this theosophical-nationalist discourse and soon recognizes it to be as restrictive a threat to intellectual and artistic license as any of Catholicism's doctrines of sin and punishment. Stephen's ultimate disbelief of the materialist aspect of his theory is indicative of the remnants of his own romanticism; his performance here may also be read as an attempt to liberate himself from his remaining spiritual idealism as well as an effort to change the Revival's standards.

That Russell's pronouncements in "Scylla and Charybdis" emanate from his theosophical beliefs is made clear in the adverbs used to describe his speech: he "oracle[s] out of his shadow" (U 9.46–47), and his "auric egg" (a reference to the aura that the theosophists believed surrounds every object—around the human head, it was supposedly egg-shaped) "warn[s] occultly" (U 9.103–4) as he introduces and defends his theosophical aesthetic in the conversation. Art, as Russell describes it, takes on characteristics of Blavatsky's Universal Divine Principle and evokes the title of Annie Besant's 1897 treatise, The Ancient Wisdom. According to Russell, "The deepest poetry of Shelley, the words of Hamlet bring our minds into contact with the eternal wisdom, Plato's world of ideas. All the rest is the speculation of schoolboys for schoolboys" (U 9.48–53). His penname, A.E., which Gifford and Seidman have helpfully traced as meaning "an emanation from Deity," adds a godlike preponderance to his words, but while Stephen recognizes their weight, he also challenges Russell's premises to discover to what extreme Russell is willing to press them.

Stephen's silent recitation of prominent theosophical leaders' names (D. N. Dunlop, editor of the Irish Theosophist; William Q. Judge, who assisted Blavatsky in founding the society in 1875; and, of course, A.E.)

and their dogma in response to A.E.'s dismissal of his *Hamlet* theory emphasizes the secretive exclusivity of the movement and his growing sense that its esoteric beliefs will also occlude him; only true initiates, or "adepts," for instance, can know the identity of the master. The "brothers of the great white lodge," those on the path to holiness, help only one another in their quest, because the "life esoteric is not for ordinary person. O. P. must work off bad karma first" (*U* 9.65–70). Stephen's off-color joke about Blavatsky, the movement's founder—"Mrs. Cooper Oakley once glimpsed our very illustrious sister H.P.B.'s elemental. . . . You naughtn't to look, missus, so you naughtn't when a lady's ashowing of her elemental" (*U* 70–73)—signals his increasing ridicule of A.E.'s mystical aestheticism and the core beliefs that enable it, which also include a disturbing passivity.[20] When Russell indicates that he may not be able to attend Moore's gathering because of the meeting of his theosophical lodge, Stephen's reflections begin to catalog not only the troubling submission of the faithful (Louis H. Victory, T. Caulfield Irwin) as they anticipate enlightenment by their Master but also the bad poetry such experiences are likely to produce. He imagines Russell enthroned in the Dawson chamber meeting room, ringed by obedient disciples ready to be indoctrinated: "Crosslegged under an umbrel umbershoot he thrones an Aztec logos, functioning on astral levels, their oversoul, mahamahatma. The faithful hermetists await the light, ripe for chelaship, ringroundabout him. Louis H. Victory. T. Caulfield Irwin. . . . Filled with his god, he thrones, Buddh under plantain. Gulfer of souls, engulfer. Hesouls, shesouls, shoals of souls. Engulfed with wailing creecries, whirled, whirling, they bewail.

In quintessential triviality
For years in this fleshcase a shesoul dwelt" (*U* 9.280–88).

Stephen's adaptation of Louis Victory's lines here suggests his negatively evolving opinion of the poet, the Revival, and its theosophical nationalism as "quintessential triviality."

As the conversation turns to Russell's "literary surprise" and the poets he has asked to contribute are enumerated, it becomes clear to Stephen that Russell regards him not as a poet-initiate but as an "O. P."—an ordinary person—and Stephen desperately resents the exclusion, enjoining himself: "See this. Remember" (*U* 9.294). For Stephen, theosophy's misguided spiritual nationalism, cemented by its utter neglect of him, belies its professed aestheticism and signals its ultimate fraudulence; Russell's oracle reveals nothing so much as his desire to press art into the service of a multitude of causes—not only Irish nationalism but also "universal brotherhood" and "eternal wisdom." Stephen again has no recourse but to distance himself from a master discourse that will insistently reconstitute his artistic vision in its own image.

Simultaneous with his explorations of theosophy, Stephen also has attempted to forge alliances with other late-century critics of Christian teleology. Nietzsche's *Thus Spoke Zarathustra* has infused Stephen's "free thought" in its proffer of a human Christ—an *Übermensch,* or Superman—who transcends not only the psychological restraints imposed by conventional morality but also the visions of immortality that enforce them. From Buck Mulligan's invocations of him in "Telemachus," the Nietzschean prophet figures prominently in *Ulysses,* but it is Mulligan, not Stephen, who apparently succeeds in casting off the precepts of Catholicism that still reverberate in Stephen's consciousness. In Mulligan's ironic achievement of a Nietzschean ethos and Stephen's failure to fully attain it, Joyce exposes the ultimate impracticability of Nietzschean philosophy for the true artist in the modern world.

Stephen's Nietzschean indoctrination begins in *Portrait* rather than in *Ulysses;* indeed, Joseph Valente has suggested that Stephen's "farewell commitment 'to forge . . . the uncreated conscience of my race' (*P* 253) is a recognizably Zarathustrian project" ("Beyond Truth" 87). But the latter novel is where the Superman theory is revealed as finally insufficient in Stephen's hands to contest the powers it would reject.[21] As Zarathustra commands, Stephen has tried to reject the false gods of modern life, religion and the State. "It is a disgrace to pray!" Zarathustra exhorts his followers, "Not for everybody, but for you and me and whoever else has a conscience in his head" (292). Stephen will not make his Easter duty because his newly awakened conscience will not allow him to commit "false homage to a symbol behind which are massed twenty centuries of authority and veneration" (*P* 243); he has also refused to pray at his mother's deathbed, despite her plea that he do so, an obstinacy Mulligan characterizes in distinctly Nietzschean terms: "You could have knelt down, damn it, Kinch, when your dying mother asked you. . . . I'm hyperborean as much as you. But to think of your mother begging you with her last breath to kneel down and pray for her. And you refused. There is something sinister in you . . ." (*U* 1.91–94). In spite of Stephen's attempts to assume a Nietzschean posture, however, he continues to be stalked by his Catholicism; its impact on him is so evident that Mulligan incorporates it into an address, a signifier of identity: "Come up Kinch! Come up, you fearful jesuit!" (*U* 1.8). That Stephen is haunted throughout the text by the specter of his mother's ghost, a clear signifier of insistent religiosity and the guilt it still produces in him, also indicates his failure as the *Übermensch*. In "Proteus," he reflects on the disintegrating state of his teeth along with his affinity for Nietzsche and considers whether the two might be connected: "Toothless Kinch, the superman. Why is that, I wonder, or does it mean something perhaps?" (*U* 3.496–97). Certainly it does: Stephen's rendition of the *Übermensch,* in the face of his Catholicism, will be forever ineffectual.

But if Stephen Dedalus represents the failure of the Nietzschean ethos in *Ulysses,* then Buck Mulligan signifies its ironically successful manifestation. It is Buck, not Stephen, who has usurped the joy of life proclaimed by Zarathustra; Malachi the messenger is Joyce's representation of the Nietzschean prophet, subverting the scriptures, parodying ritual, blaspheming with infamy: "there is no devil and no hell" is a Zarathustrian precept (132) that Stephen desperately wants to believe and Mulligan apparently does. "You have the cursed jesuit strain in you," Mulligan tells his friend, "to me it's all mockery and beastly" (*U* 1.209–10). But Mulligan, in his patronage of Haines and his willingness to sell out Stephen, also reveals his own rendition of the *Übermensch* to be a fraud; in spite of his rejection of Catholicism, Mulligan signifies not the liberated artist but the "superfluous" people Zarathustra warned about: "They steal the works of the inventors and the treasures of the sages for themselves" (162). Though Mulligan is associated with the Literary Revival and recognized by it in a way that Stephen is not, Mulligan's own "contribution to literature" has been limited to pissing on Synge's door (*U* 9.572) and devising the blasphemously obscene ditties he calls "The Ballad of Joking Jesus" and "Medical Dick and Medical Davy"; otherwise, he pimps the work of Dedalus: "I told him [Haines] your symbol of Irish art. He says it's very clever. Touch him for a quid, will you?" (*U* 1.290–91). The true Superman, in Nietzsche's conception, must exhibit the propensity for real achievement once he achieves moral transcendence: "You call yourself free? Your dominant thought I want to hear, and not that you have escaped from a yoke. Are you one of those who had the *right* to escape from a yoke? . . . Free *from* what? As if that mattered to Zarathustra! But your eyes should tell me brightly: free *for* what?" (175). Mulligan reveals himself perhaps capable of transcendence but not of creation: "Usurper" is not only Stephen's epithet for being shut out of the tower and excluded from his poet's birthright, it also signifies his recognition of Mulligan's false appropriation of the Nietzschean ethos. Mulligan has enacted the Zarathustrian precept "not by wrath does one kill, but by laughter" (427), and with "jocoseriousness" tries to convince Stephen to play the same, ultimately servile role that he enacts: "A jester at the court of his master, indulged and disesteemed, winning a clement master's praise" (*U* 2.44). Stephen, dispirited and dispossessed, cannot serve as jester, but he remains ever a product and servant of his culture—its politics and its faith. *Portrait*'s defiant "I will not serve" (*P* 239) is resoundingly reversed in *Ulysses* as Stephen is forced to admit to Haines that he cannot, after all attempts, free himself: "I am a servant of two masters, . . . an English and an Italian. . . . And a third . . . there is who wants me for odd jobs" (*U* 1.638–41).

Gregory Castle has observed that, in *Ulysses*, "Stephen does not give up entirely the passion for intellectual dominance that characterizes him in *Stephen Hero* and *Portrait*. He still longs for the artist's power to impose form on the world, to master it and to himself" (294). But Stephen finally fails as the Superman—not because of any overt rejection of Nietzschean ethos but because the strictures of religion and state are finally too powerful for him to overcome. As *Ulysses* proceeds, Stephen's path becomes no clearer; he fails to escape the confining ideologies of either Irish politics or Irish Catholicism. We last seem him as he leaves Bloom at the door of 7 Eccles Street; fittingly, the bells of the church of St. George peal as Stephen departs and evoke for him disjointed snatches of the Prayers for the Dying (*U* 17.1230–31). Stephen last recalled the words in "Telemachus" as he remembered his mother's death (*U* 1.276–77); here, perhaps they herald his own figurative resignation to the powers that have defeated him.

Caught in the Currents: Victorian Manliness, Public Morality, and Leopold Bloom

3

"Do you call that a man?"

The Discourse of Anxious Masculinity in *Ulysses*

Critical examinations of gender in Joyce's work have, until recently, focused primarily on representations of femininity. Gerty MacDowell's self-
conscious construction of a "feminine" identity at the confluence of various
social discourses—the sentimental novels of Maria Susannah Cummins,
the mythology of the Blessed Virgin, the poetry of Louis J. Walsh ("Art
thou real, my ideal?"), and the advertisements of the *Lady's Pictorial*
—has, for instance, been well documented by scholars such as Suzette
Henke, Kimberly Devlin, and Garry Leonard.[1] Gerty becomes the signifier
of a culturally constructed and contested femininity, a surface that draws
attention to itself by continually gesturing toward its constructedness, a
facade that is constantly threatened by contentious disruptions ("little
monkeys common as ditchwater" [*U* 13.467–68]) or contradictions within
its sources themselves. Molly Bloom is similarly engaged in a process of
contested self-representation, as Devlin and Cheryl Herr have argued.[2]
Molly, like Gerty, plays out the various gender roles—replete with their
inherent contradictions—that the culture of 1904 Dublin has assigned to
her. What has received considerably less attention than these important
recontextualizations of feminine gender identities, however, is Joyce's depiction of masculinity in late-nineteenth- and early-twentieth-century Ireland as an equally constructed and deeply conflicted ideology.

In this chapter, I wish to consider the social construction of middle-class
masculinity and its various Others as they are posited within *Ulysses,*
specifically as they converge in the figures of Leopold Bloom and other
men-about-Dublin. A variety of masculinities—all of them tenuous—are
staged in the novel, including the dandified, over-the-top performances of
Blazes Boylan and Buck Mulligan; the rough-hewn, hypermasculine exag-
gerations of the Citizen; and the sensitive and intellectual "man of letters"
represented by not only Stephen Dedalus but also by Bloom himself.
Historicizing these styles of manliness allows us to understand the depth
of Joyce's cultural critique as well as the impact he believed social forces

have on individual subjectivity; Bloom's androgynous status as "the new womanly man" ultimately owes as much to his conflicted position within competing currents of nineteenth-century masculinist discourse as it owes to the psychological emasculation he experiences over the impending infidelity of his wife. The social and the psychological are in fact inextricably intertwined in Joyce's portraits; the performances of "maleness" by men like Boylan, Mulligan, and the Citizen similarly reveal their own anxiety-laden positions in relation to the gender ideologies of their age. In these depictions, Joyce de-essentializes the notion of masculinity in general by divulging its changing, constructed, and performative nature, but he also attacks in particular the ethos that had achieved an uneasy hegemony in England and Ireland by the late nineteenth century, Anglican minister Charles Kingsley's "Christian manliness." Kingsley's midcentury reinvention of masculinity within a unified frame of rock-hard, disciplined, heterosexual virility required the location—always external to the masculine self—of various feminine, racial, and sexual Others in order to preserve its illusion of wholeness; by the end of the century the Kingsleyan discourse had effectively Othered not just these concepts but also the style of masculinity most antithetical to it, that of Victorian aestheticism.

Joyce's *Ulysses* showcases the tension between these competing styles of masculinity and the confusion they caused among turn-of-the-century men, who attempted to reproduce the Kingsleyan ethos and locate its externalized Others but who simultaneously feared to discover the locus of difference *within* the masculine body. Such a fear is not to be taken lightly, as the trial and conviction of Oscar Wilde would demonstrate in 1895: when difference/Otherness is suspected or detected within the self, it exposes fissures that threaten to fracture the illusion of wholeness so vital to the maintenance of the Masculine Ideal. In accordance with the Kingsleyan ethos (which values aggression and confrontation as "proofs" of masculine identity), such ruptures often produce compensatory acts of retribution against an external Other who serves as a scapegoat for the internal collapse. In *Ulysses,* Joyce reveals not just the social constructedness and the intolerance inherent in the Kingsleyan pose, he also simultaneously exposes its ironic fragility—its internal fissures and its extraordinary, problematic dependence upon the regard of various Others for the validation and measure of its existence. More important, Joyce reveals the immense, manipulative power of this cultural force as it molds male subjectivity: the social and the psychological are fused within the psyche of the Joycean male in a manner that only careful historical analysis can unravel.

Most recent gender critics who have turned their attention to the constructed nature of masculinity would argue that the phrase "anxious masculinity" is in fact redundant, as the question of what constitutes "masculinity" or "manliness" is "always bound up with negotiations about power, and is therefore often experienced as tenuous" (Roper and Tosh 18). Definitions of manhood and masculinity in nineteenth-century England were no exceptions to this observation; they fluctuated and evolved in response to various social challenges to patriarchal authority, such as Chartism, feminism, and colonial uprisings, movements that were themselves often framed in terms of gender. Always at issue was the question, "Who should rule?" and, as David Rosen has pointed out, such disputes often "devolved into a debate over who belonged to that privileged group called 'men.'" (21). As definitions of this "privileged group" expanded or contracted in accordance with political expedience, manhood was exposed not as an "essence" but as a socially constructed—and therefore socially vulnerable—phenomenon. The vulnerability was ubiquitous: the shifting of political power from the aristocracy to the middle classes was achieved in what the *Times* would later call a "menacing" atmosphere of social unrest as Chartist agitations for universal suffrage in the 1830s to 1840s erupted into riots in London, Liverpool, and Glasgow in 1848; violent colonial uprisings rocked India during the Sepoy Rebellion in 1857; and the Irish stepped up their demands for both land reform and home rule ("The Jubilee" 9).[3] Such events at home and abroad deeply disturbed the Victorian psyche; significantly, the fears of decline that subtended the Condition of England debates at midcentury were expressed not only in terms of diminishing nationhood but also in terms of disintegrating manhood: in 1843 Thomas Carlyle conflated the two as he bemoaned the waste of poverty and workhouses—in them, Carlyle argued, were squandered "noble . . . national virtues [and] . . . valiant manful habits, soul of a nation's worth" (*Past and Present* 9). In 1848 Charles Kingsley urged Chartist agitators, the "workmen of England" toward a manly readiness to rule, imploring them to "be fit to be free" before increasing their political demands (63–64); in 1853 John Ruskin lamented British industrialization and efficiency in decidedly gendered terms: "We manufacture everything . . . except men" (87).

As a result of this sense of progressive social and political emasculation, masculinist movements of the midcentury moved self-consciously to reconstruct "manhood" as a less ambiguous and physically harder phenomenon than the reflective, emotive, and intellectual ideal epitomized by the Romantic poets and propounded by philosophers such as

Carlyle, who had proposed the cerebral "man of letters" as the hero of the age.[4] Kingsley not only advocated but also came to embody the new ideal of a virile and distinctly heterosexual manliness, one that required (in the words used by Kingsley's contemporaries to describe his public persona) "'boldness,' 'honesty,' and 'plainness'; a defiance of authority; stoic patience; and violent energy" (qtd. in Rosen 18–19). Kingsley's aim was no less than to reconfigure Christ himself as a strong, robust, "manly" figure—less passive, less pious, and less "womanish" than Kingsley believed the Church had made him out to be. In an 1857 parody of Kingsley's own rhetoric, the *Saturday Review* acknowledged Kingsley's role in revising popular perceptions of both masculinity and religion by eliding the earlier "effeminacy" of each construct; it dubbed his philosophy "muscular Christianity" and described his paragon as a man who "fears God and can walk a thousand miles in a thousand hours—who . . . breathes God's free air on God's rich earth, and at the same time can hit a woodcock, doctor a horse, and twist a poker around his fingers" ("Two Years Ago" 176).

But as this revitalized masculine body began to recognize its metaphorical status as a signifier of nationality and religiosity and began to reinvent itself to arrest their perceived degenerations, it also remained vulnerable to their destabilizations. Like the institutions of Church and State, the Masculine Ideal derives its symbolic authority from its invisible integration into the social fabric and from the widespread acceptance of its "essential" nature; thus any attempt to "reinvent" manhood (or any other cultural ideology) calls attention to itself as performance and in fact undermines the ideal it strives to preserve. Lacan, following Joan Riviere, has suggested that both masculinity and femininity are forms of masquerade;[5] Lacan observes that to masquerade is "to play not at the imaginary, but at the symbolic, level" (*Four Fundamental Concepts* 193). If such play is, as Lacan claims, an attempt to anchor the self to the symbolic order as a means to reassure the self of its own authenticity and wholeness, then such efforts also inscribe an intense subconscious fear of inauthenticity and lack. Intriguingly, Kingsley's deliberations often indicate not only the anxiety of the subject but also a fear that the symbolic order itself was crumbling: his agonized reflections in the aftermath of British brutality during the Sepoy resistance register the conflation of the national/religious/masculine subject as well as its shaken faith in the stability of the overarching symbolic order that this body in turn attempted to signify: "I can think of nothing but these Indian massacres. The moral problems they involve make me half wild. Night and day the heaven seems black to me, though I never was so prosperous and blest in my life as I am now. . . .

What does it all mean? Christ is King, nevertheless! I tell my people so. I should do—I dare not think what—if I did not believe so. But I want sorely some one to tell me that he believes it too" (207). Though intended to reassure, Kingsley's remarks instead record a remarkable anxiety over the justice of his government's actions and the ability of his God to maintain order; they also evince a deep-seated need to locate some external vindication for these foundational beliefs. Kingsley's reiteration of the manly ideal ("Christ is King, nevertheless") ostensibly restores confidence and shuts down the disruptive questioning ("What does it all mean?") that threatens to unmask the ideal's impotency and its constructedness, but such silencing is ultimately unable to erase the anxiety that subtends and threatens its authority. Neither is the wished-for validating look ("some one to tell me that he believes it too") forthcoming in this passage, and, as Leopold Bloom is well aware, when this look is withheld or withdrawn, the authority of the subject (Nation, God, Man) evaporates along with any authenticity that it had hoped to achieve inside its poses. Bloom, too, is cognizant of the masculine subject's need for vindication by external regard, though he pragmatically ratchets the ocular standard downward: if the presence of approbation is not available, Bloom will settle for the simple absence of ridicule: "See ourselves as others see us. So long as women don't mock what matter?" (*U* 13.1058–59).

As Kingsley's masculine ideal registered this intense, subconscious awareness of its own instability and its failure to reliably attract an authenticating gaze, it turned its valorizing efforts toward a difference-based measure of manhood: "muscular Christianity" also attempted to define and validate itself discursively against feminine, racial, and sexual Others. Kingsley despised what he called "Mariolatry," or worship of the Virgin Mary, and exhorted his followers to go "not to the Mother but to the Son—not to the indulgent Virgin, but to the strong *man,* Christ Jesus" (104). He valued the robust strength of Esau over the intellectual softness of Jacob but "trembled" at England's dependence on the latter (214–15); he problematically attempted to brand the colonized subject with subhuman status in order to justify British rule and affirm British manhood, not an unusual move in colonial discourse, but Kingsley's 1860 account of the Irish peasantry evinces an extraordinary agitation over racial similarity, which gestures toward the precariousness of these constructs. "I am haunted by the human chimpanzees I saw along that hundred miles of horrible country. I don't believe they are our fault. I believe there are not only many more of them than of old, but that they are happier, better, more comfortably fed and lodged under our rule than they ever were. But to see *white* chimpanzees is dreadful; if they were black, one would not feel it so much but their skins, except where tanned by exposure, are as white as ours" (236).[6] As it unsuccessfully attempts to mark racial difference, this letter also exposes the intense anxiety that lies at the heart of Othering. Kingsley's insistence here on referring to the Gaels as "chimpanzees" rather than "men" suggests the portentous dependence of masculinity on its externalized Others: if difference collapses, then dominance is lost, and so is English manhood.

As the century progressed, the Kingsleyan ethos moved to secure its hegemony in the culture at large as it focused intently on marking Otherness, but British society absorbed both the new style of masculinity and its Other-driven anxiety. A fanatical obsession with racial decay merged with an irrational fear of "womanishness" and fueled a curious cultural admixture of male purity movements and muscle-flexing:[7] organizations such as the Young Men's Christian Association (1844) aimed to show "the average Victorian. . . that religion was not really about 'feminine' piety . . . but was instead a robust and manly affair in the Kingsley mould," while the Boys' Brigade (1874) and the later Boy Scouts drilled military discipline, citizenship, and personal hygiene into their memberships (Springhall 53).[8] Masculinity became a state of muscle rather than a state of intellect as children's novels such as Thomas Hughes's *Tom Brown's School Days* (1857) and compulsory sport invaded the boys' public school curricula between 1860 and 1880, promoting the ideals of competitiveness and physical manliness: the new masculinity, as J. A. Mangan has observed, actualized "an implicit, if not explicit, crude Darwinism" embodied in aphorisms: "life is conflict, strength comes through struggle and success is the prerogative of the strong" (142).

But even as the cleansed and hardened male body rose to ideological prominence, it was not the only conception of manhood at work in the mid and late nineteenth century. Aesthetes such as Pater, Swinburne, and Wilde challenged Kingsley's notions of moral asceticism, self-discipline, and utilitarianism; they attempted to reclaim the male body, as they reclaimed art, in the name of beauty and sensuality rather than production and empire. The aesthetes' revival of Hellenism additionally enabled them not only to appreciate the artistry of the body, it also facilitated their ability to reconceive masculinity apart from a prohibitive Kingsleyan heterosexuality and instead to imagine it in terms of androgynous or male-male desire.[9] The enactment of the 1885 Criminal Law Amendment Act, a product of the social purity crusades spawned in part by the Kingsleyan ethos, attests to the sexual anxiety that the aesthetes evoked within the

Kingsleyan model: among its various provisions, the new law forbade acts of "gross indecency" between men (qtd. in Dellamora 243n). Certainly this new form of masculine discomfiture played itself out ten years later in the sensational trial and conviction of Oscar Wilde under the same law: Joyce himself noted that Wilde's ultimate "crime" had less to do with his sexuality than with the fact that he had caused a public scandal. To be sure Wilde's relationship with Lord Alfred Douglas flouted the age's dominant discourse on maleness and sexuality, but in Joyce's view it was Wilde's role in taking this sexuality public (rather than the nature of the sexuality itself) that prompted the virulence directed against him.[10] Wilde was no "perverted monster," Joyce wrote, but "the logical and inescapable product of the Anglo-Saxon college and university system, with its secrecy and restrictions"; that is, Joyce saw Wilde as having exposed English society—unforgivably so—to the fissures within its own masculine ideal and within the system constructed to perpetuate it (*CW* 204). To shore up its receding illusion of cultural manliness in the wake of the trials, the English populace branded Wilde a "deviant" and removed him to prison: Sinfield suggests that the Wilde trials in fact created the figure of the homosexual Other; after 1895 "the principal twentieth-century stereotype entered our cultures: not just the homosexual, as the lawyers and medics would have it, but the queer" (*Wilde* 3). From the standpoint of the heterosexual, Kingsleyan ideal, Wilde's incarceration and branding served at least two vital purposes: they sanctioned and exteriorized a convenient measure of difference against which the culture's "masculine" identity might gauge its own future iterations.

"Christian manliness" along with its Other-driven anxiety also suffused Ireland, establishing itself as a dominant social and political discourse as early as July 1865, when the *Dublin Review* complained of the invasion of a Kingsleyan ethos in the schools, remonstrating that manhood had been reduced "to a mere question of tissues and of tendons"—its goal "to bring out muscle, pluck, self-reliance, independence, endurance—the animal man" ("Public School Education" 36). In spite of such protestations, however, late-nineteenth- and early-twentieth-century nationalist movements in Ireland adopted this hard, masculinist ideology as they absorbed—and attempted to defy—a colonial discourse that defined them as "effeminate" and racially inferior. As their British counterparts did, the Gaels began to equate a sturdy, rugged maleness with nationhood, and as Mary Condren reports, the "recovery of 'manhood' . . . became synonymous with the discovery of the Irish national soul" ("Sacrifice" 167).[11] Like Great Britain, Ireland turned to sport to redefine the body of the nation; the Gaelic Athletic Association (1884) promoted this new muscular manhood, advocating distinctly "Irish" games such as hurling, handball, and Gaelic football over English sports such as rugby, field hockey, and polo. Literary Revivalists resurrected warrior figures from Irish mythology such as Finn MacCool and Cuchulain, while other cultural nationalists engaged in additional brands of Other-driven anxiety, defining Irish manhood against both effeminacy and ethnic impurity. The Gaelic League (1893) insisted on a return to the Irish language, while Revivalist literature proclaimed against "too many strangers in the house" (Yeats, *Cathleen ni Houlihan* 226). Such attempts to purge the Saxon influence and to assert Irish manhood and authenticity through fitness and purity movements were not only deeply ironic—they in fact validated the British ethos of middle-class manliness—they were also complicated by Ireland's persistent self-mythologization as a female figure.

Ulysses illustrates the hegemonic nature of Kingsleyan discourse in Ireland, its anxious dependence on its racial and feminine Others, and its awareness of the threat presented by the imminent collapse or inversion of this difference. The masculine self is frequently defined in the text against a feminized, Semitic Other that embodies the paradox of difference as well as reveals the intricate interconnectedness of Irish definitions with their British forms. On the one hand, the feminized Jew appears to make those men who measure themselves against him feel more "manly" (consider the convergence of the racial and feminine Others disported by J. J. O'Molloy in "Cyclops": "every jew is in a tall state of excitement . . . till he knows if he's a father or a mother" *U* 12.1647–48);[12] on the other, the figure also menaces the men who encounter it with economic emasculation. The Englishman, Haines, is the first man in the novel to register the fear of racial decay; in conversation with Stephen Dedalus, Haines slurs the "German jews," noting that they are "our national problem, I'm afraid, just now" (*U* 1.667–68). The thread is woven through the various nationalities and political persuasions represented in the novel. Garrett Deasy, the Protestant unionist, tells Stephen that the Englishman's most cherished boast is "I paid my way," and then he characterizes Britain's "jew merchants" as usurping this financial manhood and sapping "the nation's vital strength" (*U* 2.348–50); from the funeral carriage of "Hades," Parnellite Simon Dedalus and Dublin Castle clerk Martin Cunningham localize and personalize the identical sentiment as they deride a figure they judge to be an elderly Jew, "a curved hand open on his spine," ostensibly for usury (*U* 6.253). Even Bloom, who comes to embody this racial and feminine Otherness, attempts to measure his own manliness against it and locate this

Other outside himself: he notes that Reuben J. Dodd (who was in actuality a Catholic, though he is characterized by Bloom and other Dubliners as a Jew [Gifford and Seidman 110]) has been punished by a judge for his moneylending activities and is—unlike himself—"*really* what they call a dirty jew" (*U* 8.1159, my emphasis).

In spite of, or perhaps because of, the masculine Otherness that Bloom comes to inscribe within himself, he is in fact the character who provides the best example of the extent to which the tenets of British Victorian masculinity had permeated Irish social discourse in 1904; Bloom demonstrates both the cultural domination of Kingsleyan dogma and the extent of the unease that surrounded it. That Bloom has been steeped in the model of muscular manhood as well as its acute, Other-driven discomfiture is made clear throughout *Ulysses;* Bloom constantly measures himself against a standard of "hard" masculinity and continually comes up soft, a pattern that produces for him several anxious masculine moments which recur in his psyche like primal scenes. Bloom's turns as the "new womanly man"—especially his dramatic transformation in "Circe"—have been read profitably from psychoanalytic, feminist, and cultural vantage points;[13] I am arguing that the anxious androgyny associated with Bloom is also significantly indebted to broader societal apprehensions over the instability of the masculine signifier, a position supported by the evident compulsion of various Dublin men to gauge their own manhood against the racial and feminine Other that Bloom comes to embody as well as by their own anxiety-ridden masculine performances.

Bloom is the *Ulysses* character who most consciously—and anxiously —engages the question of masculinity, and he is well aware of the Kingsleyan paragon. During Paddy Dignam's funeral service, Bloom notes the rugged appearance of the presiding priest, Father Coffey, and applies to him the very term the *Saturday Review* used to describe Kingsley in 1857: "Bully about the muzzle he looks. Bosses the show. *Muscular christian.* Woe betide anyone that looks crooked at him: priest. Thou art Peter" (*U* 6.596–97, my emphasis). But Bloom himself does not meet this standard of rock-hard virility, either physically or philosophically. Bloom attempts throughout the novel to reimagine manliness outside the Kingsleyan mode, rejecting both Social Darwinism and physical violence as well as endeavoring to collapse the notion of difference so integral to masculine identity (consider, for instance, his definition of a nation: "the same people living in the same place" [*U* 12.1422]). But in spite of these efforts, Bloom is ultimately unable to escape the hegemony of the Kingsleyan discourse; that he is a much "softer" version of manhood than Victorian education aimed to produce causes him great consternation and prompts him to compensatory explanations—a revisionist history of his own masculinity—whenever possible. Throughout the day he anxiously interrogates his own physical manliness, coming up soft at every turn. He imagines the blind stripling in "Lestrygonians" to be "sizing me up . . . from my hand," but since Bloom's touch is admittedly gentle (and therefore womanish), he decides the stripling "knows I'm a man" from his voice (U 8.1098, 1102); he speculates in "Nausicaa" whether women detect a "man smell" about the male, and he inserts his nose into his waistcoat to discern his own odor which is distinctly, sweetly, feminine ("Hm . . . Hm . . . Almonds or. No. Lemons it is"), produced as it is by Molly's soap (U 13.1043); he frets throughout the novel about not having resumed Sandow's exercises and congratulates himself on not having allowed Gerty MacDowell to view him in profile, perhaps as much to elide her vision of his soft stomach as his Semitic features. Bloom even attempted in earlier years to solidify his masculine hardness by masquerading as that poet dubbed by Kingsley as the most "manly" of the Romantics—George Gordon, Lord Byron— while he courted Molly. In an essay, "Thoughts on Shelley and Byron," Kingsley touted Byron—"the sturdy peer proud of his bull neck and his boxing"—as the embodiment of rugged virility and branded the "utterly womanish" Shelley as his effeminate Other (qtd. in Houghton 202).[14] Bloom, Molly tells us, wooed as Byron, presenting her with a volume of poems and even going so far as "trying to look like" the poet (U 18.185, 209). But Bloom's Byronic self-construction is again undercut by an unmanly softness, a Shelleyan Other: Molly remembers Bloom not only as "very handsome" but also as "too beautiful for a man" (U 18.208–10), an androgynous assessment that recalls common physical descriptions of Shelley offered by women and men alike.[15] Bloom perhaps carries with him a subconscious awareness of this softness, which undermined his performance: in "Lotus Eaters," his loose allusions to both Byron's early volume, Hours of Idleness (1808), and Shelley's poem "The Sensitive Plant" (1820)—"Flowers of idleness. . . . Sensitive plants" (U 5.34–35)— conflate the two poets into a single image and neutralize the Byronic virility that Kingsley praised.

To combat this softness, Bloom has availed himself of various products that promise—either explicitly or implicitly— to "make a new man" of their purchasers, but these items are more than just ineffectual; in fact, they inscribe a pervasive gender anxiety by calling attention to the insufficiency of masculine identity and by collapsing the difference integral to its existence. Gadgets like the Wonderworker and the exercises prescribed in Eugen Sandow's *Physical Strength and How to Obtain It* trade on a profound sense of masculine inadequacy. The Wonderworker promises to make "a new man of you," peddling both flatulence relief and a reconstructed, purged, and purified masculine identity in the Kingsleyan mode (*U* 17.1829); Sandow's program is similarly engaged in shoring up hard, physical manliness, offering powerful physiques to modern men whose "sedentary occupations" have caused their muscles to soften with disuse (*U* 17.515). But even as they offer an improved male body, these cultural artifacts also manage to textualize Edwardian anxiety over the masculine signifier by compressing not only the spaces between heterosexuality and homosexuality but also those between "hard" and "soft" masculinities. The Wonderworker, advertised as being of service to women as well as to men, has been misdirected to *Mrs.* L. Bloom, rendering its promise to make "a new man" of the addressee ("Dear Madam") more than a little ironic: if women can become "new men" by "insert[ing the] long round end" into the rectum (*U* 17.1833), then, one must ask, what do men in this same position—certainly suggestive of anal intercourse—become? Just as the Wonderworker's "new man" subversively contracts the space between heterosexuality and homosexuality, so also the image of the strongman manages to conflate the notions of "hard" and "soft" masculinity: Maurizia Boscagli has observed that Sandow's hypermasculine, specularized body also inscribes an intense masculine anxiety, one that gestures toward the spaces of femininity and loss as it disperses the phallus throughout its musculature. As machines increasingly performed the labor heretofore reserved to men, muscles in the modern era had less practical use than ever before; in the figure of the strongman, then, the enhanced male body evolves from Kingsleyan utility to aesthetic pleasure. Sandow's exercises were to be performed in front of a mirror—a pose that enhances the specular nature of both process and product—in order "to bring into play the various families of muscles and produce successively a *pleasant* rigidity, a *more pleasant* relaxation and the *most pleasant* repristination of juvenile agility" (*U* 17.512–18, my emphasis). Thus the hypermasculine male body, as it becomes the pleasure-giving object, inscribes within itself a feminized—and fetishized—site of Otherness, produced by the very musculature that was intended to signify its manliness.

Bloom's investment in the Kingsleyan ethos and his anxiety over the location of difference within himself are best illustrated by his attempts to reconstruct the history of his own masculinity to make it "harder." Born in 1866, Bloom recalls school experiences that seem to affirm Victorian Ireland's emphasis on physical development, in spite of the *Dublin*

Review's protestations: "Though ringweight lifting had been beyond his strength and the full circle gyration beyond his courage yet as a High school scholar he had excelled in his stable and protracted execution of the half lever movement on the parallel bars in consequence of his abnormally developed abdominal muscles" (*U* 17.520–24). Significantly, Bloom fails to meet the specified requirement for biceps, though he here substitutes another set of muscles to atone for his deficiency. His description of this demonstration of athleticism reveals its debt to Kingsleyan manliness not only in its emphasis on physical strength but also in its assessment of the "courage" required to complete the maneuver, which Bloom noticeably lacks as well. As he reevaluates his performance, Bloom's need to assert another kind of physical potency, rather than, say, intellectual prowess (which we might reasonably expect, given the quasi-intellectualism that Bloom displays throughout the novel and for which he is disparaged by the "Cyclops" narrator), suggests the depth of his investment in this ethos. I have already noted the ambivalence with which the masculinity movement treated intellectualism, and Bloom's revision of his inadequacy in physical terms suggests his awareness that cerebral gyrations were no substitute for those performed by sinewy tendons.

The most telling evidence of Bloom's implication in the discourse of Kingsleyan manliness, however, may be his altercation with the Citizen. Here again, in the aftermath of the event, Bloom repeatedly takes stock of his performance, which, in spite of his philosophical rejection of physical violence, he perceives as deficient—he has delivered only linguistic punches rather than physical blows. In the Kingsleyan worldview, the physical contest was crucial to masculine prowess, as this excerpt from *Tom Brown's School Days* illustrates: "After all, what would life be without fighting . . . ? From the cradle to the grave, fighting, rightly understood, is the business, the real, highest, honestest [*sic*] business of every son of man. Every one who is worth his salt has his enemies, who must be beaten, be they evil thoughts and habits in himself, or spiritual wickedness in high places, or Russians, or Border-ruffians . . . who will not let him live his life in quiet till he has thrashed them" (Hughes 277). Bloom seems to have absorbed something of this ethos in that he refuses to back down from the racial confrontation in Kiernan's pub, hurling his defiant declaration, "Your God was a jew. Christ was a jew like me," back into the bar even as he is hustled out the door and into the jarvey by Martin Cunningham (*U* 12.1808). But Bloom's reflections will return to the scene's violence several times during the course of the evening; he will wonder whether by missing the physical confrontation he has somehow violated the conventions of "manliness." His anxiety is on display as he vacillates between the poles of "manly" defense of one's honor in the Kingsleyan mode and a more "effeminate" appeasement: "Got my own back there. Drunken ranters what I said about his God made him wince. Mistake to hit back. Or? No. Ought to go home and laugh at themselves. Always want to be swilling in company. Afraid to be alone like a child of two. Suppose he hit me. Look at it other way round. Not so bad then. Perhaps not to hurt he meant. Three cheers for Israel" (*U* 13.1216–20). Bloom's confused, "Mistake to hit back. Or? No" weakens the muscular ethos even as it attempts to affirm it and gestures toward another fissure contained within the Kingsleyan ideal itself; unlike Kingsley, Christ taught his followers not to "hit back" but to "turn the other cheek." Bloom's willingness to accord the Citizen the benefit of the doubt ("Perhaps not to hurt he meant") while at the same time trying to position himself in a more "masculine" light, having retaliated against the Citizen's abuse, in fact serves as an emasculation of his enemy, a linguistic sleight that reduces the Citizen's brute physicality and even his sarcasm to sentimental cheerleading: "Three cheers for Israel." Such a move enables Bloom to cast himself in the more "manly" role, one he will continue to refine throughout the day.

In "Eumaeus," Bloom continues this pattern of vacillation, first congratulating himself on his cool and manly reliance on "plain facts" in the face of the Citizen's emotional, anti-Semitic outburst, then seeking Stephen's approbation for his response, appealing to yet another precept of Christian pacificism that further undermines the Kingsleyan paragon: "A soft answer turns away wrath. He hadn't a word to say for himself as everyone saw. Am I not right?" (*U* 16.1085–87). While Bloom here asks for vindication of his action, Stephen's muttered, Latinate response ("*Ex quibus . . . Christus . . . secundum carnem*" [*U* 16.1091–93]) affirms only the fact of his claim—that Christ was indeed a Jew—and not its appropriateness. In this vacuum (in which Stephen withholds from Bloom the validating gaze that he seeks), Bloom continues to obsess over the encounter, reimagining it and recasting his response until it resonates with the appropriate level of manfulness. Declaring to Stephen with "dramatic force" that "I'm . . . as good an Irishman as that rude person I told you about at the outset" (*U* 16.1131–33), Bloom reconstructs his physical pacifism until he convinces himself that he not only avoided an engagement but also that he was its victor. Within a few more lines, Bloom has perfected his revisionist history of the encounter: "He, though often considerably misunderstood and the least pugnacious of mortals, . . . departed from his customary habit to give him (metaphorically) one in the gizzard" (*U*

16.1595–98). Bloom's use of the "manly" colloquialism here—"To give him one in the gizzard"—to describe the verbal fisticuffs in which he has engaged reveals his subconscious need to transform an intellectual victory into proof of physical prowess, according to the dominant conventions of his age.

The self-consciously performative nature of masculinity is similarly on display in other Joycean bodies throughout the text. Both Hugh "Blazes" Boylan and Malachi "Buck" Mulligan locate within themselves conflicting sites of overdetermined masculinity that betray the era's intense anxiety regarding the proof and display of its manhood. As Kimberly Devlin has written, Boylan and Mulligan strike "assertively phallic" poses—roles signified in part by their sexualized nicknames—that self-destruct by virtue of their own excess ("Castration" 133). Boylan's unusually colorful and carefully accessorized garb ("tan shoes and socks with skyblue clocks. . . . a skyblue tie, a widebrimmed straw hat . . . and a suit of indigo serge"), his "jaunty" step, and even the "rakish" tilt of his hat all mark him as a version of the Edwardian dandy (*U* 10.1241–44), that aestheticized, theatrical figure James Eli Adams has identified as a "textual mark . . . of masculine identity under stress or revision" (*Dandies* 55). While the dandy's dramatic artifice is "purged from the true hero, or gentleman, whose authenticity is manifested . . . in an absence of self-consciousness" (54), the elaborateness of Boylan's attire, his fashion-plate furnishings that rival those of even Gerty MacDowell, attests to a deep-seated need to compel the regard of others. The dandy's sole desire, Thomas Carlyle observed in the early nineteenth century, is "that you would recognise his existence; would admit him to be a living object; or even failing this, a visual object. . . . Your silver or your gold . . . he solicits not; simply the glance of your eyes. . . . Do but look at him, and he is contented" (*Sartor Resartus* 207–8). Boylan's elaborate dress thus evokes the exaggerated musculature of the strongman, in both its aestheticized excess and the intense masculine anxiety it inadvertently conveys. But Boylan's performance for the public eye goes over the top in other visual ways as well; he not only arrays himself as gazed-upon object, he also positions himself as aggressively gazing subject. The way Boylan overacts this second role— staring brazenly down the blouse of the shop girl at Thornton's, for instance, or strolling through Dublin with a red carnation between his teeth, offering the "bold admiration of his eyes" to the women in the viceregal cavalcade (*U* 10.1246)—is also indicative of masculinity in crisis rather than the healthy, heterosexual manliness it strives to convey. Boylan's habit of aggressive looking (a trait he shares with Bloom) is emblematic of the way certain men—abundant enough to warrant the nickname "male pests" in the popular press—reacted to women's increasing invasion of the public space at the turn of the century. As I will detail in chapter 8, such aggressive gazing (and worse) by men at women was a product of men's perceived loss of territory as well as an attempt to intimidate women into relinquishing their claims to this newly contested space. Thus driven by desire—itself a condition indicative of lack and anxiety—Boylan specularizes, and therefore feminizes, himself in much the same way that Sandow does; he substitutes exhibitionist clothing and an overdone ocular performance for an elaborate physique in order to attract the imaginary gaze that would validate the masculine self.

Ironically, however, neither the performance nor the gaze it elicits can shore up these fragments; the dandy's act, like the strongman's display and Leopold Bloom's uncertain vacillations, exposes this style of masculinity as yet another charade, while the judgment of the Other's gaze, far from offering approbation, frequently renders Boylan's masculine play an absurdity. Dublin's opinion of Boylan is at best ambivalent: while Nosey Flynn and his ilk applaud Boylan's duplicity in fixing the odds on the Keogh-Bennett fight ("Blazes is a hairy chap," Flynn tells Bloom [*U* 8.807–8]) and Lenehan applauds his prowess in picking winning horses ("see the conquering hero comes" [*U* 11.340]), the text also insistently corrects these temporary elevations of Boylan's star. It counters the admiration of Boylan's double-dealing with such disparaging morsels as the "Cyclops" narrator's description of Boylan as his father's progeny— "Dirty Dan the dodger's son" (*U* 12.998)—and inverts Lenehan's hyperbole with a narrative reference to Bloom as the "unconquered hero" (*U* 11.342). The regard of the women Boylan encounters is no more resolute: although Miss Douce and Miss Kennedy smile winningly at him in "Sirens," the shop clerk in Thornton's is not at all impressed by his antics. When we look through her eyes, Boylan, his costume, and his flower all appear ridiculous: "the blond girl glanced sideways at him, got up regardless, with his tie a bit crooked, blushing. –Yes, sir, she said. Bending archly she reckoned again fat pears and blushing peaches" (*U* 10.330–33). In the young woman's estimation, Boylan does not need the carnation he requests to complete his outfit—he is "got up regardless"—and he is not even suavely cool; in fact, his off-center tie makes him appear a little undone. The blush in this passage may be Boylan's as easily as it may be the young woman's: she does not smile at him at any time during their interlude; instead she is composed and professional, filling the order and taking the delivery address. From this coolness I conclude that her final "archness" is supercilious rather than playful and constitutes a refusal on her part to return to Boylan the admiring female gaze he seeks. Boylan, of course, concludes the opposite, which renders his performance here and on the street before the viceregal carriage all the more absurd.[16]

Molly Bloom's estimations of Boylan best exemplify the ambivalence his act commands throughout *Ulysses*. From one standpoint, Molly is apparently complicit in replicating/enacting the female gaze that would validate Boylan's masculine performance—and Boylan does perform for Molly every bit as much as she performs for him. Molly lavishly praises his virility and that omnipresent, displaced signifier of masculinity, his penis: "he must have come 3 or 4 times with that tremendous big red brute of a thing he has . . . I never in all my life felt anyone had one the size of that" (*U* 18.143–50). But neither is Molly's look reliably affirming; it is just as often deflatingly critical. She concludes that Boylan is probably less potent than Bloom—"Poldy has more spunk in him" (*U* 18.168)—and is displeased by other aspects of her lover's "chamber performance," such as his removing his clothing without her permission (*U* 18.1373), frightening her with a "determined vicious look" during intercourse (*U* 18.153), and slapping her on the behind as he left the house (*U* 18.122, 1368). Even more important, Molly is aware that Boylan is, in fact, performing to please the Other: she observes that, after removing his clothes, Boylan stood in his half-shirt, erection on display, waiting "to be admired" (*U* 18.1373–74); she also notes and appreciates the details of his elaborate costume. It marks him, in her eyes, as being financially successful, but it also causes her to register some perplexity at his rage at having lost twenty quid on the horserace, "tearing up the tickets and swearing blazes" (*U* 18.422–24). But the ability to fix a fight or to pick a winner is one of the markers of Boylan's masculine style; having that marker called in in Molly's presence undermines his prowess. Boylan's fit of temper serves not only as an outlet for his annoyance, it also functions as another demonstration of male virility—Boylan's display is designed to offset his dual losses (of money and Molly's esteem) and is staged for Molly's particular benefit, as she is perhaps subconsciously aware. Molly associates Boylan's cursing with his nickname ("swearing blazes") in an intuitive nod toward the constructedness of his reaction: it is apparently as staged and overdone as the rest of his masculine charade.

For his part, Buck Mulligan also inscribes a destabilized, heterosexual masculine presence that deconstructs itself through performance; in contrast to Boylan and Bloom, however, Mulligan appears to know that he is acting a role.[17] In "Telemachus," for instance, Mulligan plays for the approbation of Haines (his principal audience, the one from whom he hopes to get money) and encourages Stephen to do the same, but as he prepares to "dress the character" of the dandified Wildean aesthete (wanting his "puce gloves and green boots") (*U* 1.516), Mulligan notes the presence of a "contradiction. Do I contradict myself? Very well then, I contradict myself. Mercurial Malachi" (*U* 1.517–18). The inconsistency that Mulligan perceives within himself suggests that the role he presently dons is somehow at odds with his other enactments of masculinity—for instance, the conventional, courageous hero who "save[s] men from drowning" (*U* 1.62) or the hyperheterosexual stud who offers pronouncements designed to inflate his own sexual prowess ("redheaded women buck like goats" [*U* 1.706]) and who proposes a "national fertilizing farm" with himself as principal servicer (female patrons, Mulligan boasts, would "find in him their man" [*U* 14.684–91]). When Mulligan puts on the role of Hellenized aesthete, he apparently sees himself as subverting his other masculine machinations, which are in fact dictated by the Kingsleyan, Hebraistic model. In an 1869 essay *Culture and Anarchy*, Matthew Arnold detailed the dichotomy between the two impulses. Hellenism constituted the antithesis of Kingsleyan dogma, privileging intelligence, a "spontaneity of conscience," and "seeing things in their essence and beauty." Hebraism, on the other hand, propagated Kingsleyan tenets, valuing acting over thinking, a "strictness of conscience" (that is, behaving "rightly"), and acknowledging the presence and degradation of sin (Arnold, *Culture and Anarchy* 467–69). Although Arnold's essay carefully purges such associations in a move that indicates the era's unease with shifting sexual paradigms, Dellamora notes that the terms also inscribed sexual boundaries, with "Hellenism" connoting explorations of male homosocial desire and "Hebraism" signifying a more "manly" heterosexuality (33, 61). Garry Leonard has argued that the relationship between Stephen and Mulligan also functions as an expression of masculinity in crisis, an encoded exploration of male homosocial desire, and that Stephen is (unreasonably, in fact) breaking off the friendship because of a growing sense of confusion over what their association actually means: Leonard maintains that Mulligan's desire to "Hellenize" both Ireland and Stephen ("Ah, Dedalus, the Greeks! I must teach you" [*U* 1.79]) introduces a new dynamic into their bond, one that confounds conventional definitions of masculinity and contributes to Stephen's unease ("A Little Trouble" 16–17). It seems to me, however, that Mulligan's suggestions and Stephen's repudiations of each of Mulligan's masculinist poses—most obviously, Stephen's declaration, "I'm not a hero" (*U* 1.62) and his refusal of the "spiffing" new gray-striped trousers (*U* 1.118) that would update his own costume (as well as his role in this sideshow)—are even more significant than illustrating the confusion over what it meant to be a man and how men interacted in this society.

Mulligan's awareness that he is enacting various styles of masculinity certainly may, as Leonard argues, constitute a form of "camp" that parodies and attempts to undermine the ethos of Hebraism and the social construction of masculinity, but although Mulligan may see himself as a revolutionary, repudiating Hebraism and embracing Hellenism, Stephen certainly does not. In Stephen's eyes, all of Mulligan's mockeries are "idle" (*U* 1.661)—undirected toward any principle larger than himself and therefore useless in effecting the social change he purports to desire. The nature of the heresies that Stephen attributes to Mulligan—against the Church and against the Masculine Self—lies in Mulligan's acknowledgment and exposure of them as "performative, not normative" concepts (Leonard, "A Little Trouble" 11). But Mulligan does not manage, at least in Stephen's eyes, to subvert the authoritarian center of either discourse. This is why Stephen ultimately withdraws his approbation from Buck, and it is for this reason, rather than a moment of homosocial/sexual "panic," that Stephen decides to sever their relationship. Stephen has sought since *Portrait* to establish a homosocial alliance with another man—first Davin, then Cranly, and now Mulligan—who would support him in his struggle against the powerful social forces arrayed against both him and his art, but each has fallen short of his expectations. In yet another iteration of the trope of male-male betrayal that Stephen sees all around him, neither Cranly nor Mulligan takes Stephen's part in standing against the forces represented by his mother's demands; each friend (in choosing the woman's part) disappoints him—by failing to support Stephen's own efforts to circumvent authority or to provide him with a successful model for his emulation.

To Stephen, the forces that Mulligan mocks are not merely illusions; the power that subtends the social discourse in Stephen's belief is backed by a "malevolent reality" (*P* 243) that wants to command his obeisance. The alternative proffered by Mulligan's latest pose, Hellenism, is no option for him at all: first, it inscribes one more moment of male-male betrayal (not to mention Irish subservience) in its associations with Wilde; second, it constitutes a further example of the dichotomous, imitative thinking that Stephen is trying to escape. Artistically, a Hellenistic ethos is as proscriptive as a Hebraistic one: Hellenism dictates "seeing things as they are, and by seeing them as they are to see them in their beauty" (Arnold, *Culture and Anarchy* 468); Stephen, however, is attempting to reject such romanticism. He sees things as they are, yes, but he does not apprehend beauty—instead he perceives squalor and oppression. Finally, if this ethos is, as Leonard suggests, a product of the Oxonian culture represented by Haines and evoked in Stephen's thoughts by Mulligan's reference to the "ragging" of Clive Kempthorpe (*U* 1.165–75), it also constitutes yet another English import. As such, it becomes one more copycat masculinist/artistic pose, inauthentic in the fact that it is a pose but also in that it is not Irish nor even (any longer) Greek—it represents a further British colonization and appropriation of an external culture. As Stephen recognizes, Mulligan's desire to Hellenize the island—its politics, its masculinity, its art—is no good solution either to Stephen's own difficulties or to the problems of Ireland: Hellenism ultimately inscribes another self-betrayal that will fail to open up the authoritarian constructs it purports to dismantle—and become itself another confining ideology. Mulligan's reference to Whitman in this early passage—"Do I contradict myself? Very well then, I contradict myself"—as he rummages for a Wildean trademark costume (his source being, of course, Whitman's 1855 "Song of Myself") is appropriate in several respects to his pretended subversions and Stephen's cognizance of their impotence: the quotation evokes the male-male passion for which both Whitman and Wilde were infamous, thus "contradicting" Mulligan's own carefully constructed heterosexuality;[18] at the same time, it refuses to displace either model and allows both to coexist within his person—the next line of the passage Mulligan selects is "I am large. . . . I contain multitudes" (Whitman 51.1316). As Stephen comes to realize, Mulligan is ultimately unable to repudiate anything or to stand for any principle—to him all is playful and ineffective expedience.

The hypermasculine nationalism on display in the "Cyclops" chapter appears to contrast sharply with the masculine oscillations of Bloom, Boylan, and Mulligan, yet it also reveals the hegemony of the Kingsleyan ethos in Edwardian Dublin and the anxiety that subtended it. Like the social constructions of masculinity in Ireland, political postures owed a great deal to Kingsleyan dogma as the discourses of manhood and nationhood converged; in spite of his overtly phallic "knockmedown cigar," Bloom is transformed by the men of this episode into the exteriorized racial and feminine Other on which these discourses—and their own masculine identities—depend. Acting "like a man" preoccupies the "Cyclops" denizens as intensely as it disturbs Bloom, but the bar-stoolers repeatedly assure themselves of their collective masculinity by comparing themselves to Bloom's supposed lack. For John Wyse Nolan, behaving "like men" involves standing up to injustice "with force" (*U* 12.1475), but Bloom uses words; for the nameless narrator, acting "like a man" requires "putting up a pint of stuff" (*U* 12.1663), whereas Bloom will neither drink nor buy. To J. J. O'Molloy, Jack Power, Ned Lambert, and the Citizen, being a man evidently has something to do with fathering children and then disregarding them. They disparage Bloom for buying a tin of Neave's food six weeks before Rudy was born: "Do you call that a man?" the Citizen wants to know (*U* 12.1654).

To combat perceptions of themselves as racially inferior, the Gaels required their own racialized Other against which they could measure their manhood, and in *Ulysses* it appears they have located it in Bloom, the Irish Jew. Bloom's racial difference is overtly displayed in this episode, and anti-Semitic slurs abound: Bloom is called a "perverted jew" by Martin Cunningham (*U* 12.1635) and is suspected by the narrator of smelling like a "jewie" (*U* 12.452); he is even challenged to name his nation, which he does: "Ireland. . . . I was born here. Ireland" (*U* 12.1431). Obsessed with Bloom's ethnicity, these men are desperately trying to maintain the difference their own masculine identities require, but Bloom appears bent on erasing such difference. His definition of a nation is predicated on sameness—"a nation is the same people living in the same place" (*U* 12.1422)—and even the distinction he draws between his nation (Ireland) and his race (the Jews) seems designed to elide the difference between him and his interrogators: the Jews, according to Bloom, comprise a race "that is hated and persecuted" (*U* 12.1467), a description consistent with the Citizen's rendition of Irish mistreatment at British hands.[19] Thus Bloom's final sally—"Your God was a jew. Christ was a jew like me" (*U* 12.1808–9)—inspires such rage in the Citizen because it collapses the racial difference upon which his masculine identity depends, and he responds with a physical gesture that attempts to reinforce their remaining locus of difference: between the man who talks and the one who fights.

Certainly Dublin men besides Bloom are Othered by effeminacy in this episode: Denis Breen is branded a "bloody old pantaloon," an old man in bath slippers, feminized by his foolishness (*U* 12.253), and Bob Doran is derided by the nameless narrator for being able to control neither his tears nor his exhibitionist wife (*U* 12.394–402). But it is Bloom who comes in for the brunt of this impulse as the masculinized, nationalist body attempts to locate effeminacy outside the self and within the body of the Other. In just one example, the narrator identifies Bloom as "one of those mixed middlings. . . . Lying up in the hotel . . . once a month with headache like a totty with her courses" (*U* 12.1658–60). In contrast to these "wom-

anish" men sits the Citizen, whose "broadshouldered deepchested strong-
limbed frankeyed" manliness epitomizes the new national body, purged of
its racial impurity and its feminization (*U* 12.151). But the de-feminiza-
tion of this body does not end with Bloom; it also extends to attempts to
reimagine and repersonify the mythology of Ireland in masculine, rather
than feminine, terms. It is no coincidence that the chapter of *Ulysses* most
concerned with building Irish manhood/nationhood is also the one most
fixated on feminine betrayal. Despite the physical absence of women from
the bar, their faithless images appear repeatedly in narrative or dialogic
form, from Polly Doran's exposure of herself to her husband's associates
to the faithless wife of the *Police Gazette* and finally to the "blushing bride
elect" of Robert Emmet, who deserts him at his hanging for an Oxford
graduate with a healthy bank account (*U* 12.636). In addition, forms of
betrayal not particularly associated with women—the colt Sceptre's loss at
Ascot, for instance—are also perceived here in terms that nonetheless suggest feminine responsibility. Lenehan laments his loss in terms that lay the
blame distinctly at woman's door: "Frailty, thy name is Sceptre" (*U* 12.
1227–28). Similarly, the Citizen blames a woman (incorrectly, it seems)
for smoothing the way of Saxon invaders even as he evokes the words of
Cathleen ni Houlihan—"we want no more strangers in our house" (*U*
12.1150–51)—and undercuts the conventional heroism of this female
image: "Our own fault. We let them come in. We brought them in. The
adulteress and her paramour brought the Saxon robbers here" (*U*
12.1156–58).[20] This obsession with feminine betrayal is the manifestation
of a masculinity attempting to disassociate itself from Ireland's own self-
mythologization as a female figure, whether victim or warrior queen.
Condren has noted a misogynistic pattern in nationalist rhetoric, observing that "there was a constant fear of impotence, of 'becoming women,' or
even worse: becoming 'old women'" ("Sacrifice" 167). Such rhetoric
would have been difficult to reconcile with an Ireland that consistently
allegorized itself in just such gendered terms: Cathleen ni Houlihan and
Granuaile represented the invaded woman-nation in need of liberation,
while Caillaic Beare (the Hag of Beare) embodied its sovereignty.[21] Nationalist manhood attempted to redress this dissonance between its masculinist rhetoric and Ireland's feminine identity by characterizing the female as the tainted betrayer of manhood-nationhood; its purity lost, the
feminized image could no longer personify the nation. In its place, revisionist mythology turned, as Charles Kingsley did, from the image of the
mother to that of the Son: significantly, according to the Citizen, it is the
"*sons* of Granuaile, the *champions* of Kathleen [*sic*] ni Houlihan" who

will free Ireland and "come again . . . with a vengeance" (*U* 12.1374–75, my emphasis).

Both socially and politically, then, *Ulysses* reveals Edwardian Ireland to be ironically infused with the anxiety-ridden ethos of Kingsleyan manliness even as it attempts to throw off British hegemony. Both Bloom and the Irish nationalists endeavor to remasculinize their identities according to the Kingsleyan code, revising their personal histories and national mythologies to enable them to fulfill their culture's ideal of "manliness." Bloom himself tries to locate outside himself the racial and feminine Others so critical to masculine identity, but ultimately he is unable to do so and becomes himself the signifier of Otherness for the various men who have similarly absorbed the codes of middle-class manliness. The presence in the text of men like Boylan and Mulligan attests to the shifting nature of masculine styles; knowingly or unknowingly, each enacts a variation on the theme that reveals its performative, rather than essential, nature. Ultimately, the representation of masculine anxiety in *Ulysses* reveals "manliness" to be not a reified concept against which other social constructs can be measured but another oscillating signifier that remains paradoxically dependent on the existence of Others for its survival; it lives in perpetual fear that this difference—and finally identity itself—will collapse. Like their female counterparts, Gerty MacDowell and Molly Bloom, the "masculine" men of Dublin chase the uneasy signifiers of a gender identity that is at once culturally constructed and contested. The particular style of masculinity donned by these men is finally of little import; any choice they might make shackles them securely to the gender constructs of their age.

4

Urban Spectatorship, Victorian Vice, and the Discourse of Social Reform

Just as they attempted to reinvent the concepts of both masculinity and nationality, Victorians also engaged in rereading and reimagining the city throughout their era. The rhetoric of purity that permeated the discourse of both nationalism and masculinism similarly invaded the discourse of the Victorian city; the abundance of "social problem literature" produced during the period attests to the fact that "cleaning up the streets" had become a nearly obsessive preoccupation among Victorians and Edwardians alike. A series of governmental reports known as Blue Books was commissioned in the 1830s and 1840s by the Parliamentary Committees of Enquiry to scrutinize the conditions of factory work, child labor, education, public health, and sanitation; these reports, along with journalistic exposés on similar topics, testified to the presence of a fetid underbelly beneath the buoyant surface of Victorian progress. Friedrich Engels's *Condition of the Working Class in England in 1844* (1845), based on both parliamentary committee reports and his own direct observations, and Henry Mayhew's *London Labour and The London Poor,* a fifteen-year project that began serialization in the *Morning Chronicle* in 1849, further exposed the misery of the working classes and the squalor of life in the London streets. Midcentury novelists such as Charles Dickens and Elizabeth Gaskell also chronicled this urban pathology: Dickens turned an unflinching gaze on all facets of London life, from workhouses (*Oliver Twist*) and debtors' prisons (*Little Dorrit*) to chancery courts (*Bleak House*) and urban ash heaps (*Our Mutual Friend*), while Gaskell dramatized the plight of the factory laborer (*Mary Barton, North and South*) in the industrial towns of the north. Later in the century, this extraordinary interest in the urban condition still had not waned: in 1889 Charles Booth published the first part of what would become a seventeen-volume statistical analysis, *Life and Labour of the People in London,* and in 1890 William Booth in collaboration with W. T. Stead detailed the efforts of the Salvation Army among England's most destitute citizens in his treatise *In Darkest England and the Way Out.*

Social reform also became parliamentary priority during the period: a spate of regulatory measures such as the Factory Acts (1833, 1844, 1847, 1867, 1878) improved working conditions in textile mills by prohibiting the hire of children under age nine, reducing workday hours for children and women, and providing for safety inspections of machinery. The Public Health Act (1848) enabled the establishment of municipal boards of health to oversee the remediation of water, drainage, and sanitation problems, and the Contagious Diseases Acts (1864, 1868, 1869) mandated medical and police inspections of prostitutes in port and military garrison towns. The passage of these and similar laws codified a new regulatory gaze in the manner of Foucault's Panopticon, that foundational cultural structure that creates a sense of permanent surveillance among its citizens in order to regulate their behavior. The Panopticon "arranges power," Foucault notes, in order to strengthen social forces: "to increase production, to develop the economy, to spread education, to raise the level of public morality" (*Discipline and Punish* 208). The agitation for repeal of the Contagious Diseases Acts (finally achieved in 1886) suggests an intriguing subtext for social reform legislation in general: the regulatory gaze that increased throughout the period had finally become so intense that it was recognized—at least in this instance—as having achieved an indefensible obtrusiveness, of having overstepped its bounds. Objections to the Contagious Diseases Acts were made on several grounds: that they promoted a sexual double standard by requiring examination only of women and not of the men who patronized them, that they in fact codified (though they did not legalize) prostitution by assuming it to be a "necessary evil," and that they unfairly targeted poor women while granting extraordinarily broad powers to metropolitan police regarding the identification and apprehension of women who were suspected of being prostitutes.[1] It is this final complaint, which in fact distrusts the motives of the regulatory gaze and suspects it not only of harboring a legalized, prurient look but also of committing officially sanctioned vice, that Joyce would have found most interesting. His *Ulysses* registers all of these suspicions as well as the broader ramifications such accusations held for the issue of social control in the aggregate.

This fixation on improving "the public good" not surprisingly included a vigorous (and unwittingly self-subversive) moral component; the efforts of Victorian reformers were fueled not by simple altruism but by a more complex combination of impulses that included an intense fascination with the meanness and vice that they strove to eradicate. Judith Walkowitz and others have argued compellingly that a "powerful streak of voyeurism" and a "'prolonged, fascinated gaze' from the bourgeoisie" impelled the various social reform movements that swept through Victorian England;[2] in *City of Dreadful Delight,* Walkowitz revisits the nineteenth-century figure of the flâneur, that "privileged urban spectator" with early roots in the work of Charles Baudelaire and later turns in the fiction of Henry James. In order to "experience the city as a whole," Walkowitz writes, this man "stroll[ed] across the divided spaces of the metropolis" to own its experiences, to order its narratives, and to establish his "right to the city" (*City* 16).[3] While early flâneurs treated the city as only spectacle, a source of entertainment and amusement, mid and late Victorians "roamed the city with more earnest (if still voyeuristic) intent to explain and resolve social problems" (*City* 18). In contrast to their earlier counterparts, however, these later figures—their acute urban awareness having evolved into a full-fledged social conscience—forfeit the distance and anonymity enjoyed by their predecessors and instead find themselves dangerously vulnerable to absorption by the very spectacle that they most desire to transform. Joyce perceived and appreciated this ironic link between vice and vigilance, and he appropriates this nexus in *Ulysses* as he constructs his own version of the social reformer, the prurient and perspicacious Leopold Bloom. Connected to this lampooning of the reformer in *Ulysses* is an important critique of the regulatory watchfulness that the figure both represented and inspired. Joyce exposes not just the increasing intensity of this gaze as it attempted to direct public and private behavior throughout the era, he also showcases its insidiousness: as Bloom internalizes the presence of social surveillance and subjects himself to its mechanisms of control and punishment, Joyce dramatizes its power to infuse and manipulate individual subjectivity.

Joyce was well aware of the rhetoric of social reform, especially its convergence with the discourses of nationalism and masculinism; on November 13, 1906, he wrote to Stanislaus of his irritation with the moralizing he perceived in such oratory (particularly as regards its insistence on sexual purity) and his desire to expose its hypocrisy:

> By the way, they are still at the "venereal excess" cry in *Sinn Fein.* Why does nobody compile statistics of "venereal excess" from Dublin hospitals. *What* is "venereal excess"? Perhaps Mr. Skeffington-Sheehy could write something on the subject, being, as J. J. B. [*sic*] puts it 'a *pure* man.' . . . Anyway my opinion is that if I put down a bucket into my own soul's well, sexual department, I draw up Grif-

fith's and Ibsen's and Skeffington's and Bernard Vaughan's and St. Aloysius' and Shelley's and Renan's water along with my own. And I am going to do that in my novel (inter alia) and plank the bucket down before the shades and substances above mentioned to see how they like it: and if they don't like it I can't help them. I am nauseated by their lying drivel about pure men and pure women and spiritual love and love for ever: blatant lying in the face of the truth. . . . The Irish consider England a sink: but, if cleanliness be important in this matter, what is Ireland?" (*Letters II* 191–92)

Joyce insists in this letter on Ireland's—and the reformer's—own implication and participation in the vice that each decried; later in the same letter he broadens his derision to encompass not just the reformer's rhetoric but also the reformer's handiwork. Answering a question put to him by Stanislaus about the thematic significance of the *Dublin by Lamplight Laundry,* which appears in the *Dubliners* story "Clay," Joyce tells his younger brother that he suspects the laundry of being "a Magdalen's home"—that is, an establishment for reforming prostitutes: "The phrase *Dublin by Lamplight* means that Dublin by lamplight is a wicked place full of wicked and lost women whom a kindly committee gathers together for the good work of washing my dirty shirts. I like the phrase because 'it is a gentle way of putting it'" (*Letters II* 192). Joyce's subtle mockery of the reformer's impulse constitutes a minor thematic chord even within this early story and paves the way for more extensive examinations of the trope in his later novels.

In "Clay," Joyce "gently" satirizes the reformer, represented here by Maria, who holds some undetermined administrative position at the Protestant-run laundry at Ballsbridge Terrace (the prospectus of which identified its aim as the "rescue and reform of all the outcast women of society").[4] While Maria is not by any stretch of the imagination a reformer of the public space, she does in fact style herself according to the "do-good" model and strives for the betterment of her own environment: she recalls with some pride that the women at the laundry consider her "a veritable peace-maker" (*D* 99), and she evidently prizes "proper" behavior among her associates: she judges Ginger Mooney's demeanor to be deficient ("she had the notions of a common woman," Maria thinks to herself [*D* 101]) and hopes that Joe Donnelly will not "come in drunk" to the Hallow's Eve party she plans to attend at his house later that evening (*D* 100). Joyce and Stanislaus made fun of Maria's ready application of her favorite adjective—"nice" (*Selected Letters* 93)—and the author ironizes her impulse to both judge and adjust other people's behavior by revealing her propensity for stirring up trouble. Not only does Maria "the peacemaker" annoy the children (and probably their mother as well) upon her arrival at the Donnelly house by accusing them of eating her missing plum cake, she nearly spoils the festivities altogether by trying to patch up the estrangement between Joe and his absent brother Alphy. Joe, who has been pleasant enough thus far, becomes incensed and denounces his brother when Maria mentions his name. In turn, Mrs. Donnelly begins to berate her husband for his attitude. Maria evidently has fanned the embers of a long-standing family quarrel, and it is the extraordinary efforts by others (specifically Joe himself, who determines not to lose his temper; his wife, who obligingly fetches more stout to head off the explosion; and the next-door girls, who pursue their distracting games), not Maria, that restore the order that her desire for familial betterment has fractured. Although she quickly apologizes, Maria shortly appears to have forgotten her role in instigating the near meltdown: as the games progress, the text tells us that "soon everything was merry again. Maria was delighted to see the children so merry and Joe and his wife in such good spirits" (*D* 104). Evidently oblivious to her role in producing the rancor, Maria's vision is conveniently elliptical: she sees only her own good intentions and ignores any unpleasant repercussions of her actions. Her inability to acknowledge the clay that is her lot in the blindfold game—quite likely it is the children's revenge on her for accusing them of stealing the plum cake—is connected to this occluded vision, represented most vividly by the presence of the blindfold. Norris suggests that the children are playing a juvenile prank on Maria in the midst of their game, one in which an unknown but benign substance is offered to the victim as something repulsive and disgusting: "the point of the children's joke," Norris writes, "is to make prim, 'genteel' Maria recoil in shock and disgust at the mistaken sensation of touching 'excrement'— only to reveal to her, upon removal of the blindfold, the harmless garden dirt. The embarrassment would be self-inflicted: the victim would be betrayed by her own 'dirty' mind" (*Joyce's Web* 133). I believe that the joke, as well as the garden dirt itself and the fact that Maria has soiled her hands by touching it—subtly mocks Maria's own "cleansing mission" as well as the "good work" of her laundry.

This early exploration of the correlation between occluded perception and the self-delusions of the reformer is reminiscent of Dickens's treatment of the same figure. In *Bleak House,* for instance, Mrs. Pardiggle

proselytizes the poor but is blind to every aspect of their miserable existence except their supposed heathenism; Mrs. Jellyby's vision is similarly
obscured by her own "civilizing mission": as she works toward "the cul-
tivation of the coffee berry—*and* the natives" in Africa, she fails to perceive that her own children are hungry and neglected (Dickens 35). In
Joyce's novels this occlusion gives way to a more careful examination of
the reformer's "vision." In *Portrait,* Stephen's disavowal of the utopian
programme espoused by MacCann suggests the dangers he perceives
within it: the rhetoric of "universal brotherhood" constitutes yet another
attempt to mandate the conformity of thought and social control so
threatening to Stephen's artistic independence (*P* 177, 195–99). In *Ulysses,* Joyce moves beyond the allusions of "Clay" and the simple renuncia-
tions of *Portrait* and attempts to defuse the discourse of reform by exposing its internal fissures: his portrait of Leopold Bloom reveals the
voyeurism behind such utopian plans and exposes the insidious nature of
the regulatory gaze that controlled the "public good" and endeavored to
dictate both public and private behavior.

Critics have long recognized Bloom's voyeurism and his interest in
social reform, but the connection between the two impulses has been
largely overlooked. Bonnie Kime Scott, following the lead of Richard
Ellmann, has helpfully examined Joyce's relationship with social activists Francis and Hanna Sheehy-Skeffington, arguing that Francis's progressive positions on socialism and feminism provided Joyce with the
model for MacCann/McCann of *Portrait* and *Stephen Hero.*[5] Scott also
suggests that Joyce continued his representation of Francis in Bloom,
though she does not elaborate ("Hanna and Francis" 84). Grace Eckley
has argued that Bloom's reformism has its source in the life of crusading
journalist William T. Stead, and still other critics have examined Bloom's
utopian desires outside a biographical context, choosing instead to repo-
liticize them.[6] Cheryl Herr, in a discussion of the debt to the pantomime in
"Circe," argues that Bloom "both projects the culture's Utopian fantasies
and exhibits its ideological insufficiencies" (*Joyce's Anatomy of Culture*
173), and more recently, Vincent J. Cheng has elucidated the political
bases of Bloom's Circean phantasmics. Important as these discussions are,
however, they have missed Joyce's implicit—and gleeful—critique of the
antivice crusader.

To fully appreciate Bloom's highly ironized status as social reformer,
some understanding of his predecessors—their concerns as well as their
vulnerabilities—is helpful. Antivice organizations were not a nineteenth-

century innovation; in fact, they thrived in England from at least the late seventeenth century when the Society for the Reformation of Public Manners agitated against such "immoralities" as Sabbath violation, profanity, prostitution, and homosexuality. In 1802 the Society for the Suppression of Vice (popularly known as the Vice Society) was founded and ultimately dedicated itself to the eradication of "sexual vice," namely obscenity and prostitution. By the 1880s, another spate of reform organizations—now numerous enough to be dubbed the "social purity movement"—began to manifest themselves. These groups pursued a variety of agendas—among them suppression of obscene materials, the "rescue" of prostitutes, and the repeal of the Contagious Diseases Acts. The Salvation Army inaugurated its "rescue" mission in the mid-1880s; less long-lived (but highly influential) organizations included Josephine Butler's Ladies' National Association for Repeal of the Contagious Diseases Acts, Ellice Hopkins's White Cross Society, and William Coote's National Vigilance Association. In the years between 1875 and 1885 Hopkins alone founded more than two hundred women's rescue committees and men's chastity leagues in the British Isles; by 1885, nearly fifteen thousand men had taken the "purity pledge," which required of its adherents:

1. To treat all women with respect, and endeavour to protect them from wrong and degradation.
2. To use every possible means to fulfil [sic] the command, "keep THYSELF pure."
3. To endeavour to put down all indecent language and coarse jests.
4. To maintain the law of purity as equally binding upon men and women.
5. To endeavour to spread these principles among my companions, and to try and help my younger brothers. (rpt. in Bristow 103)

The Dublin White Cross Vigilance Association was also established in 1885, and by 1891 the Dublin sects alone numbered fourteen and counted 530 men who busied themselves by accosting brothel patrons by lantern-light and driving them away (Luddy, *Women* 143–44).[7]

The Dublin experience was not unusual. Reformers did more than distribute pamphlets on street corners; they took an active and personal role in exposing illegal activities. Vice Society members frequently acted as police informers by going undercover and purchasing obscene materials and then turning them over to the police; according to Bristow, by the time of its financial demise in 1880, the Vice Society had seized more than

"385,000 obscene prints and photographs; 80,000 books and pamphlets; five tons of other printed matter; [and] 28,000 sheets of obscene songs and circulars" (49). This personal involvement extended to the dramatic "street rescue" of prostitutes, as both male and female workers patrolled the city's red-light districts and entered brothels to entice women to return with them to one of many Magdalen asylums in operation by the turn of the century. Ireland's first such establishment was founded in 1766; the "penitents" admitted to these refuges were generally under age thirty and worked—as they do in the Dublin by Lamplight Laundry in "Clay"—to support the institutions that housed them, generally by taking in either needlework or washing. During the nineteenth century, Maria Luddy reports, at least fourteen such asylums were operational in Dublin alone (*Women* 109). Antivice reformers also broadened their influence by capturing the regulatory gaze, which produced laws that scrutinized public and private morality: the Obscene Publications Act (1857) granted magistrates the power to issue search warrants of premises suspected of dealing in prurient materials, and the Criminal Law Amendment Act (1885) raised the female age of consent from thirteen to sixteen years, provided penalties for indecent assault, prohibited public solicitation of and by women for the purposes of prostitution, and forbade homosexual conduct between men in both public and private venues.

The personal contact of the reformers with the vice they were attempting to eradicate often placed them in a precarious position; it was feared that female reformers could be trapped inside brothels and that males would fall prey to seduction. Indeed, critics frequently suspected male reformers of variously ignoble or selfish motives, including lasciviousness, and the reformers themselves often admitted to an interest in their work that crossed the line between compassion and titillation. Bristow reports that rescue manuals frequently contained warnings such as the one to male workers not to "kneel down with women at midnight [prayer] meetings, especially behind a pew" (70), and William E. Gladstone recorded in his *Diaries* not only the events of his extensive political career but also his compulsion for rescue work and the moral (and later political) jeopardy in which such contact placed him. On January 20, 1854, for instance, Gladstone reflected on the many prostitutes he had spoken with over the years (eighty to ninety, he estimated) and the one rehabilitation he believed his influence to have achieved: "Yet this were much more than enough for all the labour and time, *had it been purely spent* on my part. But the case is far otherwise . . ." (*Diaries* 4:586, my emphasis). Much later, on July 16,

1886, Gladstone's friends convinced him to give up his "nocturnal activities," warning of a "conspiracy on foot to blacken your private character" (*Diaries* 11:593n).

Perhaps the era's most notorious example of the male reformer's vulnerability—whether in fact or in public perception—to the vice he endeavored to expose was the prosecution of journalist-editor William T. Stead following the July 1885 publication of his exposé of child prostitution within the environs of London. The provocatively titled series, "The Maiden Tribute of Modern Babylon," appeared in the *Pall Mall Gazette* over a week-long period and chronicled Stead's personal investigation into the world of juvenile prostitution, an exploration that included the procurement (though not the violation) of thirteen-year-old Eliza Armstrong. Stead employed Rebecca Jarrett, a reformed prostitute, to purchase Eliza from her mother. Eliza was taken to a midwife to be certified "*intacta*" (that is, a virgin) then escorted to a brothel where she was put to bed and chloroformed. She awoke to find Stead in the room with her; he melodramatically recounted her reaction at the end of his first installment: "And then there rose a wild and piteous cry—not a loud shriek, but a helpless, startled scream like the bleat of a frightened lamb. And the child's voice was heard crying in accents of terror, 'There's a man in the room. Take me home; oh, take me home!'" ("Maiden Tribute" 6). Stead never touched Eliza, and after the incident she was again examined by a doctor, Heywood Smith, who recertified her virginity.

Calculated to spur the passage of the stalled Criminal Law Amendment Bill (first introduced in 1883), Stead's articles were preceded by his somewhat self-incriminating preface that predicted "a shuddering horror that will thrill throughout the world" ("Maiden Tribute" 1). Headings such as "The Violation of Virgins," "The Confessions of a Brothel-Keeper," "How Girls Are Bought and Ruined," and "A Child of Thirteen Bought for £5" punctuated the text. The reports caused an incredible sensation; crowds gathered daily before the *Pall Mall Gazette* offices, and police had to be called in to keep the peace. Stead's detractors excoriated him in the press for "posing as a hero and a martyr" (rpt. in Schults 184), for reaping personal profit (in increased newspaper sales) from the revelations, and for degrading public morality. The *London Standard* opined on July 17: "We venture to say that no other capital in Europe would tolerate for an hour the spectacle presented in the main thoroughfares of London at the present moment of men, women, and children offering to men, women, and children copies of a newspaper containing the most offensive, highly-coloured and disgusting details concerning the vicious ways of a small section of the population" (rpt. in Schults 151).[8] Even Gladstone indicated his unease with Stead's methods, noting in his diary on July 15: "Am not well satisfied with the mode in which this mass of horrors has been collected, or as to the moral effect of its general dispersion by sale in the streets" (11:371). Suspicion turned to sanction, however, in November, when several months after Mrs. Armstrong reappeared (July 11) to report her daughter missing, Stead was convicted of abduction under the new Criminal Law Amendment Act, passed into law in August. During his trial, Stead's detractors believed their suspicions of his motives vindicated when he admitted to feeling "intense excitement" during his investigations and, though a teetotaler, to partaking of "champagne and cigars in order to pass as a veteran participant in the world of vice" (Schults 180). Such confessions, coupled with the procurement of Eliza, brought both moral and legal judgments to bear against him, and Stead served three months in Holloway Prison for violating the very law his investigations had helped to enact.

Considered in this context, then, it appears to be no coincidence that Joyce's Leopold Bloom, who exercises his visual acuity in order to reimagine his city as he traverses Edwardian Dublin, is also an aficionado (albeit an often frustrated one) of women's ankles and undergarments: like his nineteenth-century predecessors, Bloom is endowed with a capacious vision that ironically fuels his reformer's conscience. Seeing is an endless preoccupation of Bloom's, and he takes covert pleasure—both libidinous and philanthropic—in that which he observes. Though he is seemingly indefatigable in his attempts to glimpse a flash of stocking as women climb into cabs or settle their garters, Bloom's regard is not reserved solely for the female form. He also exercises his look on behalf of social problem solving, an impulse evidently subtended by an intense desire for approbation, given his Circean fantasies of grandeur. Bloom recognizes the pollution of the river Liffey, the economic potential of the railway, and the suffering (physical and emotional) of his fellow Dubliners. Because little escapes his notice, his speculations on reform are extraordinary in their range: trams could carry cattle to the quays and the dead to the cemeteries (U 6.400–408); vertical burials would save room in graveyards (U 6.764); small birth annuities would ensure a new generation's financial comfort (U 8.384); anesthesia's widespread use could ease the agonies of childbirth (U 8.382–83); prostitutes and food should be medically inspected and the former licensed to prevent the spread of disease (U 16.743, 804). A pacifist, Bloom even may be characterized as an early-twentieth-century advocate of gun control; he is disturbed by "children playing battle" and marvels, "How can people aim guns at each other. Sometimes they go off" (*U* 13.1192–94).

True to historical type, however, Joyce insists on undermining the selfless transcendence of the reformer's vision from its very first appearance in the novel: that moment when Bloom begins to skim the pages of *Ruby: the Pride of the Ring*. Mary Power has, of course, demonstrated the subject of Amye Reade's 1889 novel, slightly renamed by Joyce, to be circus reform;[9] the "flamboyantly illustrated" text exposed the "cruelty rather than the glamour of circus life and shows how young performers were exploited" (Power 115). Significantly, however, both Leopold and Molly have other, more prurient expectations of the book; in fact, Bloom's reaction to it registers the sexual suspicion that underlies the reform movement: "He turned over the smudged pages. *Ruby: the Pride of the Ring.* Hello. Illustration. Fierce Italian with carriagewhip. Must be Ruby pride of the on the floor naked. Sheet kindly lent. *The monster Maffei desisted and flung his victim from him with an oath.* Cruelty behind it all. Doped animals. Trapeze at Hengler's. Had to look the other way. Mob gaping. Break your neck and we'll break our sides" (*U* 4.345–51). Layers of spectacle converge in this passage: Reade verbally depicts the scene of the circus master's cruelty, and her illustrator, Talbot Hughes, has drawn it, inviting such eyes as Bloom's (and ours) to look on in shock and horror. But what Bloom sees first is not the "cruelty behind it all"; what arrests his glance ("Hello"!) is the depiction of the whip-wielding tyrant threatening the nearly naked young woman (her form cloaked only by a sheet)—a scene of potential sadomasochism and a particular textual taste of Bloom's. Only after this reading of masochistic sensuality does Bloom's attention shift to the didactic purpose of the novel, circus reform. The passage now evokes Bloom's own experience as circus spectator watching a trapeze accident, and his description of the circus mob's callous voyeurism provides yet more evidence to suggest that reformism may not be as selfless as it pretends. Although Bloom certainly abhors the cruelty of circus life to both human and animal performers, he is initially drawn to the picture because of its sadomasochistic overtones, and like the crowds that eagerly gathered to await subsequent installments of "The Maiden Tribute," the mob Bloom remembers gapes in enjoyment (horrified enjoyment perhaps, but enjoyment nonetheless) at the accident, not in outrage. The spectacle that creates the reformist impulse, then, has covert

pleasure at its source: "Break your neck and we'll break our sides"—
laughing.

Reformers frequently couched their antivice rhetoric in terms of class,
which, taking their cues from Friedrich Engels, they often perceived in
ocular terms.[10] Engels excoriated an upper class that refused even to look
at its poor, segregating them in slums where they "struggle through life
as best they can *out of sight* of the more fortunate classes of society" (33,
my emphasis). In "The Maiden Tribute," Stead borrows Engels's discourse and applies it to juvenile prostitution, declaring it an "evil" that
had been "hidden out of sight," an act in which "the daughters of the
people" are compelled as "sacrifice to the vices of the rich" ("Maiden
Tribute" 1). Stead goes on to assert that of democracy and socialism, the
latter "will find the most powerful stimulus in this revelation of the
extent to which under our present social system the wealthy are able to
exercise all the worst abuses of power. . . . Wealth is power, Poverty is
weakness" ("Maiden Tribute" 1).

The obliteration of class stratification may also be found at the egalitar-
ian heart of Bloom's reformer's vision. Like his predecessors, Bloom often
perceives issues of class in voyeuristic terms. Listening to Bob Cowley play
the minuet from *Don Giovanni* in the Ormond Hotel, for instance, Bloom
connects visual perception to class recognition as he recalls a scene from
the opera that dramatizes the unbridgeable fissure between upper and
lower classes: "Court dresses of all descriptions in castle chambers dancing. Misery. Peasants outside. Green starving faces eating dockleaves. Nice
that is. Look: Look, look, look, look, look: you look at us" (*U* 11.966–
68). Significantly, Bloom alters this scene in a way that intensifies class
boundaries and betrays his socialist preoccupations. Mozart's peasants,
unlike Bloom's, are also dancing, and Bloom's addition of "dockleaves"
and "green starving faces"—both emblematic of the Great Famine, according to Gifford and Seidman (306)—affixes to Mozart's creation a
particularly Irish tint. But it is the passage's ocular ambiguity that ultimately is most intriguing. We are not quite sure who is compelling whose
look, and such obscurity simultaneously suggests multiple possibilities:
one, that the richly dressed dancers consciously and ostentatiously display
their splendor to the view of the less fortunate who watch and starve; two,
that Bloom's hungry, miserable peasants desperately desire to be seen (in
this they would gain affirmation not only of their plight but also of their
very existence); and three, that some mutual obligation is incurred on the
part of each to notice the other—that is, the wealthy and the poor each are

able to compel one another's vision. At the same time, Bloom conjures his own spectacle of affluence and squalor; however, he is insensible neither to the beauty of the music nor to the joy that it expresses: "Nice that is." Such dissonance links this passage to Bloom's observations regarding *Ruby* and the trapeze accident—"break your neck and we'll break our sides" (laughing)—and once again evokes the covert pleasure that resides at the heart of the reformer's vision.

These scenes, along with his own "programme" (articulated more fully in "Circe" and subtly deployed in "Eumaeus"), establish Bloom as heir to the Victorian reform tradition and its ironic, voyeuristic implications. Certainly novelists such as Charles Dickens and Wilkie Collins suspected their own infamous reformers of motives more self-indulgent than noble (Mrs. Pardiggle and Mrs. Jellyby of *Bleak House* spring immediately to mind, along with Miss Clack and Godfrey Ablewhite of *The Moonstone*), but the reprehensibility of these characters, like those citizens criticized by Engels and Stead, seems to lie primarily in their collective inability to see comprehensively. By contrast, such selective seeing is not a flaw of which Joyce's Bloom (unlike his Maria) could ever be accused: Bloom fits, then, into the reformer's camp populated by writers such as Engels, Mayhew, and Stead who made it their business to explore and expose the taboo. In his preface to "The Maiden Tribute," Stead proclaims "an end to that conspiracy of silence" perpetuated by "the Home, the School, the Church, the Press": "It is a veritable slave trade that is going on around us; but, as it takes place in the heart of London, it is a scandal—an outrage on public morality—even to allude to it. We have kept silence far too long" ("Maiden Tribute" 1). The "scandal" first of discovering and then of publicizing issues such as juvenile prostitution rendered the reformer extremely vulnerable to societal disapprobation, and Joyce illustrates this susceptibility of the reformer to both submersion and censure by endowing Bloom with an intense self-awareness. As he covertly peers at others throughout the course of the novel, Bloom frequently feels himself subjected to the societal gaze, as well as to its implied judgments.[11] This duality of vision helps to demonstrate the complex relationship of voyeurism to reform: the reformer's look is necessarily captivated by the urban spectacle in order to imagine its transformation, but at the moment of enthrallment, the reformer is absorbed by the spectacle. Thus reformers may be at once lauded for their vision and vilified for it as the gaze catches them watching. As Bloom thrills to the social spectacle, he becomes the object of the gaze; he is conscious both of being observed ("see ourselves as others see us" [*U* 13.1058]) and of avoiding detection ("see, not be seen" [*U* 11.357–58]). Like those urban reformers who preceded him, Bloom's voyeurism renders him continually vulnerable to becoming awash in spectacle himself, a wave that will crest in the novel's "Circe" episode, where he will be both condemned and lauded for the inclusivity of his vision.

"Circe" plays itself out in Dublin's phantasmagoric red-light district, certainly a significant locale for the social reformer. Indeed, Herr has observed that "Circe" is the space in the novel most in need of reform: "the atmosphere projected from the beginning of the chapter describes a violent culture in which life is almost unsupportable. . . . The fact is that what we read as expressionistic exaggeration is in some cases more faithful to the reality of life in an Irish tenement district that one would like to admit" (*Joyce's Anatomy of Culture* 167). As the episode progresses, it enacts not only the reformer's absorption in vice but also the legal and moral judgments that might potentially be levied against the reformer. Here, a solicitous Bloom pursues a drunken Stephen Dedalus into nighttown, "watching" out for the young man. Bloom, ever the good Samaritan, is also scheming to effect his own version of a "street rescue," not of a prostitute but of another dispossessed youth—Stephen himself. Having entered the very core of urban vice, Bloom mutates into spectacle—just as Stead did with his makeup, champagne, and cigars—a transformation underscored by the episode's playlike configuration, complete with parts and stage directions. As Bloom searches for Stephen (who, with Lynch, has arrived in nighttown ahead of him), reality and imagination collide in his perception as bawds, conscious of "the polis in plain clothes" (*U* 15.370–1), hawk maidenheads while various Others appear to query Bloom regarding his presence in the district. His father, Rudolph, wants to know, "What you making down this place? Have you no soul?" (*U* 15.259). Although he will offer many false identities, addresses, and excuses to the Watch, Bloom does not answer his father. Instead, he offers his first accounting of his activities to the image of Mrs. Breen, presenting himself as an antivice crusader and claiming to be in nighttown on particular business: "Interesting quarter. Rescue of fallen women. Magdalen asylum. I am the secretary . . . " (*U* 15.401–2, ellipses Joyce's).

As Mrs. Breen fades from his imagination, Bloom's subconscious now conjures a trial that proceeds to scrutinize his look; this scene in many ways parallels the legal and moral judgments levied against the reformer and attests to the increasing intrusiveness of the regulatory gaze upon private behavior as well as within the individual psyche. As the day's images flood in upon him, Bloom imagines he is put on trial for "unlawfully watching and besetting" (*U* 15.733–34), accused by various Others who now represent the gaze: Gerty MacDowell charges he has seen "all the secrets of [her] bottom drawer (*U* 15.384); Martha Clifford sues him for "breach of promise" (*U* 15.765); Philip Beaufoy accuses him of being a "street angel and house devil" (*U* 15.854) and exhorts the "court," "Why, look at the man's private life!" (*U* 15.853). Now, Mary Driscoll, a former house servant of the Blooms, comes forward to testify to Bloom's lecherousness, and Mrs. Yeverton Barry (among other women) charges he has written anonymous, offensive letters to her and covertly admired her "peerless globes" (*U* 15.1019). Bloom's look here is exposed by the gaze as undeniably prurient: he has been "caught in the act" of looking (*U* 15.680) and is judged guilty by all; only Paddy Dignam's corroboration of his alibi saves him from a fictitious hanging, a sentence pronounced by the Recorder in terms used to describe the child prostitution exposed by Stead's "Maiden Tribute": "I will put an end to this *white slave traffic* and rid Dublin of this odious pest. Scandalous!" (*U* 15.1167, my emphasis).

Reality intrudes as Bloom reaches Mrs. Cohen's establishment, the house in which he will finally locate Stephen and Lynch. Accosted out front by Zoe Higgins, Bloom exhibits a curious mixture of titillation and disinterest in the prostitute, caressing her right breast "mechanically" but making a lascivious reply when she asks him for a cigarette: "Rarely smoke, dear. Cigar now and then. Childish device. (*lewdly*) The mouth can be better engaged than with a cylinder of rank weed" (*U* 15.1349–51). Ironically, it is this remark, suggestive of fellatio, that leads to the novel's fullest exposition of Bloom's reformist fantasy.

In this scene, the obsessive look for which Bloom was condemned during his trial now empowers him. Looking is what Bloom does best, and fittingly, the reformer's vision is introduced by an exhortation to scrutiny that parallels but modifies Beaufoy's: "Why, look at our *public* life!" (*U* 15.1361, my emphasis). Bloom is installed as the new Lord Mayor of Dublin because of his perspicacity; his first speech reveals what he has seen—a society divided by deep economic inequities—and his words conjure the same spectacle of working-class exploitation that Engels evokes. As Lord Mayor, Bloom is an advocate of progress but not of dehumanizing mechanization. He rouses the crowd's applause by proclaiming his opposition to the capitalistic exploitation of the common worker: "Machines is their cry, their chimera, their panacea. Laboursaving apparatuses, supplanters . . . manufactured monsters for our mutual murder, hideous hobgoblins produced by a horde of capitalistic lusts upon our prostituted labour. The poor man starves while they are grassing their royal mountain stags or shooting peasants and phartridges . . ." (*U* 15.1391–97). A variety of discourses converge in this passage. The alliteration and the concern with "prostituted labor" perhaps have their roots in the sensationalism perpetrated by the *Pall Mall Gazette,* and the visions of class Otherness and even class warfare ("shooting peasants and phartridges") certainly have a source in Engels, who wrote of exploitation of the poor by wealthy capitalists and predicted the ultimate demise of such an economic structure. The intent of Bloom's Nova Hibernia, of course, is to end all such conflicts by perpetuating utopia through economic equality.

When Bloom puts on his ruby ring (*U* 15.1490), the act may very well resonate with colonial and imperial associations as Gifford and Seidman claim, but the appearance of a ruby ring in this scene also evokes the Amye Reade novel that Bloom skimmed earlier in the day and symbolizes the connection of voyeurism to reform so critical to Bloom's character.[12] Thus "Leopold the First" is hailed as "the world's greatest reformer" (*U* 15.1459) and is applauded for his vision: "All that man has seen!" (*U* 15.1464). But the "new Bloomusalem" appears to be not so much benevolent as it is disaster-prone; its construction creates homelessness, destroys monuments, and results in the death of several innocent bystanders. Bloom survives this temporary failure, however, and the episode now moves to illustrate the "covert pleasure" that Bloom the Reformer takes in his endeavor. As Bloom renders his pronouncements—"I stand for the reform of municipal morals and the plain ten commandments" (*U* 15.1685–86)—he continues to wink and whisper lewdly to and about various women in his audience. Even more enjoyable for Bloom, perhaps, is the consequent personal glory that the enactment of reform has brought him. Bloom, the dispossessed, the quintessential outsider, now belongs, and he revels in his newfound identities. For a brief time Bloom imagines he is beloved of Dubliners from all classes, genders, and ideologies, including a blacksmith, a millionairess, and a bishop; even the vituperative Citizen of "Cyclops" blesses him (*U* 15.1617–18). Bloom now presides over the "Court of Conscience" and parades his new selves, all of which enhance his stature among his "subjects": alternately he becomes Bloom the Wise, advising Paddy Leonard to pay his taxes and Nosey Flynn his insurance; Bloom the Generous, refusing three shillings from Hynes and giving his coat to a beggar; and even Bloom the Ladykiller, his wit prompting the suicide of the veiled sibyl and several other attractive women in the audience.

As dissenting voices begin to plague his utopia, Bloom's private life is probed again in a scene that recalls the aftermath of the social purity movements. Public leaders came to be held to a higher moral standard in their private lives, and those who failed to achieve it, including Charles Stewart Parnell and Sir Charles Dilke, fell from power.[13] Bloom's contributions to the public welfare now are similarly forgotten as he is accused of "infantile debauchery" and of worshipping "the Scarlet woman" (U 15.1756, 1758). To vindicate himself, Bloom calls for medical testimony to affirm his sexual innocence. Robert Byrnes has argued that Joyce drew on the nineteenth-century medical stereotype of the "degenerate" Jew for the purposes of high comedy (305), but his analysis, in focusing on the stigmata of the Jew, overlooks the conflation of Bloom's Jewishness with the figure of the prostitute—another important image of both disease and sexual difference. The "pervaginal examination" that Bloom undergoes operates on at least two levels: it evokes both the medical certifications of virginity that were performed by midwives and doctors on behalf of brothel keepers, and, although none of Bloom's diseases is sexually transmitted, the examination recalls the reform-minded investigations of the prostitute's body mandated by the Contagious Diseases Acts.[14] Here the regulatory gaze is turned against Bloom in one of the closest possible looks at the human body: Dr. Mulligan's verdict is delivered in the language of the brothel keeper's medical cohort—"*virgo intacta*"—but the pathological analysis of Bloom suggests the government-sponsored public health examinations of the prostitute. The collapse of these two examinations onto one another—one designed to perpetuate vice and the other intended ostensibly to curb it—exposes each as the other's ironic counterpart; they become equal partners in violation and degradation. Such irony was not lost on the detractors of the Contagious Diseases Acts (foremost among them Josephine Butler), who branded the compulsory examinations "instrumental rape" (qtd. in Walkowitz, *Prostitution* 101).

In his discussion of panopticism, Michel Foucault equates the gaze with surveillance and with punishment, observing that the viceless, utopian society, or "perfectly governed" community, is sustained by subjects who internalize as self-surveillance the State's formal disciplinary powers.[15] Foucault argues that the individual who is "subjected to a field of visibility, and who knows it, . . . inscribes in himself the power relation in which he simultaneously plays both roles; he becomes the principle of his own subjection" (*Discipline and Punish* 202–3). "Circe" dramatizes Foucault's point as Bloom, within the confines of his own psyche, "plays both roles": watcher and watched, castigator and castigated. As his Circean encounters unfold, Bloom gravitates between these positions; guilty of looking, he imagines himself as the object of the gaze and subjects himself to both its judgment and its punishment. His metamorphoses—from voyeur to reformer to victim—dramatize not only the crusader's role in attracting the regulatory gaze and his vulnerability to immersion in the spectacle he seeks to expose, they also testify to the intensity of the internalized gaze and the disciplinary power it wields over the individual psyche. Vincent J. Cheng has observed that Bloom becomes a messianic figure who appears to be sacrificed in martyrdom in the final moments of this scene, and certainly the litany that closes it would support this conclusion. However, we must overlook neither the fact that pain and punishment are integral components of self-sacrifice nor the detail of immolation, an act that implies purgation as well as martyrdom: diseased corpses were often burned to prevent the further spread of illness. Bloom's imagined immolation is clearly connected to the unrelenting scrutiny he has undergone in this episode; he burns in much the same way that a combustible object placed beneath a magnifying glass in bright light will shortly ignite. Bloom's immolation, a result of his internalization of the regulatory gaze as self-surveillance, thus functions also as self-inflicted punishment, and Bloom ends this scene "mute, shrunken, and carbonised" (U 15.1956), his reformer's voice (temporarily) silenced, his stature reduced, his body blackened with soot—an external manifestation of the reformer's ironically tainted vision.

In the closing moments of the larger episode, Bloom recovers his reformer's persona and begins to effect the originally intended rescue of Stephen Dedalus, who, terrified by his own hallucinations, has broken a lamp in Mrs. Cohen's establishment and fled into the night. Bloom tries desperately but unsuccessfully to extract the drunken young man from the dangerous predicament that immediately engulfs him, that of having run afoul of two belligerent British soldiers, Privates Carr and Compton. Bloom's efforts here in fact become a literal "street" rescue, as Stephen is soon lying prone on the pavement, "his face to the sky, his hat rolling to the wall," having been punched in the face by Private Carr ostensibly for insulting Edward VII (U 15.4749). With Corny Kelleher's assistance, Bloom prevents Stephen from being written up by the police, ensures he has not been injured, and stands watch over his insensible form until

Stephen revives enough to walk to shelter. The final phantasm of the episode, Bloom's dead son, Rudy, appears to Bloom as he bustles protectively around Stephen and suggests yet another personal motive that may propel the reformer's concern for the less fortunate: the satiation of some deep yet unfulfilled emotional need. Josephine Butler, in fact, entered rescue work after the accidental death of her five-year-old daughter in 1863; shortly thereafter, she began to visit workhouses and opened her first home for terminally ill prostitutes. Of Butler's continuing efforts on behalf of these women, Stead wrote, "other labours in this most difficult field have been impelled thither by a desire to save souls, or to rescue women. Mrs. Butler always wanted to save daughters" (qtd. in Bristow 80). Bloom, it seems, would like to save a son.

If "Circe" exposes the voyeuristic elements of the reformer's vision, then "Eumaeus" suspects it of decidedly mercenary motives.[16] Or as Bloom so succinctly puts it in a reflection on Dublin's temperance shelters, "the idea . . . was to do good and net a profit" (U 16.800). Here Bloom continues his attempted rehabilitation of Stephen Dedalus, escorting the young man to a cabman's shelter (which he associates with temperance shelters such as the Coffee Palace [U 16.792–93]) and lecturing him en route on "the dangers of nighttown, women of ill fame," and drinking (U 16.63). Once arrived at the shelter, Bloom attempts to sober up Stephen with coffee and a roll. Critics such as Gilbert and Ellmann have suggested that the redundant, cliché-ridden verbosity of this chapter reflects Bloom's mind-numbing weariness;[17] my own belief is that the syntax of this episode suggests not exhaustion but rather a superhuman attempt to control and exorcise the accusatory demons of "Circe." For if "Circe" is the hallucinating mind's dream of reform, then "Eumaeus" presents the rational mind's recapitulation of that vision. Still smarting from its Circean exposure and censure, Bloom's look in this episode is more consciously surreptitious here than anywhere else in the novel; he throws a "guarded glance" at Stephen (U 16.300), tries to steal a look at Skin-the-Goat "so as not to appear to" (U 16.358), and glimpses the episode's lone streetwalker (whom he suspects of having just been released from a Lock Hospital [U 16.729]) from behind the pages of the Evening Telegraph. His reformer's conscience will not be so easily quashed, however, and in a torrential narrative attempt to drown the voices of self-doubt, Bloom spins out his utopian fantasy once again, this time for Stephen's edification and—perhaps —his participation.

"Improvements"—both municipal and personal—occupy Bloom's

thoughts in this episode. He thinks of visiting London for "an instructive tour of the sights of the great metropolis, the spectacle of our modern Babylon where doubtless he would see the greatest improvement"—perhaps, given the reference here to Stead, in eradication of prostitution (*U* 16.513–15), and considers that D. B. Murphy, when he steps outside to use the urinal (itself a municipal improvement, having been "erected by the cleansing committee") would note that the Loop Line elevated railway bridge had been "greatly improved" (*U* 16.935–36). Bloom's own additions to these municipal improvements are again rehearsed in this episode in a slightly more coherent form than they appeared in "Circe":[18] he argues for a guaranteed income (around £300 per annum) as a guarantor of "universal brotherhood" for all who work and seems to advocate a return of the Contagious Diseases Acts, telling Stephen of his own support for licensing and medical inspection of prostitutes (*U* 16.1134–35, 743).

But it is in his "Utopian plans" involving Stephen that the reformer's profit motive is most clearly revealed. Fearing in Stephen's patronage of local prostitutes not only disease but also the possibility of his running afoul of the Criminal Law Amendment Act (*U* 16.1193), Bloom determines on a larger plan for Stephen's rehabilitation, one that will also, not coincidentally, benefit himself. Realizing he already has made an investment in Stephen (his reparation for the damaged lamp shade in "Circe" as well as the current coffee and roll), Bloom decides he might "profit by the unlookedfor occasion" (*U* 16.1217). Stephen, he believes, would be a stimulating intellectual companion for himself; he might give Molly Italian lessons; he and Molly might even form a highly lucrative musical partnership: Bloom envisions "concert tours in English watering resorts packed with hydros and seaside theatres, turning money away, duets in Italian with the accent perfectly true to nature" (*U* 16.1654–56). Both partners would benefit from the association; Stephen would enjoy a distinctly better existence involving nicer clothes, regular meals, a better social circle, and the ability "to practise literature in his spare moments" (*U* 16.1861); the Blooms would benefit financially and intellectually from the arrangement. To enhance his "shining hour" even further, Bloom imagines he might even make a few extra guineas (one per column, to be exact) by recounting his underworld rescue of Stephen and the rest of his encounters that evening with "the lives of the submerged tenth" (*U* 16.1225–27), a phrase he lifts from William Booth's 1890 Salvation Army publication, *In Darkest England and the Way Out*. Bloom's working title for his own exposé is somewhat less dramatic, *My Experiences in a Cabman's Shelter*

(*U* 16.1231), but his plan to record his experience for profit suggests the avarice of which journalists like Stead were often suspected.

Critics have often suggested—with little actual evidence or contextualization—that the overblown language of "Eumaeus" perhaps constitutes this very missive. Certainly the episode's preoccupation with the crusader and the crusader's vision, as well as its predilection for borrowing stock phrases and exaggerated rhetoric from the discourse of the day, indicates the plausibility of this theory. More important, however, it appears that Bloom's head is literally filled (as Bloom himself might say) with this type of rhetoric; it is little wonder that Stephen eventually departs 7 Eccles Street with no evident plans to return. Bloom's advocacy of the Contagious Diseases Acts and "universal brotherhood," not to mention his plans for the "improvement" of Stephen, mark him as complicit in maintaining the internalized, regulatory gaze that the younger man desires so desperately to escape. Stephen no doubt intuits that he is being "furtively scrutinised" (*U* 16.1180) by Bloom and perceives in these utopian visions a reflection of the propagandist agitations he repudiated in *Portrait;* when Stephen sobers up, he notably and "openly" dissents from Bloom's views on "civic selfhelp" (*U* 17.29) in a manner that recalls his earlier refusal to countenance MacCann's positions. Foucault encapsulates the import of such pervasive surveillance in the name of reform; Bloom's attempt to "watch out" for Stephen, though well intended, is not a benign activity. Foucault argues: "Our society is not one of spectacle, but of surveillance . . . ; it is not that the beautiful totality of the individual is amputated, repressed or altered by our social order, it is rather that the individual is carefully fabricated in it. . . . We are neither in the amphitheatre, nor on the stage, but in the panoptic machine, invested by its effects of power, which we bring to ourselves since we are part of its mechanism" (*Discipline and Punish* 217). Stephen well understands that Bloom, like himself, has been absorbed into his culture's self-regulating mechanism; such schemes for betterment (his own, Ireland's, or the world's), no matter how potentially well meaning, imply a cultural surveillance that is both insidious and ubiquitous as it internalizes itself within the individual and seals off all possible routes of escape.

Joyceans are fond of observing that the "three smoking globes of turds" that emanate from the rear of the street-sweeper's horse serve as commentary on the episode. I would suggest that this defecation—as well as its imminent expurgation by the "brush [that] would soon brush up and polish" (*U* 16.1876–77)—functions more specifically as Joyce's excremental metaphor for social reform, deployed for the first time in "Clay"; it represents the era's pervasive preoccupation with "cleaning up the streets" and again offers silent testimony to the reformer's ironically tainted vision. The watchful presence of the sweeper himself, observing the progress of Stephen and Bloom as they make their way up Lower Gardiner Street, signifies the omnipresent, surveillant gaze invoked by reformers and intensified by their work: whether the sweeper actually dozes or not (as the text speculates) is in fact immaterial; what is significant is that he is perceived to be ever-watchful of all that transpires around him.

Fracturing the Discursive Feminine: Joyce
and the "Woman Question"

5

Deconstructing the Discourse of Domesticity

Joyce was well aware of the Victorian era's complex and contested representations of gender, as well as its vigorous debate over the "essential"
nature of women and their role in society. The author's personal aversion
to the ideological constraints of matrimony has been well documented;
James Joyce and Nora Barnacle did not legalize their union until July 4,
1931, two children and nearly twenty-seven years after they first departed
Ireland together in the fall of 1904.[1] In September 1904, a month before
they sailed, Joyce wrote to Nora of both the difficulties in, and his reasons
for, flouting propriety: "It seemed to me that I was fighting a battle with
every religious and social force in Ireland for you. . . . There is no life
here—no naturalness or honesty. People live together in the same houses
all their lives and at the end they are as far apart as ever" (*Letters II* 53).
What is less evident than Joyce's rejection of religious and familial conventions are his insistent attempts to dismantle the underlying cultural mores
that enabled their existence. Joyce's belief that marrying Nora Barnacle
would ensnare them both should be reexamined in the context of a slightly
earlier missive, one that suggests he understood the aftermath of marriage
in Ireland to be more stiflingly restrictive for her than for himself. In an
August 1904 letter to Nora, Joyce blamed his mother's death of the previous year not on cancer but on her powerlessness as a woman within Irish
society:[2] her existence, Joyce charged, was circumscribed by a social order—"home, the recognised virtues, classes of life, and religious doctrines"—that he would attempt, in his own life, to reject. Joyce wrote:
"My mother was slowly killed, I think, by my father's ill-treatment, by
years of trouble, and by my cynical frankness of conduct. When I looked
on her face as she lay in her coffin . . . I understood that I was looking on
the face of a victim and I cursed the system which had made her a victim"
(*Letters II* 48). Joyce's sense that his mother had been trapped within an
insidious ideological mesh that not only dictated her confinement but also
may have expedited her death is corroborated by the cultural discourse
that governed the lives of nineteenth- and early-twentieth-century women
in England and Ireland. Joyce's fiction continues to reproach the "system"

that victimized women like Mary Jane Murray and from which he tried to deliver both Nora Barnacle and himself; in his work, Joyce attempts to fracture the idols of gender that perpetuated feminine subjugation.

An extraordinary dissonance, one that is laid bare in Joyce's fiction, divided the predominant cultural image of nineteenth-century womanhood—the domestic angel—from the sexual and legal facts of her existence. Coventry Patmore's 1854–56 glorification of domestic femininity, *The Angel in the House,* sold more copies than any other poetic work of the era except Tennyson's *Idylls of the King* and instilled within the discursive figure of the virtuous wife-mother a near-absolute moral authority and ability to rule the domestic realm. Possessed of modesty, "pure dignity, composure, ease" and "marr'd less than man by mortal fall," this woman necessarily and inevitably sacrifices her virginity on the altar of married love, and any sexual impulses that she previously may have possessed summarily dissipate when she becomes a wife (Patmore 135–36). This sublimation of desire, sourced in the punishment assigned to Eve's hunger ("Thy desire shall be to thy husband, and he shall rule over thee" [Genesis 3:16]) and the passivity with which the Virgin Mary embraced her fate at the announcement that she would conceive a son ("Behold the handmaid of the Lord; be it done unto me" [Luke 1:38]), is encoded in the perfect wife's ideological makeup; not only her desire but also her individuality is subsumed by her husband-master: she "makes all the sum of her desires to be devotion unto his" and submits to her husband's will in a "rapture of submission" (Patmore 137–38). Midcentury medical discourse similarly colluded with this view of wifely frigidity, which continued to operate throughout the period. Physician William Acton wrote in 1857 that "a modest woman seldom desires any sexual gratification for herself. She submits to her husband, but only to please him, and, but for the desire of maternity, would far rather be relieved of his attention" (101–2).

But the domestic angel, in an important discursive parallel to the Church's exaltation of the Virgin, is considered to derive from these sacrifices a powerful moral authority.[3] Patmore's poem acknowledges and ennobles a wife's ability to employ an elutriated kind of artifice—"cunning," "deceit," and "wiles"—to keep her husband, without his knowledge and "against his nature," on the path of righteousness by manipulating his desire for her (Patmore 139). Such stratagems would seem to undermine the Virgin-Angel's claim to innocence, but here they are apparently neutered by their containment within the wifely role that directs their proper exercise. So powerful is this woman's resultant purity of body, mind, and spirit that "wrong dares not in her presence speak" (Patmore 135), and even her husband respectfully realizes in the poem's last lines that when she calls him "lord," it is only a courtesy. His wife's true allegiance, he observes, is to her heavenly master, and in this commitment she also figuratively retrieves her virginity: her "Temple keeps its shrine / Sacred to Heaven; because in short, / She's not and never can be mine" (Patmore 141). This discourse of domesticity thus elevated the Victorian angel to a position that transcended her own carnality even within the marriage union; it is this sublimation of her own desire that propelled her ascendancy and formulated the locus of her authority.

Absolutely essential to the exercise of the domestic angel's power was her position within the home. It is the wife, and not the woman, who is necessarily bereft of desire in this discourse; unattached females or other women who ventured outside their homes were regarded as having potentially dangerous sexual natures. Most late Victorians appeared paradoxically convinced that what they believed to be the "essence" of womanhood—sexual purity—would dissolve outside the supposedly protective sphere of the husband's or father's abode. Certainly the era's domestic fiction, perhaps in spite of itself, perpetuated such fears. When the Victorian heroine ventures away from her family and into the world, she frequently encounters new sexual knowledge that renders her "fallen" in the eyes of her community: novels such as Elizabeth Gaskell's *Ruth* (1853), Thomas Hardy's *Tess of the D'Urbervilles* (1891), and Grant Allen's *The Woman Who Did* (1895), all found in Joyce's library, try to imagine new possibilities for constructing womanhood outside of a perpetual asexual virginity, but their writers ultimately stop short of repudiating the discourse of domesticity. Instead, they attempt to contest only the domestic angel's determining criterion of sexual purity, and even in this they are not entirely successful. While Ruth Hilton, Tess Durbeyfield, and even Herminia Barton insistently retain their moral authority (and their angelic demeanors) in spite of their sexual transgressions, each is also ultimately purged from the text: the deaths of these women rectify the disruption to the domestic discourse that their lives have symbolized, whether they unwillingly succumbed to desire (as do Ruth and Tess) or openly embraced it (as does Herminia).[4] John George Cox's remarks in the *Dublin Review* in April 1883 are similarly emblematic of a deep-seated societal need to contain and sublimate female sexuality within marriage and the home. Though a proponent of the additional rights the new Married Women's Property Act extended to women, Cox voices concern about the "evil" that might derive from allowing a wife both property and a means to support herself if her marriage foundered; in Cox's view, if a woman could "leave her home" with some measure of pecuniary ease, the door to sexual desire might swing wide as well. According to Cox, "Formerly the knowledge that the false step [adultery] would leave her destitute must have helped many a woman to turn aside from the first whisperings of temptation" (438–39), but now that a wife was financially freer to leave her husband's house, her sexual nature rose menacingly to the foreground of cultural discourse. In the same article, Cox cautions against extending the right to vote to women on a national level. Such a change would precipitate their dangerous, mass movement out of the domestic sphere and result in the diminishment of woman's moral ascendancy to the point of retarding the course of civilization itself: "If women come to be regarded as men, rivals to be trampled down, or past [sic] in the race, their old power will perish. But something more is at stake . . . , for the same process will result in a sure weakening of the spiritual forces of the world —our very ideals are in danger" (441–42).

All too often, however, the dangers that confronted the Victorian and Edwardian wife came not from outside the home but from within it. The insidious image of feminine domestic power perpetuated within the popular discourse stands in sobering and ironic contrast to the way in which this same woman was construed within both English Common Law— extended to Ireland in approximately 1603—and the statute books of the period.[5] Legal discourse canonized the wife's sexual containment and her selflessness but not her authority; in fact, the powerful domestic angel was rendered nearly impotent under the law. While a single woman enjoyed a modicum of rights, a married woman forfeited her autonomy at the altar.[6] If a husband chose to drink his weekly wages and beat, starve, or otherwise beggar his wife, he would have been well within his rights to do so throughout most of the period, because, contrary to Patmore's final epiphany of wifely transcendence, in the eyes of both the Church and State, a wife's very existence in fact devolved onto that of her husband upon their marriage.[7] A husband was responsible under English Common Law for the behavior and "discipline" of his wife and had "the right, for due cause, to chastise his wife with a stick as thick as the thumb" ("Women and Work" 671); it would not be until the passage of the 1878 Matrimonial Causes Act that a wife who had been the victim of aggravated assault perpetrated by her husband could obtain a legal separation from him. In spite of this law, however, wife beating continued as a socially acceptable practice among the working classes in Ireland; as late as February 1913 a writer for the *Irish Homestead* notes that many husbands still "drink and beat their wives" and actually proposes that these men ought to "beat [their wives] a great deal more, until they served proper meals, and kept the children in order" (qtd. in Bourke 267). Certainly Joyce illustrates this propensity toward domestic violence in his fiction; probable and actual wife-beaters abound in his work—they include Mr. Hill, who mistreated his wife during her life and now physically threatens his daughter; Mr. Mooney, who "went for his wife with the cleaver" (D 61); Farrington, whose wife "bullied her husband when he was sober and was bullied by him when he was drunk" (D 97); Tom Kernan, whose violence toward his wife ended only after his sons grew up (D156); and Mr. MacDowell, whose "deeds of violence" toward his wife have likely contributed to her migraines (U 13.298). While some women—Annie Chandler and Ada Farrington, for instance—abuse their husbands emotionally, the source of physical violence in Joyce's work is always masculine, and it is always directed against a weaker presence—physically and legally—than itself.

Not only did proprietorship of a woman's physical person cede to her husband unless a previous settlement declared otherwise, she also automatically forfeited to him any property she previously may have owned;[8] it was not until the enactment of a series of Married Women's Property Acts beginning in 1870 that the law gradually began to consider women as separate individuals with rights and responsibilities independent of their husbands.[9] Before the passage of these laws, a wife's property remained her husband's to dispose of even in cases of desertion, divorce, or death: a husband could live with his paramour on his wife's income or legally disinherit his wife of everything she possessed before the marriage as well as all that she (or they) had acquired afterward by leaving the entire estate to someone else. Thus, in spite of the canonical fiction perpetuated by the Anglican husband's marriage vow to his wife, "With all my worldly goods I thee endow," the legal reality of marriage was just the opposite. In return for this potential windfall, a husband incurred no fiduciary obligation under the law to support either his wife or their children.[10] Certainly Maria, the unmarried protagonist of "Clay," understands that as a single woman she is at least financially better off than her married counterparts: as she prepares to go out for the evening, she ponders "how much better it was to be independent and to have your own money in your pocket" (D 102).[11]

In matters of female sexuality, gender inequities reinforced the idea that women's bodies could not be divorced from their husbands' other possessions; the female body was subjected to multiple regulating authorities that did not attempt similarly to constrain men. The Contagious Diseases

Acts of 1864, 1868, and 1869 (repealed in 1886) ostensibly were designed to curb an epidemic of venereal disease in garrison and dock towns in England and Ireland, but in practice these laws were more about regulating and containing the sexuality of working-class women than about public health.[12] The C.D. acts (as they were then known) dramatically expanded the powers of the metropolitan police forces by providing for the apprehension and physical examination of any woman even suspected of being a prostitute (evidence was not required), as well as her mandatory confinement for several months in a "lock" hospital if she were found to be infected with a venereal disease; the law required no such confinement of soldiers and sailors who were equally culpable in the spread of these illnesses. The right of married men to visit prostitutes or take mistresses had been legislated (if not explicitly, then certainly tacitly) by the 1857 Divorce Act and was still in force at the fin de siècle; an English husband could legally divorce his wife for adultery (euphemistically known as "criminal conversation") although her entitlement to the same remedy required proof of desertion or cruelty in addition to his infidelity. In Ireland, the situation was more dismal: as late as 1905 divorce still could be granted only by a private Act of Parliament, as courts for that purpose had not been established there as they had been in England; thus this remedy was unreachable for any but the wealthiest and most well-connected citizens (Ignota 524).[13]

Joyce recognized the slavish dominance that the image of enshrined, domestic womanhood wielded in the popular discourse of Victorian and Edwardian Ireland as well as the realities that belied its iconography. His disaffection for the system he blamed for his mother's death perhaps explains part of the appeal Henrik Ibsen's work held for him; his early fascination with Ibsen's plays surely reveals not only Joyce's appreciation for the Norwegian's unembellished art but also his interest in the playwright's attempts to awaken his own culture to the devastating effects of domestic confinement: in Ibsen's work, a destabilizing female dissidence frequently attempts to undercut male institutionalized power. In his essay "Ibsen's New Drama," Joyce focuses his praise for *When We Dead Awaken* primarily on artistic technique, but when he compares this play with other Ibsen dramas, Joyce notes that Nora Helmer "capture[s] our sympathy" (*CW* 65) and that Hedda Gabler is a "tragic" figure (*CW* 64). Certainly the oppressive social and marital situations of these women in no small part produce these impressions: one resorts to forgery to save her husband's life because she had no legal right to secure a loan for his medical treatment (and discovers in the exposure of this act that she is married to a "stranger"); the other marries a man whom she does not love in order to satisfy a craving for professional, social, and personal power that, as a woman in her society, she is unable to sate in any other way. Hedda Gabler's suicide and Nora Helmer's departure from her doll's house are the shocking results of these ultimately unbearable lives; their final acts signal the devastating social oppression of women as well as the need for cultural change. In his turn, Joyce not only suggests that the discourse of domesticity unfairly confines women and stifles their sexuality, he also implies that the realities of marriage and home frequently—and ironically—constituted physically dangerous spaces for the "angel of the house."

Given Joyce's own coming of age amid the turbulent gender reformulations of the late nineteenth century, as well as the volume of texts at his disposal that register these conflicts, it should come as no surprise that residues of Victorian gender constructs—domestic angels, "mad"women, and New Women—manifest themselves throughout his canon. But Joyce engages these questions of gender not by constructing female characters that reflect nineteenth-century typologies; instead, he creates women who refract them. The difference in terms is critical: according to *Webster's New Universal Unabridged Dictionary,* "to reflect" is to "bend or throw back . . . to give back an image of; to mirror or reproduce." "To refract," on the other hand, springs from the Latin "refractus" or "refringere," meaning "to turn aside, to bend aside, from 're-' and 'frangere,' to break." Though they remain always confined by ideology, Joyce's women do not simply mirror the feminine ideals explored, contested, and perpetuated in Victorian discourse; his female characters also expose the fissures and contradictions that exist within the discourse of domesticity and warp the icon beamed at them, often beyond recognition.

Like many of his predecessors in Victorian literature, Joyce challenges conventional notions of femininity, but his work registers none of their tormented ambivalence toward the subject. Instead, in Joyce's portraits of the desiring "Araby" boy as well as *Ulysses'* mutual voyeurs, Gerty Mac-Dowell and Leopold Bloom, the author unapologetically depicts the restrictions and dangers perpetuated by the cult of domesticity. But as Joyce unmasks the fraudulence of the discourse that specifies the icon's chastity and her moral authority, he does not condemn the woman who attempts to enact such codes; instead, he savages the society that perpetuates such improbable paradigms of feminine perfection. As Bonnie Kime Scott has observed, several of the *Dubliners* women at first appear to resonate an angelic transcendence; they frequently occupy "self-sacrificing, nursing, serving roles" that admit "a parallel between the female protagonist and the Virgin Mary" (*Joyce and Feminism* 16). But we must not fail to notice that Joyce nearly always subtends these portraits with hints of illicit sexuality; he chooses the Dublin by Lamplight Laundry—in actuality a home for reforming prostitutes—as the home for the nunlike Maria and presents the service that Polly Mooney (a "little perverse madonna" [D 62]) renders to the men of her mother's establishment as sexually suspect long before she ensnares Bob Doran.[14] As we have seen, in the common parlance the domestic angel possessed no overt impulses of her own, sexual or otherwise, and submitted to the sexual act only in order to satisfy her conjugal obligations and to fulfill her maternal role. The Virgin-Mother paradox hinges on the elision of female desire, but in Joyce's work, females may be both desired and desiring: as agents of desire as well as its objects, the women of "Araby" and "Nausicaa" set the charge for their archetype's ironic implosion.

In the girl of "Araby," Joyce attempts his earliest—and subtlest—subversion of the cult of the domestic angel. We watch the "Araby" girl through the eyes of the story's impressionable young narrator, whose vision of her and their subsequent relationship reveals nothing so much as the extent to which he himself has been mesmerized by the cultural icon. As the boy first glimpses Mangan's sister, she seems to him to resonate a virginal purity, much like Gaskell's Ruth or Hardy's Tess; she appears backlit, in an aura, her figure always awash in light, "defined" by a glow that emanates from behind her (D 30) or simply "touched discreetly" by the incandescence of a street lamp (D 33). Her innocence is further emphasized by that fact that she is young enough to still wear petticoats; the light also catches the "white border" of this undergarment as the girl talks with her admirer for the first time (D 32). The girl's virginal stasis evokes the moral authority of both Patmore's domestic angel and the Blessed Mother: as the boy immobilizes the object of his desire upon her proverbial pedestal, he literally looks up to her—he watches her from the shadows as she stands above him on the porch and calls to her brother, or he lies on the floor of his front parlor so he can watch her movements without being observed. His admiration fuses with religious obsession: "I imagined that I bore my chalice safely through a throng of foes. Her name sprang to my lips at moments in strange prayers and praises which I myself did not understand. My eyes were often full of tears (I could not tell why) and at times a flood from my heart seemed to pour itself out into my bosom. . . . I did not know . . . how I could tell her of my confused adoration" (D 31).

Worship of the Victorian virgin significantly metamorphoses into adulation of the Catholic Virgin, as this passage's extensive religious metaphors make clear: love becomes the sacred chalice, and the beloved's name—which we do not know—becomes a prayerful mantra. The girl's namelessness in the boy's recounting may signal both the iconic passivity and the moral authority he imagines for her: without identity she becomes selfless, to be sure, but the obscurity of her name also recalls the Hebrew tradition that holds the holy name of god to be unrepresentable. At the very least, the girl's anonymity indicates her status in the boy's imagination as an icon: she is to him an "image" of feminine perfection, an archetype rather than an individual woman.

In the boy's characterization—though not in Joyce's—the agency of the look and the desire that it signals are largely denied to Mangan's sister: when she appears on the stoop of the house and attempts to look for the boys, they spy on her instead; when she speaks with the protagonist to ask whether he is going to the bazaar, he first reports his own embarrassing confusion then coolly intimates that she demurely failed to return his glance, focusing either on the silver bracelet she turned "round and round her wrist" or "bowing her head" toward him (D 32). But the boy's intense disorientation at the girl's initial approach ("I was so confused that I did not know what to answer. . . . I forget whether I answered yes or no") and the evident straightforwardness of her query ("She asked me was I going to *Araby*. . . . It would be a splendid bazaar, she said; she would love to go" [D 31]) suggest that her gaze was in fact more direct and discomfiting than his accounting relates; accordingly, the boy has attempted to revise their encounter to deny the girl's look and negate the awkwardness that her directness has caused him. His alterations in fact displace his own shyness onto her in order to fit her more precisely into the narrative vision that he endeavors to construct throughout the tale: the image of the domestic angel. Garry Leonard has observed that the girl's desire to attend the bazaar is appropriated by the male narrator and represented as his own: it is Mangan's sister, not the boy, who originates the wish to visit Araby (*Reading* 73). To be completely accurate, however, we must also acknowledge that the boy does not elide the possibility of feminine desire altogether: he simply ratchets its scope downward to a more manageable level, one he believes that he himself might satisfy and control: if the girl cannot attend the bazaar because of her convent's retreat, then he will ride out in her place to secure her a souvenir.

By attributing to Mangan's sister a lesser aspiration than the one she actually expresses— that is, not the desire for the quest itself but for the trinket that it might produce (which might be supplied by him)—the narrator sublimates the girl's desire in a manner that neatly fits his conception of her as the domestic angel. Undoubtedly influenced by the conventions of courtly love described in one of the books he has found among the dead priest's possessions (Walter Scott's romance *The Abbot*) as well as by the cult of the Victorian virgin, the boy has wished to enact chivalrous deeds to win the affection of his "stainless lady" even before she speaks to him: "Her image accompanied me even in places the most hostile to romance. . . . I imagined that I bore my chalice safely through a throng of foes" (*D* 31). The medieval tradition is consistent with the nineteenth-century discourse of domesticity in that both conventions required the beloved female to remain safely ensconced at home while her male lover forayed into the world on her behalf; once the boy carefully alters the girl's wish to make her own pilgrimage into a desire that he might perform the feat in her place, the narrator finally possesses the charge that he has imagined: he determines to visit the bazaar in order to win both his trophy and his love. Mangan's sister is thus perceived by her young admirer as a lady to be sequestered, worshiped, and won; all the models of ideal Victorian womanhood at this boy's disposal require that the girl never admit to, much less venture forth to slake, her own desires. In his construction of their encounter, then, the boy determines to satisfy the girl's aspiration in her place and thereby sublimates her desire; the souvenir he plans to bring back thus becomes a symbol of himself as woman's ultimate—and only possible—fulfillment within the domestic discourse.

But Joyce also provides in this story a paradox of innocence and sexuality that subverts the boy's efforts to suppress the girl's look and to redirect her desire; his wary attempts to reshape her disruptive frankness into the Victorian angel's submissive satiation are undermined by his own narrative. Just as the boy carefully revises the girl's wish to attend the bazaar, he also attempts to ignore the sensuality of her appearance: however, the narration itself again gives the boy away; it subtly disrupts his discursive production of her idealized, asexual image. Ironically, the narration appropriates the very motifs that Victorian fiction and the boy's account employ to convey purity; it then subverts these tropes to formulate Joyce's critique of a social order that must either disavow or condemn female desire. First, the narration undercuts both the light and the childish innocence that lend Mangan's sister her angelic and innocent aura—the same light also lets the boy see the lines of her body through the fabric of her dress. "She was waiting for us, her figure defined by the light from the half-opened door. Her brother always teased her before he obeyed and I stood by the railings looking at her. Her dress swung as she moved her body and the soft rope of her hair tossed from side to side" (*D* 30). Even more significantly, this scene radiates a cinema-like quality that softens and sensualizes the female form; the backlit girl waits, then positions herself to receive what Laura Mulvey has called in the terms of film theory, "the intimidating look of the camera in its role as sculptor of passive femininity" (ix). Onto this image the narration manages to graft both the boy's—and his society's—conflicted suppression of female sexuality that exists within the Virgin-Wife-Mother paradigm. Joyce invokes such sexual dissonance throughout the story: *The Abbot,* as Harry Stone and R. B. Kershner have observed, is not only the tale of Roland Graeme's idealistic, youthful chivalry on behalf of Mary, his "idealized Catholic" monarch, it is also the story of Mary, Queen of Scots, a woman known also as "a 'harlot queen,' a passionate thrice-married woman who was regarded by many of her contemporaries as the 'Whore of Babylon,' as a murderess who murdered to satisfy her lust" (Stone 350).[15] This image of voracious and unsatisfied female desire is further underscored in the boy's uncle's allusion to Caroline Norton's poem "The Arab's Farewell to His Steed," as he finally hands over money for the excursion. In their annotations to *Dubliners,* John Wyse Jackson and Bernard McGinley provide the opening lines to Norton's poem and point out that Joyce's use of equine references throughout the story are appropriate to its motif of "knightly chivalry." Here is "The Arab's Farewell":

> My beautiful! my beautiful! that standest meekly by,
> With thy proudly arch'd and glossy neck, and dark and fiery eye,
> Fret not to roam the desert now with all thy wingèd speed!
> I may not mount on thee again—thou art sold, my Arab steed;
> Fret not with that impatient hoof, snuff not the breezy wind—
> The further that thou fliest now, so far am I behind. (rpt. in Jackson and McGinley 25)

Jackson and McGinley note the similarities of equine anatomy to Mangan's sister's "curved neck" (*D* 32, 33). They also point out that the woman at the bazaar resides in a "stall" (*D* 35); indeed, the entire bazaar area takes on a drafty, barnlike aura. But presenting women as horses suggests something besides the story's chivalric quest, especially in the context of these lines. In "The Arab's Farewell," horses may be bought or sold as property and "mounted" at will by their owners; they stand obediently under the gaze only for the moment—in fact, they are impatient to run wild once again. That this horse is eager to be off with a new owner implies the presence of a perpetually unsated, untamed desire—evocative, perhaps, of that attributed to Mary, Queen of Scots and suggestive of the ever-unfulfilled wish of Mangan's sister.

The equine imagery works well for Joyce; it allows him to strengthen the undertones of sensuality that threaten to erupt throughout the boy's story, and it manages to suggest the boy's underlying (and well-founded) fear of his own insufficiency as he attempts to satisfy the girl's desire. The imagery also knits together the important tropes of sensuality and commerce: the logic of the boy's discourse unwittingly implies that the affection of Mangan's sister, like the loyalty of the Arab steed, is also for sale to the highest bidder; that is, the man who brings her the souvenir from Araby. The biography of the poem's author, Caroline Norton, deepens and complicates the allusion by introducing the motifs of male duplicity and acquisitiveness in relation to female sexuality: in 1836, in hopes of obtaining a handsome financial settlement, Norton's abusive husband falsely accused her of committing "criminal conversation"—that is, infidelity—with the prime minister and sued him for alienating her "wifely affections." When Norton and her husband separated, she was left with almost nothing: under the law he retained custody of their children, secured an inheritance left to her by her father, and attempted to claim as his own the income she generated from her literary works. Norton's case—and her subsequent activism to remedy her legal powerlessness to impede her husband's petitions—dramatically illustrates the commodified status of women and their sexuality throughout most of the nineteenth century. The embedded biography also allows Joyce to suggest that residing within the boy's childish adulations and usurpations is a deeper menace—his presumptions are grounded in the same forms of institutionalized power that permitted the exploitation of Caroline Norton.

These unsettling tropes of female desire and male acquisitiveness begin to surface in the boy's consciousness as he slowly recognizes the irreparable fragility of the illusions that he has constructed. Until the moment he arrives at its gates, *Araby* has possessed in the boy's imagination a "magical name" (D 34); its image in fact converges with the girl's own as the source of his distraction and enthrallment. She, too, has an evocative name that he has repeated to himself in prayer, and now, "[a]t night in my bedroom and by day in the classroom her image came between me and the page I strove to read. The syllables of the word *Araby* were called to me through the silence in which my soul luxuriated" (D 32). But once the boy passes through the bazaar entrance, he senses that he has been duped; instead of the "Eastern enchantment" (D 32) he has anticipated, he finds only darkness, weariness, and English accents. Not surprisingly, the sullied image of the bazaar begins to debase that of the beloved. The reason for the quest itself evaporates, and the image of virginal perfection also begins to dissolve: suddenly the boy can hardly remember why he has come to Araby; he does so only "with difficulty" (D 35). His impression of the next woman he sees is colored by this changing perspective: in the shop girl (whom the narrator scrupulously refers to as "the young lady," perhaps in a final narrative effort to sustain the feminine icon) and the "two young gentlemen" with whom she flirts, he discerns triviality as well as female desire and male cupidity; their conversation invades his consciousness and begins to melt another of his illusions, the quest of courtship. The emphasis on money that distracts the boy throughout the story's final pages—he clutches a "florin," looks in vain for a "sixpenny entrance," hands over a "shilling" to the gatekeeper, sees two men "counting money," hears the "fall of coins," and feels the "two pennies" and "sixpence" that remain in his pocket (D 34–35)— not only suggests his painful awareness that he is short of cash, it also underscores his emerging realization that the ritual of courtship, in which men woo women with gifts and flowers, in fact constitutes a form of simony.

The narrator now begins to perceive what Joyce has been suggesting all along, that women—including Mangan's sister—may be both desired and desiring in their own right. The shop girl gazes at the boy in a scene that parallels his first conversation with Mangan's sister, and he is again discomfited, his posture of (financial) sufficiency exposed: when "the young lady came over and asked me did I wish to buy anything" the narrator is forced to answer, "No, thank you" (D 35). Without the souvenir from Araby, he knows he will be unable to satisfy the modified (and more modest) desire he has fabricated on behalf of Mangan's sister; amid this realization, the angelic paradigm the boy has constructed around her figure begins to collapse. The previously suppressed image of voracious and unsatiated female desire now emerges in the boy's consciousness and underscores his own inadequacy as the agent of feminine fulfillment; instead of a virtuous angel, the boy now sees—both in Mangan's sister and in the "young lady"—her nemesis: the fallen woman. Hugh Kenner has argued that in the bazaar scene, "The chalice of youthful confident enterprise is broken against deglamourizing inadequacy—the late arrival, the empty bazaar, impractical porcelain vases and flowered tea-sets, two pennies and sixpence. . . . The great empty hall is a female symbol, entered at last; and it contains only sparse goods, the clink of money, and tittering banalities" (Dublin's Joyce 54). But it is not the female form itself that disappoints here; it is the image of the ideal, angelic woman—who does not exist—that has been tarnished. The fall of Mangan's sister—of all female forms, including the Catholic Virgin—from their brilliance-bathed pedestals is clear; the light in the bazaar gallery is not the only one that has gone out. But Joyce makes clear that the women are not at fault: the narrator has duped himself and he knows it; his own "vanity" and not Mangan's sister is the target of his "anguish and anger" (D 35) as he now turns his gaze inward, upon himself. What is not clear from these closing lines is exactly what the narrator now perceives—does he understand only his miscalculations and his ultimate failure to satisfy the girl? Or has he been disabused of his view of women generally, seeing in them now not angelic transcendence but a baser, more desiring existence? Or are his "anguish and anger" the product of both realizations?

What finally does emerge from the boy's self-rebuke is his failure to apprehend the power of the cultural discourse to perpetuate the icon that has colored his perspective and crippled his intuition. If the boy equates feminine desire with female unworthiness, or if he is disturbed by anything other than his own failure to acknowledge the girl's real want—to attend the bazaar herself—then his epiphany constitutes yet another attempt to obscure and sublimate the need that lies at the heart of this story: no amount of money could have purchased a souvenir to content this woman; what she seeks is the quest itself. It is significant, however, that while Joyce refuses to purge feminine desire from this text, he also leaves it frustrated. As long as the Virgin-Angel survives, as long as Mangan's sister is perceived through the lens of a discourse that must either sublimate or condemn her desire, her wish never will be requited. Unless the boy's final realization encompasses the larger folly of attempting to elide, usurp, or disavow a woman's desire by offering himself as the sole means to its fulfillment, then his epiphany is worthless; it serves only to perpetuate the discourse of domesticity that has controlled his subjectivity throughout the tale.

While in "Araby" Joyce subtly tweaks the Victorian need to obscure feminine desire within the discourse of domesticity, in Ulysses he constructs a more overt dichotomy that continues the dissolution of the domestic angel and extends his critique of "Society with a big ess" (U 13.666). Here again Joyce's text rejects any essentialist view of woman's "nature" and instead presents the feminine ideal as a culturally determined construct. In Ulysses' "Nausicaa" episode, Joyce exposes the fissures contained within three of the major discursive influences on late-nineteenth- and early-twentieth-century women: the cult of the Virgin, popular fiction, and contemporary advertising (all, to some degree, still operative influences in early-twenty-first-century life). Joyce does not find fault with Gerty MacDowell's attempts to synthesize these models (although her attempts do produce decidedly odd conflations); he does, however, condemn her prototypes as flawed and impractical. He also suggests—through the unsuccessful elisions in Gerty's own domestic fiction—that romantic adherence to such idealizations can in fact be dangerous, especially if an individual or a society is so intent upon constructing an idyll that it ignores the injustice and even the brutality that often sustain such visions. Just as there is an unacknowledged female truth at the heart of "Araby," so also there is an unrecognized darkness at the center of Gerty's tale; like the "Araby" boy, Gerty thrills to the discourse of domesticity, and she, too, attempts either to alter or to obscure any details of life or character that fail to conform to its indoctrinating image of perfection. While Joyce's display of female desire is much more overt in "Nausicaa" than it is in "Araby"—we encounter Gerty on the beach at Sandymount Strand, for instance, a locale that Thomas Richards has argued is necessarily invested with an illicit sexuality by virtue of its association with the fin de siècle seaside resort—Joyce also makes clear that Gerty's longings are in fact extremely conventional; she wants, more than anything, to become the domestic angel, presiding over her own idealized hearth.

Gerty's subjectivity is shaped not only by the icon manifest in the church that looms above the Strand—Mary, Star of the Sea—her thoughts also are formulated through her ingestion of Maria Cummins's sentimental fiction. *The Lamplighter* and *Mabel Vaughan* are didactic novels that promoted the era's discourse of domesticity; they are tales of young women (orphan Gertrude Flint and privileged, but parentally neglected, Mabel Vaughan) who vanquish the evils of self-love and the dangers of Dame Fashion to be rewarded with woman's supposed dearest wish: marriage to a loving man and her own happy hearth. "There is nothing so insidious as self-love, nothing so noble and womanly as that divine love which finds its happiness in duty," opines Mabel Vaughan's tutor, Mrs. Herbert (Cummins, *Mabel Vaughan* 1.10). To make sure her readers do not trip lightly over this lesson, the narrator interjects: "And is it not so? Is not woman's mission truly a mission of love?" (*Mabel Vaughan* 1.11). Such heavy-handedness is also characteristic of *The Lamplighter* and the Louis J. Walsh poem Gerty tries to remember ("Art thou real, my ideal?" [U 13.646]), as well as the fiction published in *Lady's Pictorial*, another nineteenth-century publication she peruses. But the magazine's appearance in "Nausicaa" serves as more than just a conduit for didacticism; it also overtly showcases the paradox of competing cultural discourses. On the one hand, the sentimental fiction that *Lady's Pictorial* publishes preaches resistance to vanity; on the other, the magazine encourages women to worship at the high altar of fashion. Kimberly Devlin has pointed out that sentimental fiction requires its heroines to be unconscious of their beauty and their ability to attract the male look ("The Romance Heroine Exposed"); Richards and Leonard have noted that Gerty, as the quintessential female consumer, in fact arrays herself to capture it.[16] All three critics have averred the irony implicit in Gerty's employment of "iron jelloids," "Widow Welch's female pills," and "lemonjuice and queen of ointments" (*U* 13.84–90); as she self-consciously constructs her "allure," Gerty also manifests the decidedly unidealistic traits *Lady's Pictorial* fiction warns against: vanity and materialism. But Joyce insists that Gerty is not the only "sell-out" as she ponders her "neat blouse of electric blue selftinted by dolly dyes (because it was expected in the *Lady's Pictorial* that electric blue would be worn) with a smart vee opening down to the division and kerchief pocket (in which she always kept a piece of cottonwool scented with her favourite perfume because the handkerchief spoiled the sit) and a navy threequarter skirt cut to the stride [which] showed off her slim graceful figure to perfection" (*U* 13.150–55). Joyce also implies that the women created by Cummins—both the heroines of the novels as well as the women who read them—are as fraudulent as Gerty. In the face of contradictory discourses, one advocating unselfconscious beauty and the other providing advice on acquiring it, Louis J. Walsh's poetic query, "Art thou real, my ideal?" resonates special significance; this question and its resounding "NO" frame the entire "Nausicaa" episode and its representation of Edwardian domesticity.

Joyce's first task in this chapter is to undermine the period's cardinal paragon of womanhood, the myth of the Blessed Virgin. The structure of the episode—its interweaving of Gerty's fantasies with the Mass of the Blessed Sacrament and the parallel positions of the Virgin Mary and Gerty as objects of adulation—encourages us to read Gerty and the Catholic icon alongside one another and to consider the mutual and highly ironic implosion that occurs as a result of their association.

Gerty's attempts to cast herself in the role of the Madonna are evident throughout the episode, perhaps nowhere so overtly as in her characterization of Bloom as "literally worshipping at her shrine" (*U* 13.564). The litany that emanates from Mary, Star of the Sea enumerates the specific qualities of the Blessed Virgin in language that has been strained through the gushing formulations of sentimental fiction. First, Mary offers salvation and mercy; she is "pure radiance a beacon ever to the stormtossed heart of man" (U 13.7–8), extending hope to those who have "erred and wandered" (U 13.375–76). Gerty, in her turn, imagines herself as the agent of Bloom's redemption: "Even, even, if he had been himself a sinner, a wicked man, she cared not. Even if he was a protestant or methodist she could convert him easily if he truly loved her. There were wounds that wanted healing with heartbalm. She was a womanly woman . . . and she just yearned to know all, to forgive all" (U 13.432–37). Second, the Virgin is prepotent and powerful. "Queen of angels, queen of patriarchs, queen of prophets, of all saints" (U 13.489), she compels fear as well as adoration; supplicants kneel before her in hopes of currying favor to win her "powerful protection" (U 13.380). Gerty emanates a "languid queenly hauteur" (U 13.97), her hair her "crowning glory" (U 13.116); she also understands the power of the icon she mimics. She plots vengeance on one of her own wayward supplicants, fallen from favor for lacking proper deference—young Reggy Wylie. "She could just chuck him aside as if he was so much filth. . . . And if ever after he dared to presume she could give him one look of measured scorn that would make him shrivel up on the spot" (U 13.594–98). Gerty knows that the Virgin's power derives from the moral high ground she occupies; her mere gaze trained on the sinner exposes his transgressions and produces shame and remorse.

As a model for the emulation of Edwardian womanhood, however, the image of the Madonna is as replete with contradictions as women's magazines are. Her prepotency is tinged with submission; she exists as the only female figure in a male-orchestrated catechism. God, Christ, the Pope, and all ordained officials of the Catholic Church are men; a papal edict of November 22, 1903, had forbidden women to sing in the church choir. In the "Nausicaa" service, even the worshippers are exclusively male; this is a men's temperance retreat. Father Conroy impressed the Virgin's submissiveness upon Gerty when she confessed her menstruation: "That was no sin because that came from the nature of woman instituted by God, he said, and that Our Blessed Lady herself said to the archangel Gabriel *be it done unto me* according to Thy Word" (U 13.456–59, my emphasis). The most evident contradiction within the cult of the Virgin, of course, is her claim to sexual purity; by all conventional definitions, the birth of her child out of wedlock renders this "holy Mary, holy virgin of virgins" (U 13.289) a fallen woman. While the litany may gloss over this paradox by proclaiming a miracle, Joyce's text does not. Devlin has suggested Gerty's mimicry of the sentimental heroine is defective ("Romance Heroine"

384); I am arguing that her imitation of the Virgin Mary is not so much flawed as it is faithful to the contradictions inherent in the Blessed Virgin mythology.

The inconsistencies of this icon present Gerty with the need to perform some intriguing reconciliations. On the one hand, Gerty attempts to accept the narratives of submission offered to her—that woman is biologically destined to care for children (that biology determined by God, the male figurehead) and that she is physically and intellectually ordained to acquiesce to men. On the other hand, Gerty wants to exercise the Virgin's womanly authority, which she formulates as resistance to these narratives. Thus Gerty's romanticized descriptions of childcare are interrupted by her decidedly exasperated observations about the Caffrey twins and Baby Boardman: "Little monkeys common as ditchwater" (U 13.467–68). Similarly, Gerty's evident satisfaction with Father Conroy's reaction to her confession of menstruation is belied a few pages later by her reflection, "There ought to be women priests that would understand without your telling out" (U 13.710–11). Gerty here sounds surprisingly like Molly Bloom, who will contest the authority of male priests even more directly, complaining about their prurient inquisitiveness during her own confession: "what did he want to know for when I already confessed it to God[?]" (U 18.113). The point, of course, is that Gerty's contradictory impulses toward obeisance and resistance do not conflict with the image of the Madonna offered by the litany that washes over the strand; instead, they showcase the contest that such a narrative posits within itself between power and submission.

Perhaps the strangest revisions of all occur when Gerty tries to assimilate the Virgin's conflicting messages of love, sacrifice, and sexual purity to her own unfolding experience. Aside from representing the love of God and obedience to God's will, the Virgin's "Be it done unto me" also enjoins the attitudes of Victorian women toward their marital "responsibilities"; as we have seen, sex was commonly held to be something sacrificed to men, to be suffered passively in order to obtain the "blessings" of motherhood. As Gerty ponders "the allimportant question" (U 13.656)—whether Bloom is married—she reflects on the implications of becoming his mistress, reaching two very different conclusions about "the great sacrifice" (U 13.653–54) in the same train of thought.

She loathed that sort of person, the fallen women off the accommodation walk beside the Dodder that went with the soldiers and coarse men with no respect for a girl's honour, degrading the sex.

. . . No, no: not that. *They would be just good friends like a big brother and sister without all that other* in spite of the conventions of Society with a big ess. . . . She thought she understood. She would try to understand him because men were so different. . . . . Heart of mine! She would follow, her dream of love, the dictates of her heart that told her he was her all in all, the only man in all the world for her for *love was the master guide. Nothing else mattered. Come what might she would be wild, untrammelled, free.* (U 13.661–73, my emphases)

The key to this passage's apparent discrepancies—does Gerty want a sexless relationship with Bloom or a "wild" and "free" one?—is (to risk a Cummins-like phrase appropriate to Gerty's perspective) love. That Gerty's reflections immediately precede the benedictory scene at Mary, Star of the Sea is no accident; the final words of the service are about eternal love and adulation (Gifford and Seidman 394). Love is the greatest of the gifts, according to the Scriptures; it was for love of God that Mary sacrificed at least her reputation, if not her actual virginity. In the first half of Gerty's reflection, she visualizes a scene of sex for sale in which love plays no part; therefore, her reading of the Blessed Virgin narrative and didactic fiction requires her to "recoil" and beat a hasty retreat from such a scenario. Like Mary and Joseph, Gerty and Bloom will be "just good friends like a big brother and sister without all that other." The second half of Gerty's rationalization, however, focuses on the feelings she and Bloom would have for one another; the words "heart" and "love" collectively appear five times in four lines. Like Mary before her and Patmore's submissive wife, Gerty is also willing—in the gooey language of sentimental fiction—to "make the great sacrifice" for the sake of love, "the master guide."

Although Gerty does not consciously appear to suspect the Virgin Mary of physical impurity, Joyce certainly does. His virgin is endowed with specular agency: looked upon, she gazes back, an active participant in her own pleasure as well as in Bloom's. Gerty's look enables her to create in Bloom a vision of her own fantasy man—"no prince charming . . . her beau ideal . . . but rather a manly man" (U 13.209–10)—a conception, which Devlin points out, is "wonderfully ironic, for he [Bloom] bears as much resemblance to the conventional romance hero as she [Gerty] bears to the romance heroine" ("Romance" 394). The intensity of Gerty's look makes Bloom self-conscious about his own status: he worries how he appeared to her ("Ought to attend to my appearance my age" [U 13.835–

36]) and congratulates himself that he did not allow her a side view, thus eliding exposure of his soft stomach.

Gerty's reconstructions of the cult of the Virgin ultimately carry her farther away from her original text than she intends; determining to be "wild, untrammelled, free" (U 13.673), she slips into unscripted territory as her voyeuristic encounter with Bloom reaches its climax. Left without a text, then, Gerty quickly retreats to one she knows best: "She glanced at him as she bent forward quickly, a pathetic little glance of piteous protest, of shy reproach under which he coloured like a girl. He was . . . silent, with bowed head before those young guileless eyes. What a brute he had been! . . . He of all men! But there was an infinite store of mercy in those eyes, for him too a word of pardon even though he had erred and sinned and wandered" (U 13.741–49). Gerty's reproachful glance has its source in the righteous displays of Patmore's angel and Victorian fiction's virtuous heroines: while Gerty here casts herself as the victim of Bloom's ungentlemanly designs, she also believes she retains the power implicit in the angel's gaze. Gerty imagines—incorrectly—that her glance produces contrition in Bloom (in fact, his sensations are relief and gratitude: "Goodbye, dear. Thanks. Made me feel so young [U 13.1272–73]); Gerty also claims the authority of forgiveness derived from the Virgin Mary when she offers "the infinite store of mercy . . . for him . . . [who] had erred and sinned and wandered." The connection between Gerty and Bloom thus parallels the relationship of the Virgin to the penitents in the Church above the strand on a deeper, more ironic level: Gerty offers a forgiveness that Bloom does not desire; Mary offers a salvation to men who, like Gerty's father, most likely will booze and abuse again. The final impotence of these icons and the insufficiency of their moral suasion are underscored by the connection Bloom makes between litany and advertisement as he listens to the congregation's recitation: "Pray for us. And pray for us. And pray for us. Good idea the repetition. Same thing with ads. Buy from us. And buy from us" (U 13.1122–24). Leonard has noted the similarity between the "miracle cures" guaranteed by contemporary advertising and those promised by religion ("The Virgin Mary" 13); in the juxtapositions of "Nausicaa," Joyce exposes not only the powerful influence of such discourses but also the inherent fraudulence of their claims.

Joyce moves from his attack on the Victorian angel in this chapter to a methodical deconstruction of her primary handiwork, the "happy hearth." From Austen to Dickens to Eliot, the image of a loving family nestled by the fire represents warmth and harmony. As Walter Houghton describes it, "At the center of Victorian life was the family. Its ritual is well known: the gathering of the whole household for family prayers, the attendance together at church on Sunday morning, the reading aloud in the evenings, the annual family vacation" (341). But Victorian fiction also attempted, on occasion, to interrogate the peaceful rituals it represented; Wood's *East Lynne* and Collins's *Woman in White* (both mentioned in *Ulysses*) depict a discomfiting dark side to the domestic vision. Wood's Isabel Vane is made desperately unhappy in her own home by an interfering sister-in-law and suspects her husband of an affair, so she deserts him for another man; in Collins's novel, Lady Laura Glyde's freedom, if not her very life, becomes vulnerable to Sir Percival's designs on her fortune. Even Cummins's *Mabel Vaughan* presents a distinctly unhappy hearth, Mr. Vaughan's desires for domestic tranquillity notwithstanding; his wife, it appears, is more interested in fashion and society than in homebound ministrations. The tentative critique of Victorian domesticity that appears in these novels, however, is often subtended by the same ambivalence that marks their representation of feminine sexuality; coupled with depictions of oppression within the familial circle is the suggestion that these women (and men, in Mr. Vaughan's case) have brought misery upon themselves either by marrying for the wrong reasons or wedding the wrong spouses.[17]

Cummins's novel, more overtly than the other two, faults the female figure for the disintegration of the household. Without its "ministering angel" the novel implies, a family provides none of the emotional sustenance that shelters its members from the cold misery of the outside world. No nurturing female exists in this household; Mrs. Vaughan may be legally a wife and biologically a mother, but she shirks the moral responsibilities of caregiving dictated by each role. In "Nausicaa" and throughout his canon, Joyce implies that the vision of the happy hearth is a sham—as well as physically dangerous—even when its "angel" actively participates in the fiction.

By juxtaposing Gerty's sentimental vision of domesticity with the realities of life as it is lived in *Ulysses,* Joyce ironizes Cummins's critique of the maternally neglected Victorian family. Even though Gerty's own mother seems to have opted out of the fiction, Gerty's home does contain a replacement figure—a "sterling good daughter . . . just like a second mother in the house, a ministering angel" (*U* 13.325–26)—Gerty herself. She cares for her mother's migraines, never forgets the chlorate of lime for the outhouse, and tries to construct for her home that sentimental narrative she believes will produce an idyllic reality. Gerty's descriptors either carefully reconfigure or attempt to elide the mention of any unpleasant facts regarding her home life. We find obfuscation in her mention of the toilet and of menstruation (she calls the privy "that place" [*U* 13.332]; her period is simply "that" or "that thing" [*U* 13.453, 455, 561–62]) and cliché in the few happy childhood memories she relates: her "Poor father! With all his faults she loved him still" (*U* 13.311–12) is itself the title of a popular song (Gifford and Seidman 389) and suggests the same selective production of experience that Eveline Hill practices in *Dubliners*.[18] Gerty tacks a "picture of halcyon days" from the Christmas almanac onto the inside of the outhouse door, and when she goes there "for a certain purpose" she gazes "dreamily" at the image, desperately wishing that her own family life would replicate the romantic tranquillity the drawing depicts. The picture of the young, aristocratic lovers practicing their "old-time chivalry" (*U* 13.336), however, stands in stark contrast to the violent realities of Gerty's own home where an abusive alcoholic husband/father terrorizes his wife and daughter. Instead of watching gentlemanly behavior "in the home circle," Gerty has witnessed "deeds of violence caused by intemperance and had seen her own father, a prey to the fumes of intoxication, forget himself completely for if there was one thing of all things that Gerty knew it was that the man who lifts his hand to a woman save in the way of kindness, deserves to be branded as the lowest of the low" (*U* 13.298–302). Her euphemistic substitutes—in this case, for wife beating—again derive from the agreeable language of sentimental fiction, but this time they attempt to conceal behavior that is both menacing and aggressive, not conduct that is merely unpleasant. Gerty's language notably displaces the blame for her father's actions from himself onto the liquor he consumes; her diction effectively renders him the scene's most visible victim. As it does so, Gerty's narrative actually enables the violence that lurks at the heart of this domestic discourse—by obscuring once again the suffering of the women who are its most vulnerable casualties. Just as Joyce pronounces *Ruby: the Pride of the Ring* to be excrement by allowing it to fall down "sufficiently appropriately beside the domestic chamberpot" (*U* 16.1474), so also he adjudges the myth of the happy hearth by causing Gerty to hang her picture of "halcyon days" on the wall of the outhouse and to there dream her dream of domestic tranquillity.

Deterred by neither her own reality nor Joyce's judgment of her domestic fantasy (heroines of sentimental fiction often hailed from less-than-desirable family situations before making their own happy matches, as Gerty is no doubt aware), Gerty daydreams about the home she will create for her future husband: she plans to provide those "creature comforts" (*U* 13.222) and the "feeling of hominess" (*U* 13.224) that Mabel Vaughan's father misses, cooking perfect griddlecakes and "queen Ann's pudding of delightful creaminess" (*U* 13.224–25). When Gerty's vision extends beyond griddlecakes, however, it begins to unravel: "They would have a beautifully appointed drawingroom with pictures and engravings and the photograph of grandpapa Giltrap's lovely dog Garryowen that almost talked it was so human. . . . When they settled down in a nice snug and cosy little homely house, every morning they would both have brekky, simple but perfectly served, for their own two selves and before he went out to business he would give his dear little wifey a good hearty hug and gaze for a moment deep down into her eyes" (*U* 13.231–42). The "beautifully appointed drawingroom" that figures in Gerty's domestic fiction is fitted out with the trappings of wealth and the symbol of familial fidelity, a dog. Even *Ulysses*' most financially stable couple, Leopold and Molly Bloom, fall short when their interior decoration is measured against Gerty's standard. The artwork the Blooms possess consists of a painting that hangs over their bed: *The Bath of the Nymph*, "given away with the Easter number of *Photo Bits*" (*U* 4.369–70). In a further degradation of Gerty's tasteful reverie, Bloom appreciates the painting not for any aesthetic value it may possess but for its depiction of the naked female body: he has kissed and defaced the painting (at least in fantasy) "with loving pencil shad[ing her] eyes, [her] bosom and [her] shame" (*U* 15.3264–66). Gerty's choice of dogs is ironic as well. First, the animal she considers will be only a photograph of a dog, not a real dog; as such, it allows Gerty to perform some aesthetic alterations of reality, similar to the ones she could have constructed around the planned family portrait of the MacDowells and the Dignams. The subject of this photo, "grandpapa Giltrap's lovely dog Garryowen" is in actuality the menacing, "mangy mongrel" who spends his day pub hopping with the vituperative Citizen of "Cyclops" (*U* 12.120, 12.752–54). Gerty's idyllic notion of "brekky" is belied by the only other married couple's breakfast we witness in the novel, a meal neither "perfectly served" nor daintily consumed: Leopold bumps his way up the stairs with Molly's tea tray; she criticizes his tardiness, then stuffs her mouth with bread and wipes "her fingertips smartly on the blanket" (*U* 4.334). For his part, Bloom burns the kidney he is preparing for himself and feeds the cat from the table. This decidedly unidyllic vision of the morning meal is compounded by the fact that the Blooms do not breakfast together; instead, they read their mail and ponder the secrets they imagine they have kept from each other as they eat in separate rooms. The passion implied by the deep gaze that ends Gerty's vision of marital bliss is also exposed by the problems in the Blooms' own marriage; Leopold and

Marion have not enjoyed complete sexual relations with one another since the death of their son, Rudy, "10 years, 5 months and 18 days" (*U* 17.2282) since. Gerty's house, finally, is not "homey" but "homely"—a dualism that perhaps indicates a sad, subconscious awareness that the vision is, after all, unrealizable.

Bloom's broader experience and his unromanticized reflections about Gerty's future belie her final dream of domestic bliss; he considers that her days of freedom as a single woman are in fact numbered: "Sad however because it lasts only a few years till they settle down to potwalloping and papa's pants will soon fit Willy and fuller's earth for the baby when they hold him out to do ah ah. No soft job. Saves them. Keeps them out of harm's way. Nature. Washing child, washing corpse. . . . Children's hands always round them" (*U* 13.952–57). But even Bloom apparently believes that marriage is the best place for young women and their burgeoning sexuality and that women's work—"[w]ashing child, washing corpse"—difficult though it is, also keeps them from channeling their sexual impulses into a more dangerous existence—the prostitute's. While Bloom's thoughts suggest a more realistic reason—exhaustion—than Patmore's poem gives for the sublimation of women's sexual desire within the marriage union, Bloom's idea of marriage as a safe haven for females is as fallacious as Gerty's faith in its perpetual romance. Bloom thinks of "Mrs. Breen and Mrs. Dignam once like that too, marriageable" (*U* 13.962–63), but he also knows, though he momentarily forgets it here, that their present realities, like Gerty's, are ominous: each has been saddled with an undependable husband and more children than she can adequately care for. Paddy Dignam, of course, was a drunkard: even though his sudden death is generously attributed around town to either heart trouble (*U* 8.220) or a stroke (*U* 13.316), his alcoholism no doubt contributed to his early demise; his son's most vivid memory of his father is of "the last night pa was boosed"—"bawling out for his boots to go out to Tunney's for to boose more" (*U* 10.1167–69). Although Denis Breen evidently does not have an alcohol problem, it appears that he may be violent as well as a bit "dotty"; when Bloom meets Josie earlier in the book, he notes that both her clothing and her face bear witness to the harshness of her life. As she rummages in her purse Bloom imagines a typical domestic scene: "Devils if they lose sixpence. Raise Cain. Husband barging. Where's the ten shillings I gave you on Monday?" (*U* 8.241–42). That Bloom, whose realism and pragmatism are indisputable and whose experience, like Gerty's, repeatedly indicates the perils that women faced within the domestic space, here reveals his own complicity in the deceptions of the domestic discourse indicates the startlingly far-flung influence of this dogma.

Ultimately, Joyce's most vivid comment on these idyllic, unworkable visions of Victorian virgins, domestic angels, and happy hearths that self-destruct upon contact with reality can be found in Gerty's awkward exit from the "Nausicaa" episode. Her limp is not, as Margot Norris suggests, a retraction of her beauty (*Joyce's Web* 169) or, as Leonard contends, a mark of her status as a flawed commodity ("Virgin Mary" 10). Instead, Gerty's gait functions as one of those symbolic, subversive comments on content that Joyce has perfected: the multiple myths at work on the heroine of "Nausicaa" are all irreversibly and irretrievably "lame." Both Gerty and the "Araby" boy spin out a domestic fantasy that relegates women to the home, that sphere where they were presumed to rule and to command masculine affection; as a practical matter of both law and custom, however, the home as well as the wife it contained belonged to the men who owned them. Such romantic occlusions did not protect women but endangered them by naturalizing domestic violence and encouraging women to seek (as Gerty does) their own confinement; propagating such duplicity and calling it "home," Joyce's fiction maintains, is a cultural indoctrination of the most insidious kind.

6

Female Complaints

"Mad"women, Malady, and Resistance in Joyce's Dublin

In his groundbreaking study, *Madness and Civilization: A History of Insanity in the Age of Reason,* Michel Foucault demonstrates that the asylum, from its inception in Paris in 1656 through its reform in the nineteenth century, functioned as a mechanism of social control and assimilation, its principal purpose to repress or to remove from the community noncriminal social deviance, usually in the form of indigence. In *The Female Malady: Women, Madness and English Culture, 1830–1980,* Elaine Showalter refines Foucault's thesis and argues that by the late nineteenth century, as the number of female inmates and psychiatric patients in Great Britain's asylums increased markedly, a culturally determined and intensely patriarchal discourse on mental disorder, psychiatry, had evolved to effectively confine another group as well—the feminine (6). Only two actual madhouses appear in the fiction of James Joyce, yet both attest to the role of the asylum as an instrument of social authority. The first is a cursory reference in *Stephen Hero* to a lunatic asylum standing in the Mullingar countryside: Stephen's trap driver is curiously proud of the fact that "there were a great many patients in it" (*SH* 239); his pride, one surmises, stems from the assumption that if these souls were not confined, then they would be running amok in the streets, disturbing "reasonable" people.[1] Even more significant may be the second reference, recorded in *Portrait,* which establishes a clear link between madness, the feminine, and social control. Stephen's family has moved again, and the current Dedalus dwelling is located near a church-run asylum that confines only women: late for his university classes and slowly picking his way through the lane behind his house, Stephen hears a "mad nun screeching in the nuns' madhouse beyond the wall" (*P* 175). Though he does not meditate on the possible causes of the woman's ravings, Stephen associates the sound, evocative of religious authority—"Jesus! O Jesus! Jesus!"—with attempts to subvert his own autonomy as an artist and an agnostic: "his father's whistle, his mother's mutterings, the screech of an unseen maniac were to him now so many voices offending and threatening to humble the pride of his youth" (*P* 175–76). Familial and ecclesiastical authority collapse in this scene onto the image of the madhouse, creating a synchronicity in the text between obedience and "commitment"—in all senses of the word. Though Stephen does not consider it, perhaps a life of submission has driven this nun insane.

Certainly Joyce's work, though peopled with outspoken women who actively resist the trappings of patriarchal authority—Mrs. Mooney, Molly Ivors, Emma Clery, Molly Bloom—also manifests a remarkable number of female characters who seem far less able to define or defy the domination they encounter in their daily lives.[2] Notably, these women are also beset by a mysterious litany of physical complaints or they display unsettling, sometimes compulsive, behaviors: consider the "raging splitting headaches" of Gerty MacDowell's abused mother, so severe that they evidently render her unable to fulfill her housekeeping chores (*U* 13.327); the alcoholic excess of Mrs. Martin Cunningham and her repeated pawning of household furniture; the intemperance and possible suicide of Emily Sinico after her rejection by James Duffy; the vacancy and disorientation of Julia Morkan (who "gave . . . the appearance of a woman who did not know where she was or where she was going") following her dismissal from the choir at Adam and Eve's [*D* 179]; the "palpitations" of Eveline Hill, caused, she surmises, by the "danger of her father's violence" (*D* 38); and, of course, the nonsensical ravings and "final craziness" of Eveline's mother (*D* 40). While none of these women is clinically insane by today's definitions, Joyce's literary gallery is hung with portraits of Dublin women deeply disturbed at the patriarchal frames that attempt to contain them. Even though Mrs. Hill is perhaps the only woman other than *Portrait*'s mad nun of whose lunacy we are assured, it is quite probable that late-nineteenth- and early-twentieth-century physicians would have adjudged all of the foregoing maladies to be symptoms of "female nervous disorder," a broadly defined and peculiar form of mental illness reserved exclusively to women because of the supposed "instabilities" of their reproductive systems. Of the twenty "physical" causes of insanity listed in Daniel Hack Tuke's *Dictionary of Psychological Medicine* published in 1892, for instance, five are reserved solely to women on the basis of physiology: pregnancy, parturition and the puerperal state, lactation, uterine and ovarian diseases, and change of life (2.1205).[3] Of the multiple types of insanity (ranging from "acquired" to "volitional"), the following are assigned specifically to women: amenorrheal, climacteric (for example, menopausal), hysterical, lactational, menstrual, ovarian, puerperal, postpuerperal, and uterine (Tuke 2.694–99).

Though Joyce does not generally allow his "nervous" women to be institutionalized in the sense of locking them away in lunatic asylums (the mad nun of *Portrait*'s chapter 5 is the only exception I can find to this rule), he certainly does reveal their lives to be circumscribed by the indelible scepter of male authority: husbands, fathers, priests, and popes preside over Victorian and Edwardian institutions with as much ideological power to shut women up as the asylum. The dearth of madhouses in Joyce's work perhaps signifies his rejection of both the social conformity and the conventions of "normalcy" that the asylum inversely represented: instead of quietly removing disturbed (and disturbing) women from society at large, Joyce instead exposes their symptoms, indicts the causes of their distress, and suggests that their inescapable—and unspeakable—confinement within an authoritarian system is the chief cause of their complaints.

Foucault traces the rise of the public institution in the seventeenth century to a concerted movement by power structures in Europe and England to purge and punish socially aberrant behavior rather than to care for the legitimately ill. Throughout the Renaissance, Foucault notes, the madman was considered to be a locus of ironic truth, allowed to roam freely through the cities or set to sea with willing sailors for new locales. But by the mid-seventeenth century, madness had undergone a cultural reformulation: confinement became the normative condition during the Age of Reason, not only for the mentally ill but also for those who simply deviated from norms of economic productivity. Foucault points to the establishment in 1656 of the Hôpital Général in Paris as a pivotal moment in the conflation of mental and social disorder. The precursor of similar public institutions throughout France, Germany, and England, the Hôpital Général was mandated by Louis XIII to care for the indigent by preventing "mendicancy and idleness as the source of all disorders" (*Madness* 47). Certainly the Paris hospital had more to do with policing social deviance among the lower classes than with providing refuge: a 1657 edict provided that beggars and libertines of both sexes, of all ages and from all localities, "of whatever breeding and birth, and in whatever condition they may be, able-bodied or invalid, sick or convalescent, curable or incurable" should be confined, and the militia was used to round them up (*Madness* 48). Foucault estimates that fully 1 percent of the population of Paris (some five thousand to six thousand people) was soon locked away behind the institution's door for "crimes" of idleness, poverty, and excess, as social undesirability became legally indistinguishable from mental disorder (*Madness* 49). Treatment was often brutal: "stakes, irons, prisons, and dungeons" were at the disposal of the institution's directors, who, according to its own regulations, were broadly vested with the "power of authority, of direction, of administration, of commerce, of police, of jurisdiction, of correction and punishment" (Articles XII and XIII, qtd. in *Madness* 59). Such measures continued unabated until 1793, when Philippe Pinel famously unchained the lunatics at the Bicêtre and the Salpêtrière (divisions of the Hôpital Général) and introduced a new method of managing the insane. Mechanical restraints and beatings were replaced by surveillance and a new type of authority that internalized the restrictions on the inmate's behavior: as Foucault notes, "The asylum no longer punished the madman's guilt, . . . but it did more, it organized that guilt. . . . By this guilt, the madman became an object of punishment always vulnerable to himself and to the Other. . . ." Once the policing mechanism of guilt was in place, the patient "was to return to his awareness of himself as a free and responsible subject, and consequently to reason" (*Madness* 247). Thus, Foucault concludes, "the absence of constraint in the nineteenth-century asylum is not unreason liberated, but madness long since mastered" (*Madness* 252).

Reasons for confinement retained a distinctly moralistic mien as a similar ideological shift in the treatment of mental illness took place in Great Britain. Conventional types of madness such as mania, dementia, and melancholia were often thought to be brought on by "moral causes," including unemployment, domestic troubles, jealousy, financial difficulties, and even, "over-excitement at the Great Exhibition." In the absence of these conditions, one might be committed simply on the basis of "moral insanity," defined by James Cowles Prichard in 1835 (in frighteningly broad terms) as a "morbid perversion of the natural feelings, affections, inclinations, temper, habits, moral dispositions, and natural impulses, without any remarkable disorder or defect of the intellect, or knowing and reasoning faculties, and particularly without any insane illusion or hallucination" (qtd. in Showalter 29). In England, Showalter notes, social reformers, clergy, and lay therapists "investigated the prevailing modes of treatment for the insane within private madhouses, workhouses, and prisons and began to create alternative institutions—asylums—in which paternal surveillance and religious ideals replaced physical coercion, fear, and force" (8). William Tuke exposed the brutal treatment of female patients at the York Asylum in 1793 and won public support for his humanitarian reforms; such accounts detailing the abuse of "fragile" women sparked a spate of legislative and social reforms requiring licensing and inspection of public and private institutions and codifying procedures for commitment.[4] The Lunatics Act of 1845 greatly expanded the number of public asylums in England by replicating legislation that had been in effect in Ireland since 1817: under such laws, localities were required to construct asylums rather than merely authorized to build them. In *Insanity and the Insane in Post-Famine Ireland*, Mark Finnane argues that by the end of the nineteenth century, the public asylum had outpaced both the workhouse and the prison as an instrument of social control in Ireland; census documents and annual reports by the inspectors of lunatics record increases between 113 and 308 percent in first-admission rates to district asylums during the period 1871 to 1911, while workhouse and prison populations declined during the same years (Finnane 13–14, 135 table). Coincident to these increases in facilities and admission rates, there arose another disturbing trend: as notions of "reason" and "unreason" emerged as gendered constructs in the discourse of nineteenth century psychiatry,[5] the new madhouses were increasingly populated by women.[6]

While confining a woman to the madhouse had always been a less difficult proposition than committing a man there because of her limited legal status, the feminization of madness in the mid-nineteenth century in fact coincided with the "domestication" of the English asylum.[7] Descriptions of reformed Victorian institutions reveal the newly internalized authoritarian assumptions of the contemporary model: as English asylums came to resemble country estates, sitting rooms supplanted dungeons, and relationships within the institution began to imitate those of the Victorian family. Organized social activities such as "lunatic balls," tea parties, and countryside picnics, as well as productive work and religious instruction, were foundational elements of the new "moral management"; they are also emblematic of the asylum's new mechanisms of ideological control. All asylum inmates capable of work were assigned some task deemed appropriate to their skills and social station; the director of the York West Riding Lunatic Asylum, Dr. M. Ellis, reported in an 1827 letter to Sir Andrew Halliday that his asylum boasted "spinners, bricklayers, painters, and blacksmiths" and that patients made their own clothing, bread, and beer. This work, he noted, was a "source of great saving to the institution" (rpt. in Halliday 94–95). In spite of their labor, patients were infantilized by asylum superintendents such as John Conolly, who became father figures;[8] the goal of this "moral management" in both England and Ireland was to achieve reassimilation into society at large or at least to create an existence for the patient within the asylum that approximated "normalcy." "Cured" women in theory could shift easily between paternalistic institutions, exchanging the authority of the asylum superintendent for that of the Victorian patriarch.

While Victorian psychiatrists theorized quite inconsistently about the causes of insanity in men, they were much more willing to confidently diagnose the "female malady." The female reproductive system was the culprit, according to the prevailing view: it affected women's nervous systems and rendered them more vulnerable to mental illness, creating a condition nineteenth-century physicians called "reflex insanity in women." The danger was life-long, as one physician noted: "Women become insane during pregnancy, after parturition, during lactation; at the age when the catamenia [menses] first appear and when they disappear. . . . The sympathetic connection existing between the brain and the uterus is plainly seen by the most casual observer" (qtd. in Showalter 55–56). When the evolutionary theories of Charles Darwin began to infiltrate the discourse of Victorian psychiatry in the 1870s, the predilection of women toward insanity became even easier to explain. In *The Descent of Man*, Darwin had shown woman's social position as caregiver to be her "natural" role, affixed by both biological determinants and evolutionary necessity. As the New Woman agitated for professional, educational, political, and sexual freedom in the late nineteenth century, influential English physicians like Henry Maudsley countered with warnings that pursuit of such "unnatural" female activities would lead to nervous disorders—anorexia nervosa, neurasthenia, and hysteria—and ultimately to mental breakdown. Noting the steady increase in female lunatics between the years 1888 and 1890, Daniel Hack Tuke speculated in 1892 that "the natural inference would be that . . . the increased tendency of women to enter into intellectual pursuits and to take part in political life . . . had [produced] injurious results in the direction of mental disorder" (2.1203).

Of the three principal types of disorder, Maudsley and his cohorts looked least favorably on hysteria,[9] largely because the hysterical woman's multitudinous symptoms—which could include fits, fainting, paralysis, vomiting, choking, laughing, and sobbing—precluded her from carrying out her household obligations. Perceived as rebels and suspected of fakery, these patients were frequently accused by Maudsley of "moral perversion": such women, he charged, "*believing or pretending* that they cannot stand or walk, lie in bed . . . all day . . . [become] objects of attentive sympathy on the part of their anxious relatives, when all the while their only paralysis is a paralysis of will" (qtd. in Showalter 133, my emphasis). In both England and Ireland, such sufferers were sometimes committed to the asylum until they recovered from their symptoms, but even if they remained at home, as Catherine Clement has observed, the hysterical woman was a "prisoner inside the family" (Cixous and Clement 8).[10] Maudsley's belief that hysteria was, at best, a rebellion of the conscious mind that could be simply "willed" away was, of course, being challenged in Vienna by Josef Breuer and Sigmund Freud's momentous work, *Studies on Hysteria*, published in 1895. Whereas English psychiatrists persisted in their predictions that expending energy in "unnatural" activities such as education could damage women's psyches, Breuer hypothesized that it was precisely the lack of stimulating outlets that led to hysterical symptoms. Breuer's most famous patient, twenty-year-old Bertha Pappenheim, or "Anna O.," suffered from anorexia, hallucinations, and various paralyses, as well as from a "deep, functional disorganization of her speech," a disintegration that began with a loss of grammar and syntax and progressed to a two-week period of complete mutism (Breuer and Freud 16–17). Breuer suggested that Anna O., who possessed a "keen, intuitive intellect," was bored to distraction by the "monotonous . . . existence" she led within her family circle and that her initial nonpathologic daydreams (which eventually became the foundation of her hallucinations) provided an outlet for "the unused excess of psychic activity and energy" that was denied to her in daily life (28). Thus social conditioning itself, rather than deviance from it, was proposed as the prime suspect in women's illness, though such ideas did not gain general acceptance in England until after World War I, when male hysteria—incorrectly dubbed "shell-shock"— became so prevalent that doctors had to rethink the gendered bases of their suppositions.

The theory that the body communicates, through the unconscious manifestation of hysterical symptoms, that which the voice cannot speak or cannot make heard is central to understanding James Joyce's depictions of aberrant female behavior. Whether or not he was specifically aware of Breuer and Freud's work on hysteria, Joyce's texts frequently register the symbiotic relationship between connubial or religious commitment and confinement and ultimately, for many women, between secular or spiritual marriage and malady itself.[11] In turn-of-the-century Dublin, Molly Bloom complains pointedly about the sense of containment women experience in marriage; she is uncomfortably aware of the power wedlock possesses to shut women up in a variety of ways. Molly resents being left home alone while Bloom circulates about town; she also understands that such a paternalistic arrangement does not "protect" her; in fact, she perceives her housebound position to leave her vulnerable to male violence— not from Bloom (who seems to be an exception among Dublin husbands in that he does not physically abuse his wife) but from strangers: "youd never know what old beggar at the door for a crust . . . might be a tramp and put his foot in the way to prevent me shutting it like that picture of that hardened criminal . . . in Lloyds Weekly news 20 years in jail then he comes out and murders an old woman for her money. . . . I couldnt rest easy till I bolted all the doors and windows to make sure *but its worse again being locked up like in a prison or a madhouse . . .*" (*U* 18.989–96, my emphasis). Molly's choice of simile suggests that the Dublin household clearly becomes a place of feminine isolation and confinement as surely as any madhouse; the alliance is reiterated even into *Finnegans Wake,* when Anna Livia Plurabelle recognizes, finally, that devoting her life to serving an ungrateful family has left her feeling "loonely in me loneness" (*FW* 627). Molly's further meditations expose yet another aspect of women's marital confinement: Edwardian wedlock demanded female monogamy while permitting men again to roam freely. As always, Molly's language is revealing; this time it evokes the mechanical restraints used in early asylums as well as a structure of authority that assumes male privilege: "they [men] can pick and choose what they please a married woman or a fast widow or a girl . . . *but were to be always chained up theyre not going to be chaining me up no damn fear*" (*U* 18.1388–91, my emphasis). The sanity and power of Molly Bloom and Anna Livia Plurabelle have their locus in their torrential, truthful speech, which itself enables their other acts of defiance: Molly's affair with Blazes Boylan and ALP's quittance of her still-sleeping husband.[12] Yet other women in Joyce's work appear much less capable of this kind of insubordination; powerless to make their voices heard, these women must speak instead through their bodies.

Joyce offers us multiple representations of women who exhibit hysterical proclivities; in almost all cases, he intimates that the cause of their physical complaints is social rather than biological in origin, a product of their intensely circumscribed positions within a patriarchal order. While feminist critics such as Sandra Gilbert and Susan Gubar read the trope of the madwoman in Victorian literature as an expression of rage against the domestic roles that confined her, Shoshana Felman has suggested a less romantic corrective that seems to more accurately describe Joyce's troubled women: "Quite the opposite of rebellion, madness is the *impasse* confronting those whom cultural conditioning has deprived of the very means of protest or self-affirmation" (21, my emphasis). Hysteria, in these terms, becomes a physiological manifestation of ideological constraint but not necessarily a rebellion against it; rather than a form of empowerment, hysteria becomes a sign of deadlock—in Showalter's words, a "desperate communication of the powerless" (5). The body language of the hysteric does not enable her to free herself or even to speak for herself; her symptoms and their need for interpretation bind her to another male authority, the psychoanalyst.[13] In a fascinating theoretical mediation on the sorceress and the hysteric, Clement also has argued that hysterical women are bound rather than freed by their symptoms of paralysis and speechlessness: "With their contorted faces, sore, tense muscles, and paralyzed limbs," Clement observes, "there is no need for handcuffs at all" (Cixous and Clement 11).

Eveline Hill's mother may not have been aware, as Molly Bloom is, of the link between the mental asylum and the oppressive Dublin household, but her presence, indelibly inscribed in the *Dubliners*' wallpaper, accentuates the connection: Mrs. Hill dies shut up not in a madhouse but in her own house, her world controlled by her husband (who sends away even the organ player from outside the window) and contracted to a "close dark room," her ravings the direct result of a "life of commonplace sacrifices" made on behalf of her family (D 40). The promise Mrs. Hill exacts from her daughter during the earlier, lucid days of her illness—to "keep the home together as long as she could"—illustrates the extent to which Mrs. Hill has absorbed the convenient patriarchal fiction that required women to offer themselves on the altar of home and husband: the home Eveline is asked to preserve is not only emotionally stifling, it is physically dangerous as well. Significantly, as Mrs. Hill loses her capacity for reason, she also forfeits the ability to use speech to require such pledges; when she slips into *un*reason, she desperately and insistently attempts to communicate something else to her daughter: "Derevaun Seraun! Derevaun Seraun!" (D 40). Mrs. Hill's movement out of the "male" province of reason/ordered speech allows her, in effect, to relinquish both the language and law of the Father, which require her to uphold the patriarchal order and to similarly obligate her daughter; in the "female" province of unreason, or madness, the body is free to communicate a different missive, one unintelligible to reason or to its patriarchal authority. The disordered language of delirium eventually does "speak" to Eveline, who intuits the new message: "Escape! She must escape!" (D 40).

Women like Mrs. Hill remain a subtle yet profoundly disturbing presence around Joyce's Dublin as their bodies attempt to communicate their domestic confinement. Frequently we know very little about these women and may only extrapolate the conditions of their lives: we hear of Mrs. Hill's delirium and Mrs. MacDowell's disabling headaches through their daughters, who also insinuate the abuse perpetrated by Mr. Hill and Mr.

MacDowell. While we may only hypothesize about the connection between the heavy-handed patriarch and the physical maladies experienced by these women, one fact is clear: their symptoms, like those of the hysteric, enable them to forgo the prescribed domestic role of caregiver, transforming Mrs. Hill and Mrs. MacDowell from ministering angels into suffering shut-ins, prisoners in their own homes.[14]

Although she is married to a less abusive man than either Mr. Hill or Mr. MacDowell, Mrs. Martin Cunningham nonetheless appears to register her own nonverbal complaint against her consignment to the domestic sphere. In pawning her household furniture (no less than six times), Mrs. Cunningham, that "unpresentable woman" and "incurable drunkard" of "Grace," may certainly be trying to obtain cash for liquor, but her choice of fund-raisers also suggests that she may be acting out a grudge against "housekeeping," as her efforts appear primarily geared to achieve house disposal (D 157). Certainly it seems that there is something unbearable—and unspeakable—about marriage in these cases, even to a decent and perhaps paternalistic man like Martin Cunningham, who neither beats nor impoverishes his family.

Intriguingly, Mrs. Cunningham's "unpresentability" is linked by the text of "Grace" to her alcoholism: a sign, possibly, of the "moral degeneracy" commonly thought by English physicians to characterize "nervous" women, because the text levies no such judgment against its all-too-visible drunken male protagonist, Tom Kernan. As the story opens, we find Kernan curled in a drunken stupor, having fallen down the steps to the pub bathroom: "His clothes were smeared with the filth and ooze of the floor on which he had lain," and blood trickles from his mouth (D 150). By contrast, the only recorded alcoholic behavior of Mrs. Cunningham other than pawning furniture is capering about the house with Martin's umbrella, singing "The Jewel of Asia" in front of Simon Dedalus, who, we learn in Ulysses, has relayed the incident to Leopold Bloom (U 6.353–57). Gifford and Seidman offer the full text of the song, which bursts with gendered and racial subtexts and is suggestive of another kind of intemperance. A "foreigner gay," presumably an Englishman, espies a virginal Japanese girl seated in a garden and teaches her "to flirt and to kiss like the little white miss / Who lives o'er the western water." When he jilts his "Jewel of Asia" for a "little white girl," the Japanese girl's laughing response simultaneously absolves the unfaithful Englishman and denigrates herself: "It is just as they say, Sir, / You love for as long as you can! / A month, or a week, or a day, Sir, / Will do for a girl of Japan" (112). The ease with which the girl releases the man in Mrs. Cunningham's song suggests a sexual looseness; hers, of course, rather than his, for the song insists that the Englishman "never even kissed" the Japanese girl (though one wonders how, if this is so, the man taught her to kiss in the first place). It seems, then, that Mrs. Cunningham's "unpresentability" derives not only from her alcohol abuse but also from an implicit sexual impropriety; like the mad songs of Shakespeare's Ophelia, Mrs. Cunningham's tune is subtended by male authority, male duplicity, and illicit female sexuality.

"Grace" proceeds to tell of the efforts of Kernan's friends, Martin Cunningham among them, to enlist his participation in a men's temperance retreat. By their intervention, Kernan's friends recognize and legitimate his condition, a fact accentuated by the eminent Dubliners also in attendance at the service. No such assistance is considered for, much less proffered with such careful foresight to, Martin's wife; the only reaction anyone registers to her intemperance is moralistic sympathy—not for her but for "poor Martin" (D 157). Even Bloom, who in *Ulysses* will exhibit a remarkable capacity to sympathize with women, feels only for Martin: "That awful drunkard of a wife of his. Setting up house for her time after time and then pawning the furniture on him every Saturday almost. Leading him the life of the damned. Wear the heart out of a stone, that" (*U* 6.349–52). In *Reading Dubliners Again,* Garry Leonard has argued convincingly that Kernan's alcoholic, anonymous position at the story's opening signifies a crisis of masculine identity that threatens his friends as well; Leonard reads their attempts to redeem Kernan's lack as an attempt to assuage their own masculine anxieties and to return Kernan (and by extension, themselves) to "the grace of an overarching Symbolic Order that imbues all their lives with meaning" (274). This valid insight helps to explain the cadre's complete dismissal of Mrs. Cunningham's problem (which Leonard also ignores). The group avoids Mrs. Cunningham either because her recovery is completely outside their project of resuscitating masculinity or because, as a woman who fails to reflect the authority of the phallus, her presence would intensify the peril of an already menaced masculine ethos. That a male priest offers to male penitents the "manly" grace of a masculine god as the story ends ironically underscores Mrs. Cunningham's complete inability to communicate her desperate protest in this male-dominated culture—"grace" is granted here by the authority of men and received by them; it is emphatically reserved to those, who, in the words of Father Purdon, "live in the world" (D 174) and not to those who exist shut up inside their own houses.

This overwhelming weight of male authority is invoked again in "The Dead." In *Joyce's Web,* Margot Norris asserts that a litany of female "back answers" provides a "disruptive feminist countertext" to the male-centered narrative of Gabriel Conroy: Lily, the caretaker's daughter; his colleague, Molly Ivors; and Gabriel's own wife, Gretta, conspire with Joyce to deny Gabriel the comfortable luxury of directing the female performance (*Joyce's Web* 98). Norris observes that Julia Morkan, a former soprano at Adam and Eve's, is "out of it" throughout the story and argues the cause may be the month-old papal edict (issued November 22, 1903) that ousted women from the choirs and ended Julia's thirty-year singing career.[15] In one of Joyce's chattiest stories, Julia Morkan's words are recorded only seven times; her longest remark is only eleven words. Significantly, it is her sister, Kate, to whom Joyce allows what Norris calls the "outraged voice" to accuse those male institutions—the Pope and the Catholic Church—that have so unjustly wronged Julia and women like her, by replacing their voices in the choirs with those of young boys: "I think it's not at all honourable for the pope to turn out the women out of the choirs that have slaved there all their lives and put little whipper-snappers of boys over their heads. I suppose it is for the good of the Church if the pope does it. But it's not just . . . and it's not right" (*D* 194). It is only in her singing that Julia seems re-animated, but even at this triumphant moment the narrative registers a disconnect between the confidence and focus of the voice and the singer's general demeanor: "To follow the voice, *without looking at the singer's face,* was to feel and share the excitement of swift and secure flight" (*D* 193, my emphasis). Denied the free exercise of her voice by the Church's patriarch, Julia appears to have abandoned other forms of utterance as well; yet her near-muteness itself speaks volumes: the narrative's description of Julia evokes forms of vacancy and brutishness common to nineteenth-century literary representations of the madwoman. Like an elder Bertha Mason, Aunt Julia "wanders" through the house and appears more bestial than human: "Her hair, drawn low over the tops of her ears, was grey; and grey also, with darker shadows, was her large flaccid face. Though she was stout in build and stood erect her slow eyes and parted lips gave her the appearance of a woman who did not know where she was or where she was going" (*D* 179). Her choir career cut short and her voice effectively silenced, Aunt Julia seems as unable as Mrs. Cunningham to adjust to an exclusively domestic existence: in just six months, Julia Morkan will be dead.[16]

Although he merely hints that madness may lurk in the future of many Dublin women, Joyce foregrounds the plight of the emotionally distraught female in both "Eveline" and "A Painful Case" and attempts to recount at length her still largely untold tale. In "Eveline," Joyce uses the title character, daughter of a madwoman, to reveal the emotional and physical paralysis that multiple authorities can inflict upon young woman; in "A Painful Case," Joyce more completely exposes the extent of male culpability for the distraught woman's condition.

"Eveline" reveals the plethora of male-orchestrated narratives at work in a young Dublin woman's life. Just as Eveline's father had controlled her mother's access to the outside world by shutting her away in a "close dark room" and sending away any "foreign" influences like the Italian organ grinder ("Damned Italians! coming over here!"), so also Mr. Hill similarly attempts to control every aspect of his daughter's existence: he compels her wages which she must coax back in order to buy the household groceries, threatens her physically and perhaps sexually, and forbids her association with her lover, who, like the organ player, comes from outside Dublin, on the basis of a father's superior information: "—I know these sailor chaps," he tells her (D 39).

For her part, Eveline attempts to resist her father's control—she learns to extract household funds from the belligerent man and meets her lover secretly—and tries to establish her own voice apart from the male-directed narratives that control her life. The text employs redundancy to ensure that we notice the effort: "she, Eveline" (D 37). But it quickly becomes clear that despite initial appearances, feminine subjectivity here continues to be manipulated by men. Frank presents Eveline with an apparent alternative to her father's domination, casting himself in the role of the manly hero who would "save" her from a life of oppression; it is a tale she desperately wishes to believe. But Frank's narrative threatens to subsume Eveline's own as yet un-authored self as thoroughly as her father's rule does. R. B. Kershner claims that *The Bohemian Girl*—a melodramatic story of forbidden love and Frank's choice for their date-night entertainment—amounts to little more than romantic brainwashing (63–64). The technique is an effective one; Eveline's determination to escape her mother's unhappy self-effacement is couched in the phrases of popular melodrama: "Frank would save her. He would give her life, perhaps love, too. But she wanted to live. Why should she be unhappy? She had a right to happiness. Frank would take her in his arms, fold her in his arms. He would save her" (D 40).

Hugh Kenner ("Molly's Masterstroke") precedes Kershner in suggesting that Frank is misrepresenting his life and possibilities in Argentina, but correct as this contention may be, both Kenner and Kershner are missing Joyce's larger point. The "narrative of entrapment" that envelops Eveline (Kershner 71) is not constructed around the veracity of Frank's claim to a home in Buenos Aires or whether his intentions regarding Eveline are "honorable." Instead, in Frank's offer and Eveline's final response we find Joyce's most evident repudiation of the confinement that turn-of-the-century marriage mandated to women. Frank has indeed constructed a fiction for Eveline, but it is not the tale a rake tells an innocent young woman, as Kenner and Kershner imply. It is the fiction of courtship, the story that every young man and woman tell each other—that they will always be so much in love, that they will live "happily ever after"—in short, it is the fiction belied by every narrative in *Dubliners*. If Frank and Eveline marry, they will not live such a fairy tale, whether they reside across the Liffey in Dublin or oceans away in Buenos Aires. This, then, is the desperate truth Eveline finally accepts. She certainly wants to believe that Frank is an entirely different man from her father; she tells herself that Frank is "very kind, manly, open-hearted" (*D* 38), but she remains uncertain of his stability. She has seen her father temporarily display similar qualities, caring for her during a recent illness and amusing the children. She simply cannot be sure that Frank will treat her differently than her father has treated either her mother or herself; perhaps Frank's offer will only relocate her hearth-bound difficulties to another, stranger, country. Eveline's fantasy of being folded in Frank's arms and whisked away in escape is tellingly interrupted by a contradiction—"He would give her life, perhaps love, too. *But* she wanted to live. Why should she be unhappy?" (*D* 40, my emphasis). The curious juxtaposition of these lines conveys Eveline's sense that receiving love and living one's life may be mutually exclusive activities; that these thoughts surface together and subtend one another signifies a momentary acknowledgment by Eveline's conscious mind of the message her subconscious has so fully absorbed: that marriage—even to a conceivably loving man—constitutes an eternally binding restraint.

On the pier by the North Wall, Eveline realizes that no flight for her exists, that the choice that appears to represent freedom emphatically does not. She has begun to conceive of her relationship with Frank in terms of "duty," just as she has previously regarded her efforts in her father's house as a fulfillment of an obligation. She appeals to a mediating male authority—one that she hopes will reconcile her conflicting obligations as daughter/wife: She "prayed to God to direct her, to show her what was her duty . . ." (*D* 40). But God cannot resolve Eveline's dilemma; the Church demands submission to both father and husband. To Frank's repeated pleas to "Come!" Eveline's own internal voice responds, "No! No! No!" (*D* 41). Yet this is a moment charged with desperation rather than hope. Although Eveline's very presence on the pier during this scene suggests her rejection of the male authoritative force—she has repudiated her father's influence by being there at all and has refused to follow the potential husband who "would drown her"—she is nonetheless unable create for herself her own narrative, her own alternative to their authority.

In the maelstrom created by this authorial void, Eveline is terrified, able to speak only through her body—its nausea, its "cry of anguish," and its frenzied immobility eloquently signal her arrival at the moment of desperate "impasse" of which Felman speaks. Unable to go back to her old world yet unequipped to move forward, Eveline is caught; and, like Julia Morkan, she becomes bestial, turning to Frank's pleas a "white face . . . passive, like a helpless animal." The story's last line registers the final response of Eveline's body: as her eyes lose their ability to signal "love or farewell or recognition," Eveline experiences a loss of cognition as well (*D* 41), and her own descent into madness in fact begins here as she makes her final "escape" according to the only model available to her—her mother's lunacy.

"A Painful Case" deals, as "Eveline" does, with the ideological constraints Victorian relationships placed on women. Emily Sinico is an intelligent, passionate woman whose husband has "dismissed his wife so sincerely from his gallery of pleasures that he did not suspect that anyone else would take an interest in her" (*D* 110). The "defiant note" in Emily Sinico's gaze and the "note of defiance" in her bearing (*D* 109) as she meets James Duffy for the first time recall Eveline Hill's subversions of her father's pronouncements; certainly it seems that Mrs. Sinico stages a rebellion against her husband's judgment, as well as against his emotional and physical abandonment of her, by initiating a relationship with another man. Like Eveline, though, Mrs. Sinico will also arrive at her own North Wall, and it is in this story that Joyce fully exposes the extent of male culpability for the disturbed woman's plight.

Although Emily Sinico instigates their first contact when she speaks to him at a concert, it is James Duffy who directs the course of their affair. As he constructs their relationship, Mr. Duffy embodies and extends Felman's claim that what man desires from woman is not "*knowledge* of [her] . . . but her *acknowledgment* of him," that his design is not to achieve cognition on her part but win recognition of himself (36). Mr. Duffy acquires Mrs. Sinico's affirmation of himself as subject, then (re)creates an Emily in his own image. Fanatical about order, he attempts to control his companion from the moment he meets her, trying first "to fix her permanently in his memory" and later to "attach [her] . . . more and more closely to him" (*D* 109, 111). Evidently Mr. Duffy desires a woman who will reflect both the power of his own intellect and his better nature: he lends Mrs. Sinico his "books, provide[s] her with ideas, share[s] his intellectual life with her," and turns her into his confessor, believing that "in her eyes he would ascend to an angelical stature" (D 110–11). Mr. Duffy monopolizes their discussions while Mrs. Sinico attends; he listens, too, but not to her—what he hears is predominantly "the sound of his *own* voice" (D 111, my emphasis). In order to make herself heard within the confines of this male-authored space, Mrs. Sinico must speak through the body, and she does: one evening as they sat together in the gathering twilight, she "caught up his hand passionately and pressed it to her cheek" (D 111).

The message Mrs. Sinico communicates through her gesture is as life altering and dramatic as the one Mrs. Hill conveys to Eveline. Up to this moment, Mr. Duffy has dictated the nature of their relationship to be strictly intellectual rather than sexual; Mrs. Sinico is, after all, a married woman. Mr. Duffy tolerates, even encourages, an "entanglement" of thoughts but will not countenance similarly entwined limbs. He intuits that the latter is just what Mrs. Sinico's touch has proposed, in contrast to the roles he has established for them: the chaste "confessor" is required to maintain celibacy, just as the married woman is compelled to remain monogamous. Mrs. Sinico sullies both herself and her penitent when she touches him; theirs is now a "ruined confessional" (D 112). When faced with a female Other who no longer reflects his own inflated self-image or responds to his control, a "disillusioned" Mr. Duffy severs their tie. Mrs. Sinico either has misunderstood him or has acted on an impulse independent of him; either way she is no longer capable of mirroring "James" because she has dared to project "Emily." At their final meeting, another physical response, rather than a verbal one, greets Mr. Duffy's rejection of her: Mrs. Sinico "began to tremble so violently" that Mr. Duffy fears "another collapse" and scuttles quickly away (D 112). Joyce's word choice foreshadows the precipitating factor in Mrs. Sinico's demise: the breakdown Duffy fears is at once moral and physical in that another touch might further transgress the abstemious boundaries he has established for their relationship. But far more harrowing for Joyce and ultimately, even for James Duffy, is a collapse of another kind—the emotional disintegration of Emily Sinico.

Mr. Duffy's rebuff plunges Mrs. Sinico into a spiral of suicidal melancholia; four years later, she falls to her death under a slow-moving train on the tracks at Sidney Parade. Even the narrative of her final act—a cautiously worded newspaper account constructed by an anonymous reporter—is dominated by authorial and authoritative voices that try, as Mr.

Duffy did, to submerge her desire: Captain Sinico testified that his wife had become "intemperate in her habits" during the two years that preceded her death;[17] their daughter, Mary, deposed that her mother "had been in the habit of going out at night to buy spirits"; railway representative H. B. Patterson Finlay stated that Mrs. Sinico had "been in the habit of crossing the lines late at night from platform to platform" (D 114–15). These voices, including that of the reporter "won over to conceal the details of a commonplace vulgar death," nearly obscure the despondent body language of Emily Sinico, who regularly endangered herself on these tracks, either with a reckless disregard for or apathetic inattentiveness to her personal safety. The difference between the two conditions is slight; one signifies an angry woman and the other a despairing one, yet each mood communicates a vehement disdain for continued existence. Dr. Halpin's statement that Mrs. Sinico's injuries "were not sufficient to have caused death in a *normal* person" and his carefully worded finding that death resulted "probably due to shock and sudden failure of the heart's action" (D 114, my emphasis) implicates, almost in spite of itself, both heart attack and suicidal intent in Emily Sinico's untimely death: she lacked the heart to go on living.

As James Duffy peruses this account of his former companion's death and final days, his initial reaction similarly threatens to obscure the cause of her malady as he validates the narrative authority of the newspaper's voices. He is "revolted" at the circumstances of Emily's death and decides that her disturbed and disturbing conduct reflects upon himself: "Not merely had she degraded herself; she had degraded him. He saw the squalid tract of her vice, miserable and malodorous. His soul's companion!" (D 115). The "vice" Mr. Duffy perceives may include Emily's excessive consumption of spirits and her evening streetwalking, but certainly the immoral shadow of suicide, and by extension, madness, also hovers behind this judgment. Individually, each of these behaviors would have constituted grounds in Ireland to commit Emily Sinico as suffering from either "melancholia" or "mania": more than 10 percent of the admissions to the district asylums in 1901 were precipitated by "intemperance in drink," and habitual "wandering" in and of itself was evidently considered to be a form of mania (Finnane 146, 110).[18] Most serious among Emily's behaviors, though, is the possibility of her suicide: an act forbidden by both the Church and the law, a suicide attempt or even a threat was considered "irrefutable evidence of a person's insanity" (Finnane 151). It is clear, however, that even as he perceives Mrs. Sinico's final emotional degradation, Mr. Duffy continues to expect her to represent for him that "narcissistic self-image" that Felman identifies, and she again fails to do so. Faced with Emily's continued inability to serve as his own flattering mirror, Mr. Duffy attempts to sever anew the tie that existed between them: "He had no difficulty now in approving of the course he had taken" (D 115–16).

This self-exoneration is only temporary, however; Joyce requires that Mr. Duffy finally acknowledge Emily Sinico as a being apart from himself. In the process, Joyce subverts the authority of the "official" account of her death as well as the authority Mr. Duffy had wielded to construct her life. Significantly, it is the speech of Emily's body that Mr. Duffy now "hears"; it is Emily's touch, not her words, that continues to haunt him:

> As the light failed and his memory began to wander *he thought her hand touched his.* The shock which had first attacked his stomach was now attacking his nerves. (D 116, my emphasis)

> He walked through the bleak alleys where they had walked four years before. She seemed to be near him in the darkness. At *moments he seemed to feel her voice touch his ear, her hand touch his.* He stood still to listen. (D 116–17, my emphasis)

This newfound ability of Mr. Duffy's to listen to something besides the sound of his own voice results in an understanding of his former companion that he never achieved during their association; it is only now that he senses the tormented abyss of Mrs. Sinico's loneliness and the emotional depths that she possessed beyond a surface that reflected himself. Mr. Duffy's own body begins to react in sympathetic collusion—he worries about his nerves—and he comes to see Emily in "two images": as both the object that reflected his intellectual likeness and as a subject that insistently, desperately, attempted to project itself. When Mr. Duffy senses "his moral nature falling to pieces," it is because he has realized that it is his self-absorption, his refusal to listen, and his insistence on "rectitude" in the face of another's suffering that are in fact immoral; he recognizes that the ponderous weight of these indecencies overbears the slight of committing adultery with a woman whose husband cares nothing about her. He goes on to directly acknowledge his complicity in Emily's fate: "Why had he withheld life from her? Why had he sentenced her to death?" (D 117). While some critics have argued that this passage is merely another example of Duffy overinflating his own importance, I agree with Kershner's view that Emily's death has affected Duffy profoundly and that he undergoes a "revulsion against his entire mode of experience" (Kershner 117).[19]

Finally, Duffy is left utterly alone; he has learned to listen, but no one speaks to him now: "He could not feel her near him in the darkness nor her voice touch his ear. He waited for some minutes listening. He could hear nothing: the night was perfectly silent. He listened again: perfectly silent. He felt that he was alone" (*D* 117). Duffy now feels the intensity of isolation as acutely as Emily Sinico felt it, and like her, he must now learn to exist within its confines.

Feminist critics rightfully have succeeded in shifting Joyce studies toward the view that Joyce also portrays the lives of real women and men, rather than merely depicting archetypal figures. The emotionally distraught women of Dublin, caught in the proscriptive nets of family and Church, continue this trend. Unable to speak their oppression or to make their voices heard within institutions that confine them as effectively as any asylum, these women find themselves at a juncture of silent impasse and register, through physical malady, an overwhelming sense of powerlessness. Ultimately, however, Joyce's disturbed and disturbing women do not go quietly. In what may be his most powerful indictment of patriarchal structures, Joyce refuses to shut these women away from public view; they are neither quietly assimilated into the trappings of domesticity nor are they elided and forgotten by the text. Instead, they remain a haunting presence in his Dublin, a permanent and profoundly unsettling testament to the forces of social authority that confine them.

7

New Women, Male Pests, and Gender
in the Public Eye

While the domestic angel and her disturbed counterpart might be contained within the home or the asylum, another style of woman emerged in the late nineteenth century, one who refused to sublimate herself to patriarchal authority and was less easily suppressed as she persistently demystified her discursive predecessors. By the 1890s, the urban landscape had been transformed by the presence of increasing numbers of women who worked in a growing variety of professions, shopped in the new department stores, performed in the music halls, or agitated for political and social reform. This "New Woman," as she was dubbed in the popular press, invaded public, previously male-dominated spaces and radically altered them: consider the small but instructive example of the discursive fracas that ensued in the *Pall Mall Gazette* in 1883 as correspondents bewailed and defended women's "intrusion into men's places at the British Museum": two "ladies only" tables had been established in the Great Reading Room, but, wrote one exasperated male, "There the ladies will not go—if they can help it." Instead, women frequently "invaded the men's tables," requiring their usual occupants to stand about without a seat or to demand the eviction of the offending woman—which no man had yet been "bold enough" to do, the writer noted ("Intrusive Woman" 2). In the following day's newspaper, one of the offending women responded, refusing to give way: "Your correspondent does not specify in what manner the women-students have rendered themselves obnoxious to him. Why are women to be tabooed in this way? Is it wholly impossible for a man to study alongside of a petticoat? . . . Is he so great a hater of women that he cannot endure their silent presence?" ("Intrusive Woman" 2).

This effrontery of the New Woman in expropriating "men's places" caused both indignity and anxiety on the part of her detractors; her incursions were perceived as a menace to patriarchal control and disruptive to the fabric of society itself. In an 1897 issue of the *Fortnightly Review,* Janet E. Hogarth lamented the "alarming increase of that monstrous regiment of women which threatens before very long to spread throughout the length and breadth of . . . London" (926); Hogarth's text urged the establishment of a women's employment bureau to locate "fresh markets" for female workers in order to minimize their usurpation of men's jobs (936), but her argument as well as her military metaphor exposes the apprehension that surrounded the specter of male economic displacement within the metropolis. Florence Walzl has helpfully detailed the extensive ingress of women onto the public scene in Ireland during the late nineteenth and early twentieth centuries;[1] however, these feminine encroachments often were similarly perceived as imperiling masculine agents of social control. Public education reforms such as the Intermediate Education Act (1878) and the Royal University of Ireland Act (1879) that, respectively, enabled women to sit for intermediate examinations and to take university degrees (though not classes) at affiliated institutions often were denounced on grounds that such opportunities neglected to instill in young women the proper subservience to male principals: God, father, or husband.[2] As late as 1901, a writer in the *Dublin Review* decried university education for women on just these grounds: "T. F. W." suggested the ill-fated Tennysonian brigade—silent and ever-obedient—as the appropriate paradigm for feminine behavior ("'Theirs not to make reply, theirs not to reason why, theirs but to do and die'") and asserted woman's "destiny" as wife and mother to be a position readily conceded "by all except the New Woman and a few wrong-headed men" ("Notes on Higher Education" 149). The appearance of platform orators posed another insidious threat to social authority in both England and Ireland;[3] this female activist asserted her agency, appropriated her pedestal, and publicly climbed atop it to demand still more access to higher education, professions, and political suffrage. In 1890 writers in contemporary journals such as the *Nineteenth Century* denounced the widespread "decline of reserve among women" who agitated to obtain a "share of what has hitherto belonged exclusively to men": "Where in the history of the past can one recall the spectacle of women standing upon a public platform and addressing a public assembly? And now they claim an equal right with the men to be there" (Cowper 66, 70). As late as 1911, the year Irish women obtained the right to vote in county and borough elections and hold office there, some Catholic priests still condemned from the pulpits what they perceived as the cultural degradation perpetuated by women who had offended the public eye by transforming themselves into speaking subjects: a priest in County Kerry pronounced to his parish that "it was a sure sign of the break up of the planet when women took to leaving their homes and talking in public" (qtd. in Mac Curtain 49). Such remarks are startling in their seeming anticipation of Luce Irigaray's observation more than fifty years later: "As soon as a woman leaves the house, someone starts to wonder . . . how can you be a woman and be out here at the same time? And if, as a woman who is also in public, you have the audacity to say something about *your* desire, the result is scandal and repression. You are disturbing the peace, disrupting the order of discourse" (144–45). In 1904 Dublin, James Joyce's Molly Bloom evidently has heard similar rhetoric about the disruptive habits of the New Woman from an "old Bishop": "God send him sense and me more money" is Molly's dismissive response (*U* 18.839–40).

It is clear from these and other contemporary observations that the New Woman transgressed her society's operative ideal of itself as a unified, carefully organized entity in two important ways. First, her speech— which constitutes what Irigaray might term a "disruptive excess" in its denial of "autological presuppositions"—made it impossible for the masculine principle to "all by itself define, circumvene, circumscribe, the properties of any thing and everything" (Irigaray 80). Second, the New Woman's open expression of desire (for more education, professions, and political rights)—her "self-abandonment to the public gaze" (Cowper 66)—also challenged the regulating function of social surveillance. The gaze, in Lacan's conception, functions as a powerful mechanism for social control, producing sensations of guilt, shame, and contrition in the subject it captures; when this regulating authority operates properly, Lacan observes that the desiring subject becomes acquiescent: "From the moment that this gaze appears, the subject tries to adapt himself to it" (*Four Fundamental Concepts* 83). Certainly the foregoing ill-regard of the New Woman attempts to approximate the gaze in just this way but fails in its intent to shame her: though occasionally discomfited, the New Woman refused to moderate her behavior in accordance with the implied strictures of social disapprobation. Gazed upon, she either stared back defiantly or ignored the disproving look; as she did so, she exposed both the fragility of phallic authority and the fear of impotence that subtended it.

As the frontal assault by women on "men's places" continued unabated, another important character emerged on the scene, one who emphasized the immense propensity of the New Woman to rout the primacy of urban masculinity: the male pest. Already the plague of working-class and destitute women, this figure began to harass middle- and upper-class women as they window-shopped, waited at tram stops, or strolled along the city's streets. A more intrusive variant of the flâneur, this ubiquitous figure (now as often a "gentleman" as a newsboy or "street urchin") denied to women the freedom of anonymity that enabled his own undisturbed ocularity within the metropolis. Between 1886 and 1905, the National Vigilance Association provided solicitors not only to prosecute "innumerable cases of rape and attempted rape, sexual assault or indecent exposure" but also to pursue "non-judicial action in cases such as the sending of obscene letters to young girls and the sexual harassment of women in the street" (Jeffreys, "Free" 634). The male pest's predilection toward lascivious correspondence recalls Stephen Dedalus's penning of "foul long letters" that he would leave beneath doors or in hedges so that unsuspecting young women might discover and read them (P 116), as well as Leopold Bloom's clandestine communications with Martha Clifford, Mrs. Yelverton Barry, Mrs. Bellingham, and the Honourable Mrs. Mervyn Talboys. It is, of course, the latter triumvirate, led by Mrs. Yelverton Barry, that in "Circe" subverts Bloom's gaze by exposing his harassments and demanding that he be taken into custody:

MRS. YELVERTON BARRY

Arrest him, constable. He wrote me an anonymous letter in prentice backhand . . . signed James Lovebirch. He said that he had seen from the gods my peerless globes as I sat in a box of the Theatre Royal. . . . He made improper overtures to me to misconduct myself at half past four p.m. on the following Thursday. . . . (U 15.1016–22)

Certainly this scene reveals more than Bloom's sadomasochistic fantasies as it progresses to the suggestion that he should be horsewhipped (in fact, it exposes these desires as rather insincere, as Bloom quickly retreats from the threat of a painful flogging); it also makes clear that an immense castration anxiety subtends Bloom's voyeuristic regard of women. As they escape the imagined confinement of his look, Mrs. Barry, Mrs. Bellingham, and Mrs. Talboys become menacing emasculators who appropriate the phallic authority of the whip while they terrorize Bloom with both literal and figurative threats of neutering. They promise to "geld him. Vivisect him . . . flog him black and blue in the public streets" (U 15.1105, 1115–16). Bloom's excitement turns to fear as he realizes that these women are out of his control; significantly, he wants to avoid not just the physical pain of punishment but also the public humiliation of forfeiting his authority—and consequently his manhood—before "all these people" (U 15.1095). By linking images of accusing, castrating women to Bloom's own recollections of harassing them, Joyce suggests both Bloom's guilty voyeurism and the intense masculine anxiety that underpinned the behavior of the male pest.

The *Pall Mall Gazette* first reported the male pest phenomenon in July 1887 in a series of first-person accounts that echo uncannily throughout the language of Bloom's Circean accusers. The first installment ("How Ladies Are Annoyed in London Streets") describes "the experiences of three out of thousands" who are "hunted in this fashion into hansoms and shops and omnibuses to escape the insults of these pests" (1). Two anonymous victims and a Mrs. Ormiston Chant recounted their experiences on the newspaper's front page: all reported employing various evasions to escape the unwanted attention (Mrs. Chant refers to such encounters as "do[ing] battle"), but it is Mrs. Chant who most vigorously exposes the artifice of "manliness" displayed by the perpetrators of this outrage: "I am middle aged, well-known enough in the country to have no fear of any imputation being cast on my character by being seen, followed, and leered at by a *profligate parody of manhood;* but what of thousands of other women who have not my advantages and who are just as much entitled to protection from annoyance, and the use of streets and public places, as I or any one else?" ("How Ladies Are Annoyed" 2, my emphasis). Mrs. Chant's observation contains an important recognition of the protection that her reputation afforded her from being mistaken as a prostitute: although the 1885 Criminal Law Amendment Act provided for the arrest of both men and women who solicited publicly for sex, in reality it was most often women who were detained. Even Mrs. Chant, who followed a man who had been "making eyes" at a twelve-year-old girl to ensure he did no more mischief, noted that "he might have complained to a policeman, if there had been one near, and I, in the white dress in which I had come from Buffalo Bill's with my husband, have been marched off to the police-station as a well-known prostitute!" ("How Ladies Are Annoyed" 2). In five subsequent articles on the subject (including "The Male Pest of the Streets" and "What the 'Male Pests' Have to Say for Themselves") over the next eleven days, other women wrote in to corroborate these stories with tales of their own, while men wrote to both deplore and endorse such conduct. Among the notable defenses of the pest is this one: "Is it possible to prevent men from following women and staring at them? Yes, by locking women up as they do in the East" ("How Ladies Fare" 3). Only one woman wrote to praise the conduct of London men as exemplary; the editors printed her letter "with pleasure," while unwittingly pinpointing the very cause of the problem they had uncovered: "It is really time some good word should be spoken in defence of those who in bygone times were described, not ironically, as the lords of creation" ("How Ladies Fare" 3).

According to these accounts, the pest attempted to intimidate his victims by staring, brushing against them, or stopping short to produce face-to-face confrontations; such behavior was sometimes prelude to indecent exposure and sexual propositions. The "commonest form of annoyance" proceeded as follows, according to the report of one victim: "A man would stare, walk aggressively close, humming some tune, sometimes for a considerable distance, never attempting to speak, then suddenly wheel round with a suddenness almost to bring our faces together, and I would be obliged to jerk back; then, seeing it hopeless to expect encouragement he would walk quietly away. I never spoke, but always felt it hard to be subjected to such insolence" ("How Ladies Are Annoyed" 1). Elizabeth Wilson has argued astutely that the flâneur of the modern city does not represent an "embodiment of the male gaze" or "men's visual and voyeuristic mastery over women" as Janet Wolff previously claimed; instead, he signifies the presence of an unstable masculinity, one "caught up in the violent dislocations that characterized urbanization" (Wilson 109). Certainly the odd aggressivity of the male pest also signals the presence of masculine anxiety and a fear of diminishment, but it is not unreasonable to assume that this figure may have intended his surveillance to function as a regulating force, an approximation of the societal gaze, and in this the male pest shares common ground with the New Woman's discursive detractors. That is, he meant his look, just as they designed their judgments, to surprise, shame, or embarrass its object, the female transgressor, in an attempt to counter and neutralize her perceived assault on his territory, either by transfixing the offending woman within his gaze or by driving her back to her "proper" place, the domestic sphere. Deborah Epstein Nord has theorized that such bellicosity functioned as an (unsuccessful) attempt to contain and control "public" women in lieu of a system of feminine domestic confinement now perceived to be impotent. Certainly women's advice papers of the era bear out this supposition; they understood such harassment of women by men to be aggressive assertions of patriarchal power and recommended the appearance of a new public reticence to placate the harassers; in 1890 the Girl's Own Paper suggested that its readers "avoid strolls where you are annoyed, and always look straight before you, or on the opposite side when passing any man. Never look at them when near enough to be stared at in any impertinent and abrasive way" (qtd. in Walkowitz, City 51). Although a practical reason existed for this type of advice—it kept afflicted women from themselves being charged as prostitutes—it also constitutes an important form of resistance to male authority: disregard. Other women countered the molestations with more confrontational strategies as they, too, declined to be "driven away from the public streets" ("How Ladies Fare" 2); these women appropriated or fractured the gaze that attempted to contain them by offering either verbal or ocular resistance (for example, speaking up or staring back defiantly). More often than not, these women reported, such measures proved effective: the pest usually moved on to his next victim.

Joyce was fascinated by the shifting gender relationships and the contests for sexual primacy that marked city life at the turn of the century; his writing manifests these struggles for agency and authority in an androgynous, urban terrain. The city of Joyce's early works, *Dubliners, Stephen Hero,* and *Portrait,* often signals the menace that the New Woman— ambitious, visible, often political, always vocal—posed to men's places. Women such as Mrs. Kearney, Molly Ivors, and Emma Clery, when encountered by men in a public space, illustrate the profound discomfiture experienced by masculine authority—as well as the fragility of the masculine construct itself—when it discovers an uncontrollable woman in its midst. The metropolis of *Ulysses* reveals a similarly contested terrain populated by "public" women—typists, shop girls, barmaids, performers, prostitutes—and men who manifest a visually aggressive response to them —certainly Leopold Bloom and Hugh Boylan both qualify on some level, as do many of the so-called suitors of Molly Bloom.[4] But it is Molly's dialogic subjectivity that finally de-establishes the primacy of patriarchal control in *Ulysses.* While many critics have remarked that Molly's concerns are more "personal" than political, I will argue that Molly's disruptive ruminations (along with those of Anna Livia Plurabelle in *Finnegans Wake*) render her heir apparent to the New Woman's ability to fracture the hegemonic discourse of gender. Forming the penultimate link in a matriarchal line that extends from *Dubliners* to *Finnegans Wake,* Molly Bloom perceives the efforts of the gaze to regulate her behavior and diminishes the men who attempt to hold her there, countering their visions with her own; she muses herself into existence and denies the primacy of phallic authority, though she herself is never entirely free of its bonds. No feminine ascendancy, no new ideological order, is called into existence by Joyce's final novels; he offers us, in indeterminacy, more than Ibsenian relationships that have run themselves aground on the shoals of engendered absolutisms. As Joyce demystifies and deconstructs cultural idealizations of the Masculine and the Feminine, he also fractures the mythic, unified subjectivity of a social order that bases itself upon these constructs.

As early as *Dubliners,* Joyce introduces the issues of masculine anxiety and the ability of certain women to disrupt, or even appropriate, the patriarchal center: certainly the discomfiting effect of the "Araby" bazaar clerk on that story's narrator as she returns his stare and precipitates his epiphanic, inward gaze, as well as the decisive determination of Mrs. Mooney to convert a private home (where a husband might threaten his wife with a meat cleaver) into a public lodging house, a sphere where women might rule and systematically emasculate men like Bob Doran, foreshadow Joyce's fuller expositions of the theme. The public presence of women, for instance, contributes to the combative landscape of "Counterparts"; the humiliations of a man like Farrington, whose diminishment is most obviously attributable to the disapprobation of his boss, Mr. Alleyne, are compounded not only because they occur in front of other men but also because they transpire before the figurative or actual presence of women, whose look Joyce represents in this story as vital to the illusion of masculine selfhood. Farrington tries to supplant his boss's authority before the office secretary, Miss Parker—he has mimicked Alleyne's northern accent for both her amusement and for that of Higgins —but it is in fact Miss Parker who summons him to the first chastisement in Alleyne's office, so it must be quite clear to her and to Farrington that in spite of his secret insubordination, Farrington will never be more than a disfavored underling. It is the scene in front of the client Miss Delacour, however, that most clearly underscores the importance of the female look to the performance of manliness. Farrington watches carefully as Alleyne solicits Miss Delacour's visual approval for his confrontation of Farrington, but the clerk manages—for just an instant—to intercept the woman's admiring gaze with a witty retort of his own; his boss's rage owes as much, if not more, to this usurpation as it does to Farrington's insolence. But the victory is fleeting: Farrington has to offer an "abject apology to Mr. Alleyne for his impertinence" (D 92), no doubt in the presence of Miss Delacour, as Alleyne is not likely to have passed up this chance to recapture her admiration for himself. Nor does Farrington's clever repartee increase his standing among the cashiers, from whom he still cannot obtain an advance on his pay. It is in this diminished condition, then, that Farrington heads out on a mission subconsciously calculated to refurbish his ebbing manhood:[5] pawning his watch provides him with enough money (he erroneously believes) to become his own master for the evening; he also begins to rehearse a "manly" version of the confrontation with Alleyne that he will share with the other men, a narrative that emphasizes his triumph and makes no mention of the subsequent apology.

As he makes his way toward Davy Byrne's, Farrington begins to exercise an aggressive male gaze directed specifically against public women:

though the streets are crowded with "young men and women returning from business," he begins "staring masterfully at the office-girls" in Westmoreland Street (D 93) and continues this behavior in Mulligan's pub as he ogles a well-dressed woman from the Tivoli who glances back at him "once or twice" then brushes against his chair as she leaves the bar (D 95). No doubt Farrington is attempting with these looks to assert his figurative authority over the female gaze that witnessed his earlier attenuation, but he fails miserably in this effort. Believing the woman from the Tivoli to be a prostitute, he realizes he hasn't enough money to compel either her interest or her validating look, though he finds himself fascinated by her "oblique staring expression" (D 95). Farrington is both disappointed and angered by her disregard, though he refuses to name it to himself—just as he fails to register Miss Delacour's presence at his apology to Alleyne. Such elisions are unintentionally revealing, however: Farrington attempts to suppress these incidents involving the disregard or disapprobation of women because they threaten to deconstruct the very illusion of masculine integrity that he is attempting to hold together. His recollection of the incident with the Tivoli woman two pages after it occurs now conveniently obscures the fact that she failed to favor him with even a backward glance as she left the room (D 95), for her refusal to notice him is indicative of the same inequitable power relationships evident earlier in the story: neither Mr. Alleyne nor Miss Delacour, for instance, "took any notice" of Farrington when he brought the troublesome folder that led to the confrontation with Alleyne (D 90). The well-dressed woman's lack of regard for Farrington thus underscores his ineffectuality even before he loses the arm-wrestling match to Weathers. Farrington's rage is intensified, apparently, by the fact of the woman's speech ("Pardon!") and her uninvited touch; as usurpations of his own presumed authority to pursue women and to establish the terms of their engagement, they are further reminders of his impotence.

As "Counterparts" systematically knocks the props out from under the masculine stage, it reveals the role of the public woman in bringing about its demise. Farrington's impotence has been displayed in the office, and now it becomes evident at the bar: "he had lost his reputation as a strong man" in the penultimate space where he might pose as one (D 96). Although we are not told that women actually witness Farrington's humiliations in either venue, they remain a figurative, negating presence that reminds Farrington of his failure as a man: "He felt humiliated and discontented; he did not even feel drunk. . . . He had lost his reputation as a strong man, having been defeated twice by a mere boy. His heart swelled with fury and, when he thought of the woman in the big hat who had brushed against him and said *Pardon!* his fury nearly choked him" (*D* 96–97). Though the Tivoli woman did not observe the arm-wrestling match, he partially recalls her earlier brush-off and here appears to associate it with that loss; in Farrington's mind, her disregard also becomes disapprobation. In this context it is notable that the first thing Farrington does when he gets home is to shout for his wife: "Ada! Ada!" (*D* 97); a woman safely ensconced at home should represent for Farrington a movement from the unsettling fractiousness of the public arena into the orderly, private environment of domesticity, the final place in the story where he might still expect to play the "strong man," before a fearful or otherwise validating female gaze. But no such look is available here either: Ada fails to respond to his summons because she has gone out.

Farrington's final rage, then, is directed neither at the child who has allowed the fire to die nor at the missing wife: instead it is aimed at the absence that has pervaded the story—that of the authenticating female gaze. As Farrington beats his son, who desperately and unfortunately tries to ward off the blows by offering to "say a Hail Mary" for his father, this absence is transformed into a disproving female presence that once again bears figurative witness to his failure as a "strong man." Unable to vanquish real competitors—Alleyne, Weathers, the well-dressed woman, his wife—Farrington flails the only person he knows he can defeat: a child. Having himself played the part of the boy all day long, Farrington now tries to act the role of castigating man by whipping his son, but the gaze of the Virgin Mary nullifies this final attempt at manliness and once again exposes his lack. Joyce once wrote to Stanislaus about this story: "I am no friend of tyranny, as you know, but if many husbands are brutal the atmosphere in which they live (vide Counterparts) is brutal and few wives and homes can satisfy the desire for happiness" (*Selected Letters* 130). Surely the brutal environment that here demolishes the illusion of masculinity is constituted at least in part by this struggle for the regard of women who, like Ada Farrington, Miss Parker, Miss Delacour, and the Tivoli performer, have themselves exited the home and entered the public space where neither their gaze nor their speech can be reliably commanded or regulated by the men who encounter them.

Other *Dubliners* stories similarly depict a destabilized phallic order menaced by the subversive behavior of unruly women.[6] In "Ivy Day in the Committee Room," "Grace," and "A Mother," the controlling civic force—respectively, political, religious, and cultural—is represented as being overwhelmingly male; in each story, masculine authority is threatened and weakened by female defiance. "Ivy Day" suggests the dangers that disinclined females pose to the phallic order; the women who are mentioned in conversation here are not flattering mirrors, reflecting back the prowess of the male who stands before them, but phallic females who emasculate the masculine subject: the mother of Old Jack's impudent son "cocks him up with this and that" (D 120), while Jack himself, too old to hold "the stick" (certainly an image of phallic infirmity), is no longer able to discipline the boy. Another mother, Queen Victoria, has withheld the scepter from her son, Edward VII, until he became "grey" and perhaps as impotent as Jack in the exercise of patriarchal sovereignty, in spite of the king's reputation as a "bit of a rake" (D 132). The women of "Grace" are as menacingly unmanageable as those of "Ivy Day": Mrs. Kernan openly criticizes her husband's drinking and "had very few illusions left" about either him or her marriage (D 157); Mrs. M'Coy "fulfil[s] imaginary engagements in the country" with valises her accommodating husband has secured for her (D 160); and Mrs. Cunningham, as I argued in chapter 7, is rendered "unpresentable" by the narrative not only because of her alcoholism but also because of her refusal to reflect the authority of the phallus.

In "A Mother," Joyce takes up the issue of matriarchal incursion/subversion more overtly; Mrs. Kearney insinuates herself into the masculine hierarchy of cultural nationalism by giving such an effective performance of self-effacing femininity that the men of the *Eire Abu* society fail to recognize the threat she represents to their presumed authority until it is nearly too late.[7] Leonard has convincingly demonstrated that Mrs. Kearney, the tale's ambitious protagonist, possesses a "nearly unlimited respect for what she imagines men represent (the unifying ideal of the Phallus)," but the organizers of the concerts in which her daughter is to perform are "unmanned," in Mrs. Kearney's estimation, by their own ineffectualness (*Reading* 257). In this space of phallic absence, Mrs. Kearney drops her "ladylike" demeanor and withdraws her acknowledgment of both the men and the impalpable manifestation of their authority—"the Committee." Instead, Mrs. Kearney begins to assert feminine agency in a new and startling way: she waves her contract in the faces of the men and demands—in the language of woman's suffrage—that they recognize her: "I'm asking for my rights" (D 148).

Certainly the ability to enter into a contract would have been an exciting coup for Mrs. Kearney that would have affirmed her own "masculine" worth; as a married woman, her freedom to establish a contractual relationship independent of her husband had existed for scarcely a generation (until the enactment of the Married Women's Property Act on January 1,

1883). Though this is not technically Mrs. Kearney's contract (in fact her daughter Kathleen has signed it), Mrs. Kearney imagines within it a power that legitimizes them both; in addition to protecting her own rights, she is concerned to "see that her daughter got her rights" (D 148). For Mrs. Kearney, the contract not only accords to her as a woman the legal, autonomous status that has heretofore eluded her, it also signifies the phallus, that symbolic authority that she has never been able to possess, except indirectly, through marrying it. The breach of this document, therefore, has less to do with guineas and shillings than with Mrs. Kearney herself and her (imagined) position in relation to the phallic order.

In spite of her incursion into this new masculine realm, Mrs. Kearney is still perceived by her *Eire Abu* contacts in conventionally feminine terms because her negotiations occur not in the public space of the marketplace but in the private sphere of her husband's house. Because of this fact, Mr. Holohan persists in seeing Mrs. Kearney as supportive and "homely" (D 138) rather than as overtly ambitious; he approves of her as a woman—a lady, in fact—who, to borrow the words of the *Dublin Review,* "had no wish to rule [but] through the minds or hearts of men" ("A Queen of Bluestockings" 421). Mrs. Kearney is ever tactful, "friendly and advising" as she helps Mr. Holohan to arrange the program (D 138); she is able to conceal her "masculine" zeal, then, by engaging the shroud of domesticity to encourage Mr. Holohan and the rest of the Committee to construe her subversion as submission. She continues her pretense even when her handiwork begins to unravel: the four concerts are reduced to three, and it begins to appear that her daughter may receive less than full payment. Still, Mrs. Kearney stifles the urge to mock Mr. Fitzpatrick (and thus avoids a direct challenge his authority)—because "it would not be *lady-like*"—when he tells her that "the Committee" would meet to decide the issue of remuneration (D 141, my emphasis).

But Mrs. Kearney simultaneously tries another tactic even as she continues to maintain her facade of feminine deference (and her chameleon-like shifting between roles may account for some of the confusion among the men she confronts): she attempts to meet both Mr. Holohan and Mr. Fitzpatrick on equal terms, verbally shoving her contract, the signifier of her own legitimacy and authority, into the faces of the men who try to oppose her:

—But, of course, that doesn't alter the contract, she said. The contract was for four concerts.

. . . her daughter had signed for four concerts and that, of course, *according to the terms of the contract,* she should receive the sum originally stipulated for. . . .

Her daughter had signed a contract for eight guineas and she would have to be paid. Mr. Holohan said that it wasn't his business. —Why isn't it your business? asked Mrs. Kearney. *Didn't you yourself bring her the contract?* Anyway, if it's not your business it's my business and I mean to see to it.

I have my contract, and I intend to see that it is carried out. (D 140, 141, 144)

Out of (men's) control, Mrs. Kearney manages to disrupt both the concert and this public space where men are presumed to rule. She talks so loudly that her husband asks her, evidently without result, to "lower her voice" (D 145), and she begins to attack the Committee, the locus of masculine authority, questioning its very existence and asserting her own signifier in its place. "—I haven't seen any Committee, said Mrs. Kearney angrily. *My daughter has her contract*" (D 148, my emphasis).

Significantly, as Mrs. Kearney declares her own phallic agency, she also begins to desire the approbation of the Other to affirm her tentative Subject position; she lobbies the artistes for their support, but the gendered terms she employs—"They wouldn't have dared to have treated her like that if she had been a man" (D 148)—suggest that she now begins to perceive her error in affirming the phallic order by conforming herself to it. As Irigaray has noted, such positions are carefully guarded by those who occupy them: "the phallus (Phallus) [can be viewed as] the *contemporary figure of a god jealous of his prerogatives*"; what is needed is not a replication of the patriarchal order in which woman may now function as a Subject but a modification of that order in which the terms "Subject" and "Object" would no longer exist (67–68, 78). It is the withholding of recognition by the Other and the summary judgment of the gaze in this scene—"Mrs. Kearney's conduct was condemned on all hands: everyone approved of what the Committee had done" (D 149)—that ultimately enable the patriarchal order to oust Mrs. Kearney from its midst, rather than any imperfect understanding on her part of the contract's literal terms of payment, as Gifford suggests (98–99).[8] When Mr. Holohan and the Committee realize they have been duped by Mrs. Kearney's feminine mimesis and find themselves menaced by the authority she presumes to wield within their space and in their places, they quickly move to contain her. First, they wrest back from her grasp the power of both the contract and the law: Mr. Holohan informs Mrs. Kearney that "in case her daughter did not play for the second part, the Committee would consider the contract broken and would pay nothing," effectively neutering her claim (D 148). The legalities of Mrs. Kearney's suit now out of the way, Mr. Holohan shifts the terms of their debate back to issues of gender and place, even as Mrs. Kearney continues to demand both her "rights" and a "civil answer": "—I thought you were a lady, said Mr. Holohan, walking away from her abruptly" (D 149). As the patriarchal order re-forms and consolidates itself here, Mrs. Kearney is ostracized—her "conduct was condemned on all hands"—and momentarily immobilized by this gaze as the concert continues without her: "she stood still for an instant like an angry stone image" (D 149). When Mrs. Kearney moves again, it becomes clear that the phallic order has not been annulled by her incursion, only temporarily upset; she glares at Mr. Holohan and continues to threaten him ("I'm not done with you yet") as she exits the hall, presumably to go home, but it is Holohan and O'Madden Burke who have the last words. To each other, they affirm both their act and their authority, but it is an uneasy, qualified victory: Mrs. Kearney's shifting signifier has also exposed the instability of their own.

In *Dubliners'* final story, "The Dead," Joyce reveals the extraordinary dependence of the masculine subject on the control it presupposes over the feminine Other, as well as the nullification of masculine identity that results when vociferous women refuse to cooperate in the phallic charade. The women of this story disturb what Irigaray has termed the "autological presuppositions" of the masculine principle (80). Gabriel Conroy arrives at his aunts' home certain of his privileged ability to control the discourse of femininity, as his first remark reveals: he deflects a mild reproof of his own tardiness to the party by blaming his wife, Gretta, for their late arrival and his hostesses for forgetting that Gretta "takes three mortal hours to dress herself" (D 177). It is one of the few moments in the story that Gabriel's judgments go unremarked, for, one by one, the women of "The Dead" methodically challenge and erode Gabriel's will to power, disrupting the order of discourse that he presumes to control as well as deflecting and redirecting his ocularity from a position that attempts to regulate their behavior to one that interrogates and censures his own.

Lily, the Morkans' housemaid, is the first object of Gabriel's look; he gazes at her intently, marking her "hay-coloured hair" and pale complexion as he conjures a remembered image of her as a small child, "nursing a rag doll" (D 177). In the prescribed space of Gabriel's supposition, Lily would have attended school and determined to wed, but the young woman scorns Gabriel's intimation that she ought soon to marry and his proffer of a Christmas coin; she responds to his offerings not with grateful obeisance but with an accusatory directness—"the men that is now is only all palaver and what they can get out of you" (*D* 178)—that makes him flush and avert his eyes from her countenance to his shoes, which he begins to polish with an embarrassed, energetic fervor. Molly Ivors, Gabriel's academic colleague, similarly breaks Gabriel's gaze as she publicly exposes his intellectual and political pretentiousness and escapes the party before he can counter her assault in his speech. Gretta, his wife, completes the fissure: she eludes his ocular and narrative authority by refusing to offer him the canvas of feminine passivity on which to inscribe his desire.

Molly Ivors provides the story's clearest representation of the New Woman and her ability to unsettle the masculine primacy and to expose the phallic masquerade. Gabriel trains his gaze on this Molly as intently as he looks at Lily; he notes Molly's "freckled face and prominent brown eyes," her Gaelic brooch, and her modest, unrevealing neckline. But just as Lily challenges Gabriel's assumptions about her attitudes (she would like to marry) and her position (she would be grateful for his charity), so also Molly Ivors stymies his gaze—and its intended authority—with a voice and look of her own. She behaves as the aggressor during their conversation, unmasking Gabriel's nom de plume ("G. C.") and goading him into admitting aloud the antinationalist sympathies he has concealed with it ("I'm sick of my own country, sick of it!" he declares in annoyance [*D* 189]). Her professional position, on par with his own, effectively deprives him of grounds for retort against her attack: "He wanted to say that literature was above politics. But they were friends of many years' standing and their careers had been parallel, first at the University and then as teachers: he could not risk a grandiose phrase with her" (*D* 188). Molly Ivors's ability to disrupt the order of discourse is evident in these pages; Gabriel cannot decide even how to refer to her and begins to ponder what he cannot say as well as to reconsider what he has already said: "Of course the girl or woman, or whatever she was, was an enthusiast but there was a time for all things. Perhaps he ought not to have answered her like that" (*D* 190). Although Gabriel reacts physically to Molly's assault much as he did to Lily's unanticipated disapprobation (he blushes repeatedly, becomes "inattentive," and averts his look: "he avoided her eyes for he had seen a sour expression on her face" [*D* 190]), both exchanges have a significant impact on him. Molly confronts Gabriel not in the pantry (a private and conventionally feminine space) as Lily does but in a more public venue, the drawing room. As Gabriel's reflection on their parallel careers makes clear, he is quite conscious of the fact that he and Molly occupy a contiguous space; her remarks already have encroached upon and reduced his territorial authority: he cannot "risk" a pretentious response or he might lose even more ground to her. Significantly, Gabriel fears he has been publicly humiliated: "But she had no right to call him a West Briton *before people,* even in joke. She had tried to make him ridiculous *before people, heckling him and staring at him with her rabbit's eyes*" (*D* 190, my emphases).

It is the public nature of Molly Ivors's verbal challenge that unsettles Gabriel most profoundly; he senses here that she has usurped not only his political and professional space but also his ability to direct their discourse as she appropriates the comforting authority/control of his gaze. Molly, like Lily before her, appropriates Gabriel's look with her "rabbit's eyes" and redirects it back toward him; "unnerved," he worries about the appropriateness of his antinationalist outburst and begins to consider the revenge he might take in his dinner speech against Molly's "critical quizzing eyes" (*D* 192). But Molly escapes from the party before Gabriel can retaliate, her victory underscored by her laughter. She refuses his offer to walk her home, insisting, "I'm quite well able to take care of myself" (*D* 195). It is notable that after this final sally, Gabriel grasps at any available means to restore to himself some semblance of masculine authority, just as he did when he offered the deprecating coin to Lily. Suddenly he finds himself quite excited to carve the goose at dinner, an assignment that previously produced in him no particular fervor. In fact, he now feels "ready to carve a flock of geese, if necessary" (*D* 196) and "boldly" takes his seat at the head of the table as he picks up the carving knife and fork; it is the only moment of the evening where he finds himself at entirely ease, for it is the only occasion during which his masculine place and symbolic phallus (represented here by the carving utensils) are secured from feminine incursion and appropriation. Ironically, he fails to note that these honorary scepters are bestowed upon him at female behest: the aunts Morkan, "two ignorant old women" in Gabriel's estimation (*D* 192), but the true heads of this household, have momentarily restored to him this fleeting illusion of privilege.

Gretta Conroy joins the women who subvert her husband's presumed authority; she not only resists Gabriel's overt attempts to regulate her behavior—refusing to wear the galoshes he insists on and criticizing him in front of other people ("There's a nice husband for you, Mrs. Malins," she says sarcastically when Gabriel refuses to consider Molly Ivors's suggestion of a trip to Galway [*D* 191])—she also counters his more subtle

attempts at patriarchal domination. After their departure from the Morkan house, Gabriel and Gretta journey back to their hotel, her silence
opening a void in which he tries to rewrite the narrative of their past lives
and of their immediate future; it is as romantic and sentimental a fiction as
any ever fantasized by Gerty MacDowell. Gabriel recalls three incidents:
Gretta's first letter to him ("he could not eat for happiness"), a moment
together on a "crowded platform" (perhaps during their wedding trip),
and a man making bottles before a "roaring furnace" while he and Gretta
stood watching in the cold air (D 213). That there is no response to the
question "Is the fire hot, sir?" is telling: theirs has never been a passionate
relationship. For proof, we need look no further than Gabriel's attempted
seduction of his wife later that evening; he has no idea even how to begin
and reproaches himself for his "diffidence" (D 216). In spite of this truth,
however, Gabriel insists on his power to alter the drab, passionless reality
that has been their lives; specifically, he insists on his ability to change
Gretta's conception of this reality by manipulating her narrative: "He
longed to recall to her those moments, to make her forget the years of their
dull existence together and remember only their moments of ecstasy. For
the years, he felt, had not quenched his soul or hers" (D 213). Once the
narrative of the past is palpably altered so that Gabriel appears as Gretta's
romantic champion, he turns his attention to scripting Gretta's immediate
future:

> He longed to be alone with her. When the others had gone away,
> when he and she were in the room in the hotel, then they would be
> alone together. He would call her softly:
>
> —Gretta!
>
> Perhaps she would not hear at once: she would be undressing. Then
> something in his voice would strike her. She would turn and look at
> him. . . . (D 214)

After an evening in which women have systematically challenged and
demolished his senses of authority and control, Gabriel (rather like Farrington) now fantasizes about achieving some final affirmation of his ability to dominate some woman and targets his wife. Although it seems as
though he may be ready for a woman who knows her own mind and acts
according to its preferences ("If she would only turn to him or come to him
of her own accord" [D 217]), his earlier discomfort when confronted with
women who behave in just this way betrays this sentiment. What Gabriel
really wants is the feminine ideal—that mirror that reflects and affirms the

power of the masculine Subject; he wishes for Gretta to anticipate his desire and to yield herself to it. Joyce makes this impulse to dominate clear in Gabriel's repetition of his desire to "master" and "overmaster" her and in his reflection when he believes Gretta is indeed anticipating his lust: "Perhaps she had felt the impetuous desire that was in him and then the yielding mood had come upon her" (D 217).

But Gretta here reveals a narrative of her own that effectively quashes Gabriel's surmised control. She resists her husband's lustful eye and betrays it; she trains her own loving look elsewhere, past him, outside their marriage. She is remembering her passion for Michael Furey, the man who died for love of her years before: "I was great with him at that time," she tells Gabriel (D 220). In fact, Gretta's narrative exposes the pathetic artifice of Gabriel's vision, the falsity of his domestic fiction, and the fraudulence of their marriage. Gretta succeeds in redirecting Gabriel's look/pretended gaze from one that attempts to regulate her behavior to one that powerfully interrogates his own: "While he had been full of memories of their secret life together, full of tenderness and joy and desire, she had been comparing him in her mind with another. A shameful consciousness of his own person assailed him. He saw himself as a ludicrous figure . . . the pitiable fatuous fellow he had caught a glimpse of in the mirror" (D 219–20). In the story's final moments, the power of this refocused vision becomes fully evident. Lacan has theorized that "the gaze seems to possess such a privilege that it goes so far as to have me scotomized, I who look" (Four Fundamental Concepts 84); that is, it is powerful enough to effectively obliterate the self, rendering it to nothingness. Significantly, as Gabriel senses the full impact of the gaze that Lily, Molly, and Gretta have unleashed against him, his illusion of a unified masculine self, along with the foundational assumptions of male privilege/authority that served as its basis, now slips silently away: "His own identity was fading out into a grey impalpable world: the solid world itself . . . was dissolving and dwindling" (D 223).

In Stephen Hero, Joyce's Stephen Daedalus reacts with a discomfort similar to that of Gabriel Conroy when confronted by a woman who transgresses the boundaries of feminine reticence and encroaches territory he has marked for himself. Bonnie Kime Scott (Joyce and Feminism) was one of the first critics to suggest that Stephen mistakes Emma Clery throughout most of the early fragment, but their relationship is even more complex than Scott's study indicates. Emma's "New Woman" unruliness deeply unsettles Stephen, and as she repels his attempts to direct her behavior, she in fact becomes his nemesis—contesting and breaking his discursive control. Like Gabriel, Stephen tries to ignore the complexities of the emotional/intellectual being before him and attempts instead to construct Emma in the image of the ideal Feminine, a woman onto whom he may project his physical desires and see them reflected back at him. But Emma, like the women of "The Dead," also actively resists Stephen's inscription and his idealized, constraining vision of her; she does not permit him to exercise either ocular or narrative control. Their relationship also allows Joyce to reveal the insecurity and instability of a masculine ethos founded on its ability to dominate a feminine Other.

Stephen's intense desire to construct a femininity that he can control, as well as the fragility of the construct itself, is made clear during an early assemblage at the Daniels's home, just before he is reintroduced to Emma: "Stephen sat down beside one of the [Daniels's] daughters and, while admiring the rural comeliness of her features, waited quietly for her first word which, he knew, would destroy his satisfaction" (*SH* 46). It is the vocality of the woman that fractures Stephen's gaze, just as it is the similarly voluble nature of Emma Clery that most disturbs him when he encounters her in the political arena of the Daniels's nationalist gatherings. Deprived of his authorizing look, Stephen attempts to marshal some other premise on which to base his desire for primacy and settles on masculine intellect: "Her loud forced manners shocked him at first until his mind had thoroughly mastered the stupidity of hers" (*SH* 66). But Emma is not stupid: her concerns merely fail to reflect Stephen's and thereby undermine his attempts to manipulate her image. Stephen wishes to see Emma, as Molly Bloom's recounters do, as a "warm ample body" willing and eager to pleasure him, but Emma wants to talk—about nationalist politics and the emancipation of women (*SH* 66–67, 187). Not only do Emma's language and behavior contest Stephen's ability to authorize her femininity, she also refuses to reflect back to him the admiring and desirous look with which he hopes to transfix her. Stephen is acutely aware, for instance, that, although Emma accepts his nightly escorts home, she and Father Moran appear to evince a mutual and, Stephen suspects, sexual regard for one another; he notes that "Emma stood to his [Moran's] gaze in . . . a poise of bold carelessness" but that "she did not seem to have reserved herself for him [Stephen]" (*SH* 66): as we have seen in "The Dead," a woman who returns or is transfixed by male desire affirms his control over her, but a woman who exercises her own look and trains it elsewhere—as Emma Clery and Gretta Conroy do—threatens not only masculine prowess but masculine selfhood as well.

Stephen's intense desire to control Emma and her perpetual knack for eluding and thereby diminishing the phallic authority that he presumes to wield is underscored in several additional scenes. In spite of his best efforts, Stephen perceives Emma to have the "upper hand" in the relationship and senses that she harbors within her a core of resistance directed toward him, a "point of defiant illwill" that he erroneously suspects to have resulted from his failure to pursue her in an overtly sexual manner (*SH* 67). As Emma continues to respond to Stephen in ways he cannot predict and does not expect—she controls their conversation, fails to blush at his blasphemies, makes unlooked-for "intelligent" remarks (*SH* 154), and openly interrogates his manliness even after he affirms her womanhood ("But you are not a man, are you?" she asks, teasingly [*SH* 189])—he determines to see her no more. His admission to Cranly regarding the impossibility of seducing her and his decision to move on—"I must go to where I am sure of my ground"—indicate the profoundly unsettling effect that Emma has had on Stephen's psyche as well as the territorial diminishment of phallic space her noncompliance has meant for him (*SH* 191). His concern now appears to shift from attempting to master Emma to trying to reconstruct his own masculine selfhood, but without the possibility of validation by the feminine Other, he fails miserably. Although Stephen vows repeatedly never to see or speak to Emma again (*SH* 189), the very next time he glimpses her he flings a hasty excuse at his Italian instructor, rushes out of class, and runs wildly through the streets until he catches her. Significantly, Stephen in this scene is obsessed with regaining control—of Emma and of himself. He is afraid he will say too much ("if I stand here in this stupid street beside you for much longer I shall begin to say more" [*SH* 198]), and both his approach and proposition exude more than nervous excitement: they also smack of attempted intimidation. Indeed, he tells Emma that his appearance before her has been incited by his surreptitious surveillance of her as well as the public confidence she exudes, "walking proudly through the decayed city" (*SH* 197). Like one of the male pests chronicled so vividly in the *Pall Mall Gazette,* Stephen "held her arm tightly to his side and discomposed her somewhat by speaking very close to her face" (*SH* 196) as he breathlessly propositions her: "Just live one night together, Emma, and then to say goodbye in the morning and never to see each other again" (*SH* 198). For the first time in their relationship, Emma appears "nervous" and even somewhat fearful as Stephen "fiercely" presses her arm to his side (*SH* 197), but she shortly recovers her demeanor as she comes to understand his meaning. Pulling away from his grasp, she demands, "You must not speak to me anymore. . . . Who do you think *I* am that you can speak to me like that?"

(*SH* 198, my emphasis). Here the female voice again disrupts the discursive, male-authored image and usurps from him the disproving gaze and the role of speaking subject. Significantly, Emma does not want to know who Stephen believes *he* is; such a response would acknowledge the control over her that he is attempting to reestablish. Her question instead affirms the fallacious nature of his assumptions and asserts her own Subject position. His previous attempts having failed, Stephen's free love proposal to Emma is his final chance in the fragment to contain, control, and possess her—and to solidify his own ebbing masculinity. It is also a subconscious attempt to shame her, to disabuse her of the pride that he has observed in her stride. But he fails again to approximate the regulatory gaze that might occlude Emma's "I/eye"; Emma, as E.C., continues to elude Stephen's pretenses to authority even into *Portrait,* where he repeatedly endeavors to reconstruct her image. There, Stephen's anger at her supposed dalliance with Moran "broke up violently her fair image and flung the fragments on all sides. On all sides distorted reflections of her image started from his memory" (*P* 220). Later, he tries again, but "the images he had summoned gave him no pleasure. They were secret and enflaming but her image was not entangled by them. That was not the way to think of her. It was not even the way in which he thought of her. Could his mind then not trust itself?" (*P* 233). As Karen Lawrence has written, Stephen in this passage "questions his own images, disturbed that he cannot fully represent [Emma]" ("Joyce and Feminism" 247); his failure in this effort is indicative of Joyce's fascination with fin de siècle women as "speaking subjects" and the multiple ways in which they might disrupt the order of masculine discourse.

In spite of his failures with Emma, however, Stephen never completely surrenders the prospect of controlling the feminine. In *Ulysses,* Leopold Bloom and Stephen Dedalus share an idealized fantasy of a silent, specularized woman imprisoned within a public space and a (predominantly) male gaze: Bloom's ad for Wisdom Hely's stationers, repeated to Stephen and reprised by the latter in the "Ithaca" episode, would have featured a "transparent showcart with two smart girls sitting inside writing letters, copybooks, envelopes, blottingpaper. . . . Smart girls writing something catch the eye at once. Everyone dying to know what she's writing" (*U* 8.132). "Smart girls" might be either well dressed or well educated or both; in Bloom's conception they are on the street—in men's places—but are entirely contained within the spectacle he constructs. Stephen's vision replaces Bloom's showcart with a single male voyeur who watches the writing woman from the shadows of a hotel room. The phallic appeal of either image derives from its engendered muteness; what the woman writes is not as important to the tableau as the fact that the on-looker can control her message and read into it his own meaning. Richard Pearce has observed that Bloom's ad "focuses on the dilemma of women as spectators and authors, or authors . . . of their own imaginative desires when they are trapped in the male gaze" (40); however, Bloom and Stephen merely fantasize the power of this look, which Joyce repeatedly and mercilessly ironizes as either impotent or dysfunctional. In reality the gaze conjured by the two men is much less confining than they desire it to be: Cissy Caffrey, for instance, boldly harasses Bloom and several times disrupts his look (and more) as he tries to watch Gerty MacDowell in "Nausicaa"; Stephen not only has difficulties with Emma, he even frets in *Portrait* that the young woman who attempts to sell him flowers on the street might start to heckle him if he fails to retreat quickly enough from her summons (*P* 184). That women such as these may be "trapped" in the male gaze is nothing but the figment of a masculine imagination that des-perately wishes to dam its ebbing authority; as we have seen, actual women of the period dramatically and publicly unsettled the attempts of the male voyeur to specularize and control the feminine. It is not only Joyce's fracturing of this gaze, then, but also his ironizing of it that ulti-mately reveals both its impotence and its absurdity.

Molly Bloom's transformation in *Ulysses* from constructed Other to speaking Subject mirrors the movement of women generally within the modern moment, and it is Molly's uncontrolled, dialogical presence that explodes the contained, engendered aphasia of the feminine ideal fanta-sized by Stephen and Leopold Bloom and helps to culminate Joyce's depic-tion of a destabilized masculine ethos.[9] Like the New Woman of the fin de siècle and her own predecessors in Joyce's work, Molly Bloom intrudes into men's places and unsettles the gaze that attempts to confine her (as well as the discourse it authorizes) by exposing its lack and ironizing its phallic pretentiousness. Pearce has enumerated the multiple ways in which *Ulysses* attempts to transfix Molly within a male point of view (including the reader's) as well as the role her thoughts play in dismantling the uni-fied/unitary masculine perspective conveyed by the text; in the presence of Molly's own look and her polyphonic, disruptive musings, the masculine center fails to hold: it is no longer able, in Irigaray's words, to "all by itself define, circumvene, circumscribe, the properties of any thing and every-thing" (80), especially the feminine.

As Molly's look deflects the gaze of the men who have presumed to capture her, her own "back answers" stymie their authority to manipulate

her image within their discourse. Molly counters Lenehan's pronouncement to M'Coy ("She's a gamey mare and no mistake" [*U* 10.566–67])
with her own estimation of him, colored by Boylan's curses: "that sponger
he was making free with me after the Glencree dinner" (*U* 18.426–27); she
de-fangs the salacious, mean-spirited comments of Simon Dedalus ("Mrs.
Marion Bloom has left off clothes of all descriptions" [*U* 11.496–97]) by
noting that Simon "was always turning up half screwed" and ready to
denigrate: "hed say or do something to knock the good out of it" (*U*
18.1290–91, 1299–1300). She mocks Bloom for showing her photo to
Stephen ("I wonder he didnt make him a present of it altogether and me
too" [*U* 18.1304–5]) and talks back both to the text ("I dont like books
with a Molly in them" [*U* 18.657–58]) and to the most significant authorial male of all: James Joyce himself ("O Jamesy let me up out of this
pooh" [*U* 18.1128]). Molly's ability to "resubmit herself . . . to ideas about
herself" allows her, in Irigaray's terms, not only to "recover the place of
her exploitation by discourse," it also enables her to "make visible . . .
what was supposed to remain invisible": that is, the structure and instability of the phallocratic authority that endeavors to represent her (76). Kimberly Devlin has written that Molly's polylogue destabilizes the unified
Feminine, that as Molly "does and undoes ideological gender acts," she
reveals femininity to be a socially constructed and performative act, not a
"natural" but a "naturalized" phenomenon ("Pretending"). Ultimately,
however, Molly Bloom's greatest revolt against the dominant ideologies of
gender comes not in any ability she may possess, as a woman, to reject her
externally imposed Otherness and occupy/reunify the Subject position
that she attempts to wrest from masculine control; in fact, Molly appears
to be unable to fully occupy the "men's place" for any but a brief period.
Instead, Molly's thoughts—comprising the proscriptive voices of her culture along with her assimilations and interrogations of them—inscribe a
new and vital space of gender indeterminacy. In his work on cultural
studies, Homi Bhabha has theorized that such spaces of disjunctive
multivocality produce hybridity rather than duality, and that in this shift,
those residing outside conventional structures of power/authority/ knowledge might become enfranchised: what emerges in such a space is *"neither
the One . . . nor the other . . . , but something else besides,* which contests
the terms and territories of both" ("Commitment to Theory" 28). Joyce's
Molly Bloom creates just such a space; ultimately her subjectivity posits—
for us, if not necessarily for her—a new way of looking, a transformative
vision that sees beyond the binary restraints and constructions of gender.

Well aware of the sexual, social, and political authority that men presumed to exercise over women in Irish society, Molly's personal reflections also interrogate the purveyors of public influence (lawyers, priests, doctors, and politicians) by unveiling and ridiculing the phallic apparatus through which they presume to rule.[10] She undermines with insult and innuendo the virility of John Henry Menton, the lawyer who once made a pass at her ("mouth almighty . . . of all the big stupoes I ever met and thats called a solicitor" [*U* 18.42–44]); dismisses the Church's potency with a suggestion that another, more powerful authority might dispute its views of contemporary mores ("that old Bishop that spoke off the altar his long preach about womans higher functions . . . and the new woman bloomers God send him sense and me more money" [*U* 18.839–40]); deflates the power of the medical establishment to authorize the female body by critiquing the jargon that "dry old stick" Dr. Collins uses to describe it ("where do those old fellows get all the words they have" [*U* 18.1153, 1170]); and denigrates both Home-Rule and Land-League politics by refusing to accord to them the status of rational, authorizing discourse, branding them instead (along with Bloom's support of them) as "blather" and "trash and nonsense" (*U* 18.384–85, 1187–88).

Although Molly at times invites the male look and feels empowered by her ability to attract it, she has also been its unwilling victim, and she deeply resents the predilection of men to behave as if they possess a singular right over women to occupy the public space. Molly has been harassed by male pests from Dublin to Gibraltar; as a spectator she has been both groped and ogled by strange men in Gaiety theater crowds ("theyre always trying to wiggle up to you" [*U* 18.1041]). In a similar occurrence at a performance of *The Wife of Scarli,* Molly's seat ("the one and only time we were in a box") protects her from uninvited touch, but she is now discomfited, both by the onset of her period and by the persistent eyes of an upper-class male theatergoer: "I was fit to be tied though I wouldnt give in with that gentleman of fashion staring down at me with his glasses" (*U* 18.1113–14). Molly's choice of phrase, "gentleman of fashion," not only marks her assailant as upper class, it also points to the prurience that underlies his look; the descriptor commonly appears in Victorian pornography (indeed, it is used to denote the author of *Sweets of Sin*) to denote a sexually predatory male.

Not even Molly's youth was free from such displays of patriarchal prowess. She recalls the ways in which urinating soldiers exposed themselves to her in Gibraltar as she strolled the lanes of the garrison, observing the territorial assertion behind the gesture: "that disgusting Cameron highlander behind the meat market or that other wretch with the red head behind the tree . . . when I was passing pretending he was pissing standing out for me to see it . . . theyre always trying to show it to you" (*U* 18.544–48). Susan Bazargan has suggested that this incident is encoded with the signifiers of imperial authority, but Molly in fact interprets the soldiers' gesture primarily in a gendered, rather than a colonial, context; back in Dublin, for instance, Molly intentionally passes by the men's toilet in Harcourt Street "just to try" an experiment of her own devising. She wants to see whether Irish men behave in a fashion similar to that of the queen's guard, and, in Molly's reconstruction of the scene, the Dubliners do not disappoint: "some fellow or other trying to catch my eye as if it was 1 of the 7 wonders of the world" (*U* 18.550–53). But Molly, at these moments, refuses to do homage to such scepters; in fact, she remains decidedly unimpressed by them: instead of phallic prowess, she envisions comical deflations. That Molly understands such gestures as attempts by men to procure/secure the public space against women is made irrefutably clear when she recalls that, having imbibed too much lemonade at the Comerfords' party, she and Bloom stopped off so that she might use a public toilet. It was a men's greenhouse, and Molly thinks to herself: "a pity a couple of the Camerons werent there to see me squatting *in the mens place*" (*U* 18.556–57, my emphasis). Subconsciously, at least, Molly is also aware of the implications of her symbolic incursion into the Subject position: her very next thoughts conjure not the oddity of the male member but its fragility. "I wonder theyre not afraid going about of getting a kick or a bang of something" (*U* 18.558–59). When unruly women usurp men's places, it seems, the phallus—along with its presumptions to authority—takes a beating.

It is important to note, however, that Molly's struggles against the dominant conceptions of power and knowledge, as well as her mental refusal to occupy the space of the feminine Other, are not always successful; Molly Bloom, like Stephen Dedalus, reveals herself to be deeply invested in and influenced by the beliefs she attempts to reject. In spite of her declaration, "I dont care what anybody says itd be much better for the world to be governed by the women in it," Molly also perceives women as "a dreadful lot of bitches," ready to stab each other in the back (*U* 18.1434–35, 1459). In a similar inversion, the phallic dominance that Molly at once fears and desires to subvert also enthralls her. She is fascinated by Boylan's "tremendous big red brute of a thing" and thinks appreciatively of the "fine young men" she saw "down in Margate strand bathingplace . . . *naked like a God or something* and then plunging into the sea" (*U* 18.144, 1345–47, my emphasis). She wishes for a penis herself so that she might, for once, occupy (physically, literally) the superior position in male-female relationships, fantasizing, "God I wouldnt mind being a man and get up on a lovely woman" (U 18.1146–47). But perhaps the most troubling mark of Molly's assimilation to the phallic order occurs within the context of what should be her greatest act of resistance—her affair with Blazes Boylan. On one level, this liaison is both her response to Bloom's sexual negligence and her protest against the cultural double standard that allows men to "pick and choose what they please . . . but were to be always chained up theyre not going to be chaining me up no damn fear" (U 18.1388–91). On another level, however, Molly's affair affirms not her dissent from but her complicity with the ability of masculine surveillance to dictate female behavior. The adulterous act itself, ostensibly an assertion of her own sexual agency, has been orchestrated and enabled by her husband, and even in the midst of intercourse, Molly represses aspects of her own desire because she fears Boylan's disapproval. A deep longing to "let myself go" is underscored and undermined by the intense inhibition she experiences during her afternoon tryst: "I wanted to shout out all sorts of things fuck or shit or anything at all only not to look ugly . . . who knows the way hed take it . . . some of them want you to be so nice about it" (U 18.584–92). What Molly here reveals is an inability to create herself as a fully experiencing Subject—even within the supposedly empowering context of her own recollection/imagination.

It is therefore tempting to assert that Molly's evident affinity for the British Empire is connected to a deep-seated proclivity to embrace the phallic order. Discussions of Molly's position as a colonial subject have been plagued by her pro-British politics; most critics attempt to claim either that Molly is an apolitical humanist who objects to the human costs of war, no matter who fights, or that she manifests the ambivalence of a divided colonial consciousness.[11] But unlike her reflections on gender, Molly appears to exhibit no resistance at all to the empire; indeed, she gloats over Mrs. Rubio's aversion to the presence of a British garrison on Spanish soil ("she never could get over the Atlantic fleet coming in half the ships of the world and the Union Jack flying . . . because 4 drunken English sailors took all the rock from them" [U 18.754–6]) and is extraordinarily proud of her father's service in the British army. To fully appreciate Molly's alliance, however, we must reconsider it outside the conventional binarism of colonial relations. What Molly does resist is the masculinized culture of Irish nationalism that tolerates women only so long as they do not disrupt its role as arbiter of discourse:[12] "little chits of missies" like Kathleen Kearney, therefore, are welcome, but women like Mrs. Kearney and Molly Bloom, who refuse to "get with the program" are not. Intriguingly, Molly's antinationalist stance seems to be the most consistent position of any she initiates: she and Bloom once had a "standup row over politics" (though Molly is angry at herself afterward for crying and "giving in" [U 18.175–77]); she has intentionally affronted nationalist sensibilities by signaling her support for British forces (in the Boer War, 1899–1902) during her last concert at St. Teresa's Hall, where Molly sang Kipling's "The Absentminded Beggar" and sported "a brooch for Lord Roberts" that no doubt stood out among the Gaelic devices worn by other women (U 18.377–78). Immediately after noting that Bloom has pointed out Griffiths to her as a leader of Sinn Fein, Molly complains, "I hate the mention of *their* politics after the war" (U 18.387–88, my emphasis); although she blames the war for her personal loss (Lieutenant Stanley Gardner died in South Africa of enteric fever), the remark is also a political one, directed specifically toward the nationalists, who supported the Boers in their struggle and who would have gloated—perhaps in Molly's hearing—over any British losses.[13] Like Stephen Dedalus, Molly Bloom objects to the authority of nationalist factions that presume to dictate the constitution of Irishness: she observes that, although her politics are evidently incorrect, she considers herself to look and to be as Irish as anyone else—"I had the map of it all" (U 18.378).[14] The absurdity of the nationalists' strictures is also evident in their disdain for Bloom, whose politics are above reproach, Molly notes, but who remains, with his mixed religious heritage, "not Irish enough." Molly objects to the power of the nationalist discourse to silence her voice by keeping her off the Dublin stage; it is no coincidence that, for her upcoming tour, Molly will travel to Belfast, a Protestant-unionist stronghold presumably more in sympathy with her own antinationalist politics. Ultimately, Molly's position is less protocolonial than it is antinationalist; her political stance, like her remarks on gender, indicates the ultimate insufficiency of binarism and the need for a new, hybridized discourse of Irishness.

As Joyce's Penelope weaves and unweaves her tapestry of discourse, she has often been charged with "contradicting."[15] My sense is that Molly's conundrums function in at least two ways. Their cumulative effect is one of, in Irigaray's terms, "jamming the theoretic machinery itself, of suspending its pretension to the production of a truth and a meaning that are excessively univocal" (78). First, Molly's "contradictions" testify to the ultimate difficulty of escaping the ideological mesh that contains and defines us; second, they work to deny the primacy of duality and to open spaces of possibility. That Molly simultaneously worships, fears, and diminishes the Phallus or admires, commiserates, and criticizes the Feminine is her greatest subversive strength. It is in this space of indeterminacy that resistance to the master discourse of gender is finally possible; perhaps the question of Bloom's breakfast is left open to make this very point. As her husband tries to reassert his authority and institute conventional gender norms within their relationship ("giving us his orders for eggs and tea . . . and hotbuttered toast I suppose well have him sitting up like the king of the country"/"and Im to be slooching around down in the kitchen" [U 18.930–31, 1431]), Molly is profoundly disturbed; after all, she married Bloom not only because he "understood . . . what a woman is" but because "I knew I could always get round him" (U 18.1579–80). She never decides what she will do; instead, she imagines possibilities: they range from preserving the status quo in which Bloom brings her breakfast ("I love to hear him falling up the stairs of a morning with the cups rattling on the tray" [U 18.933–34]); to reconciliation ("Ill just give him one more chance Ill get up early in the morning . . . then Ill throw him up his eggs and tea in the mustachecup she gave him" (U 18.1497–1505); to confrontation ("Ill let him know if thats what he wanted that his wife is fucked yes and damn well fucked too" [U 18.1508–11]); to entrapment and seduction ("Ill do the indifferent 1 or 2 questions Ill know by the answers when hes like that he cant keep a thing back . . . then Ill suggest about yes . . . Ill be quite gay and friendly over it O but I was forgetting this bloody pest of a thing" [U 18.1529–34]). Molly's final, syncretic vision of remembered courtship in which her former lovers converge onto the figure of Bloom may signal the most dramatic possibility of all for change within this fractured discourse. Bhabha has suggested memory can function as an attempt to circumvent oppressive structures and to reconstitute authority within the imagining self;[16] such shifting in fact constitutes Molly's most radical disruption to the confining teleology of discourse: it offers a re-beginning in which the absolutes of gender might be completely reimagined.

In the subjectivity of Anna Livia Plurabelle, Joyce continues in *Finnegans Wake* the reconstitution of gender that Molly's work has made possible. Anna Livia's letter suggests her agency as author of her own narrative; the text itself proclaims the identity inherent in such authorship: "Every word, letter, penstroke, paperspace is a perfect signature of its own" (FW 115). But the contestation and treatment of the letter—it is buried by ALP, negated as "feminine fiction" (FW 109), wounded by "numerous stabs and foliated gashes" (FW 124), and obscured by the male dreamer's psyche—again suggests the difficulty inherent in resurrecting feminine subjectivity and imagination outside a masculinized discourse.

Even the excited prattle of the washerwomen attests to the predilection of the masculine narrative to overwhelm the feminine. Although the women begin their gossip-fest announcing their prime interest to be ALP—"O tell me all about Anna Livia! I want to hear all about Anna Livia" (*FW* 196)— they quickly allow HCE's story to overwrite her tale. "She's nearly as badher as him herself" marks the moment of Anna Livia's reintroduction into the conversation by one washerwoman; the response of the other— "Who? Anna Livia? Ay, Anna Livia"—underscores that the story of ALP has almost dissolved within HCE's narrative (*FW* 198).

The feminine discourse that threatens to erupt throughout *Finnegans Wake*—ALP's letter—would expose HCE on multiple levels; it contains charges of his voyeuristic transgressions ("All schwants (schwrites) ischt tell the cock's trootabout him" [*FW* 113]); it also repudiates the phallic center that formed the basis of their marriage. The missive is filled with dreams and disillusionment: "I wrote me hopes and buried the page when I heard Thy voice," ALP recalls (*FW* 624). The biblical "Thy" in ALP's line suggests her husband has been her "lord and master," a notion confirmed by evidence found elsewhere in this section. Instead of becoming HCE's "aural eyeness" (*FW* 623), that queenly presence who would command both his ear and his monogamous gaze, ALP has been his obedient servant, even in childbearing: "Bidding me do this and that and the other. And blowing off to me, hugly Judsys, what wouldn't you give to have a girl! Your wish was mewill" (*FW* 620). Emotionally, too, she has been cheated and now arrives at the end of her marriage exhausted and drained from perpetual giving. "O bitter ending! I'll slip away before they're up. They'll never see. Nor know. Nor miss me" (*FW* 627).

Devlin has argued that the dreamer eclipses any independent presentation of ALP in her final monologue, that her voice is filtered through the still-groggy consciousness of her husband (*Wandering* 164). While this interpretation does indeed explain the graciousness with which Anna Livia initially excuses her husband's behavior ("All men has done something" [*FW* 621]), the tenderness of many of her memories, and what appears to be the preceding formal presentation of the letter itself (those five pages that begin "Dear" end with the signature, "Alma Luvia, Pollabella," and reveal disappointingly little [*FW* 615–19]), it is less satisfactory in illuminating those decidedly uncharitable reflections that culminate in ALP's desertion of her family. To suggest the latter portion of this episode is simply the manifestation of a son's or a husband's fear of abandonment overlooks the painful and overt self-revelations of the passage, which finally unearths the feminine narrative. While the letter was buried or obscured, Anna Livia played the role of the dutiful homemaker. Now, however, she metamorphoses into a woman finally able to see her family and HCE for who they are—greedy consumers of her care—and perceives her own role in perpetuating the fraudulent domestic fiction. ALP's letter is here metaphorically unburied, her voice and identity resurrected along with it: "First we feel. Then we fall. . . . I done me best when I was let. Thinking always if I go all goes. A hundred cares, a tithe of troubles and is there one who understands me? One in a thousand of years of the nights? All me life I have been lived among them but now they are becoming lothed to me. . . . How small it's all! And me letting on to meself always. And lilting on all the time. I thought you were all glittering with the noblest of carriage. You're only a bumpkin. I thought you the great in all things, in guilt and in glory. You're but a puny" (FW 627).

Anna Livia has borne the cares of wife and mother, but she has magnified her husband's significance as well as her own importance to him, both of which she here deflates as "small" and "puny." This vision of herself as an appendage of others—someone's wife, someone's else's mother—dissolves into an apparition of an Anna Livia independent of all these familial ties. She conjures a self that is "handsome," "wild," "weird," and vociferous about its freedom (FW 627), and she determines to leave this ungrateful family which has used her and taken her for granted: "I'll slip away before they're up" (FW 627). Freed from the entrapment of her marriage, the corporeal Anna Livia metamorphoses into a river and appears to abandon one patriarchal form—a husband—to return to another—a father: "sad and weary I go back to you, my cold father, my cold mad father, my cold mad feary father" (FW 628). From her description in this passage, we may expect this second relationship to prove as "cold" and unsatisfying as the first, but this return to childhood is a new beginning with a difference. The letter has been written and read; the syncretic subjectivity it symbolizes will not be easily annulled: "My leaves have drifted from me. All. But one clings still. I'll bear it on me. To remind me of" (FW 628). In this self-conscious state, ALP meets "Finn again," but she no longer needs him to "give me the keys of me heart" (FW 626); she possesses those keys herself and now freely gives them to him before proceeding on her way: "The keys to. Given! A way a lone a last a loved a long the" (FW 628). The novel's missing closure signifies not lack but promise; Anna Livia Plurabelle, James Joyce's last and newest woman, streams ever onward, her possibilities unbounded.

Joyce once remarked to Arthur Power that the "revolt of women against the idea that they are the mere instruments of men" had caused the "greatest revolution in our time and in the most important relationship there is—that between men and women. . . . The relationship between the two sexes is now on a different basis, but I do not know whether they are happier or unhappier than they were before" (Power 35). In his fiction, Joyce gives us the en-gendered contest for public space that characterized his era; his texts in fact reveal both women and men to be trapped within this cultural mêlée: Joyce depicts both feminine incursions and masculine re-assertions and suggests that the principal casualty of the struggle not only involves the Ideal Feminine but also extends to encompass the dominant masculine ethos predicated upon a silent, female Other. In the wake of this disrupted discourse, this fractured order, Joyce's characters (in keeping with their author's observation) do not know whether they are happy or unhappy in their present moment, but Joyce perhaps invites us to envision a new, hybridized space, one that renders gender not as a rigid system of confinement but rather as a fluid state of being where the "new (manly) woman" might meet the "new womanly man"—and wave the flag of truce.

Afterword

Lost in the Labyrinth

Joyce once related an anecdote to his brother about the Norwegian playwright Henrik Ibsen, who reportedly admonished an Italian interviewer as they discussed *A Doll's House:* "But you people can't understand it properly. You should have been in Norway when the Paris fashion journals first began to be on sale in Christiania." Whether Joyce believed this story or not (he was skeptical of its source, the *Irish Independent*), its implications for the importance of context to meaning had a significant impact on his own artistic method. "This is really my reason for constantly plaguing reluctant relatives at home to send me papers or cuttings from them," Joyce explained to Stanislaus (*Letters II* 166–67). Certainly Joyce's careful embedding of specific, recognizable signifiers of fin de siècle Dublin culture—the Literary Revivalist, the theosophical hermetist, the muscular Christian, the domestic angel, the hysterical woman, the New Woman, the male pest—within his texts enables us to grasp their import in millennia and places far removed from their writing. These images do not function to produce archetypal "essences" in Joyce's work; instead, they represent the impact of the cultural discourse on individual subjectivity. To understand Joyce's deployment of such discourses, it is incumbent upon us to reconstruct the beliefs and biases of a society that has long since been transformed by time and technology; resurrecting the artifacts of popular culture—newspapers, journals, advertisements, novels, poetry, medical texts, laws, letters—is the only way I know of attempting such as task.

It has been my aim in this book to reestablish facets of the cultural milieu important to Joyce's work that heretofore have escaped our notice as scholars and critics. Because of both empire and proximity, I have detailed the distinctly British nature of the ethos of nationhood, masculinity, morality, reform, and domesticity; such beliefs migrated to Ireland in the nineteenth century and suffused the social discourse to create an insidious ideological web of authority that, along with the influence of the Catholic Church, directed nearly every aspect of Dublin life. In addition to supplying these contexts for Joyce's work, I have argued that the author's specificity-laden approach signals his concern over the immense, manipulative power of these structures to formulate individual consciousness in Victorian and Edwardian Ireland. Stephen Dedalus certainly recognizes the social orthodoxies that confine his thought; his pivotal, unsettled presence in *Ulysses* draws attention to the extent to which the psyches of its other characters—Gerty MacDowell, Buck Mulligan, Blazes Boylan, Leopold Bloom, and Molly Bloom—are also owing to the social discourse, but with much less cognizance of the pressure it exerts on their subjectivities. Whether and how such structures of influence might be dismantled were questions of paramount concern to Joyce; he recognized within each discourse the ironic seeds of its own dissolution and attempted to exploit them: ideologies of "Irishness" and masculinity derived paradoxically from British forms; dogmas of public morality and social reform were subtended by a suspiciously self-pleasuring prurience; images of domestic tranquility were frequently disrupted by abusive violence and mental breakdown; masculinist illusions of dominion in the public space were fractured by the disruptive voices and disproving gazes of women who refused to relinquish these newfound venues. The Victorian predilection for social surveillance and for sequestering "undesirable" elements of the population—in workhouses, prisons, insane asylums, and Magdalen homes—becomes, in Joyce's work, an internalized and even more powerful confinement: his characters ultimately are contained by and within a social discourse that compels their obeisance; in this, ideology begins to constitute an edict whose force is inescapable. Leopold, Molly, and even Stephen have internalized the social discourses that direct their behavior as well as the gaze that reinforces it; in this atmosphere of suffusion and surveillance, no real hope of flight for them exists.

Amid all the masquerading and pretenses to authority performed by the powerless subject, Lacan explains that there is in fact "nothing false about the Law itself, or about him who assumes its authority" (*Ecrits* 311). For Joyce, the cultural discourse fomented in Victorian and Edwardian Dublin ultimately became this menacing force. Certainly there was nothing counterfeit about the influence that drove Joyce from Dublin, nearly prevented the publication of his work, and finally compelled him to marry in order to secure his estate and his copyrights to his progeny; such a force perhaps constitutes the "malevolent reality" that Stephen tells Cranly he imagines as existing behind those ideas that he fears (*P* 243). If discourse becomes the labyrinth that must be escaped, then it also must contain a Minotaur that waits to consume any being in its path.

As I worked through these arguments, I realized that theoretical approaches, while valuable, are even more useful when they are grounded in time and place—otherwise they risk asserting flawed, universal principles whose error lies in their very universality. For our beliefs—and those of our theorists—about masculinity, femininity, morality, family, sexuality, religion, political systems, labor, and wealth are all in fact bound by our own positions in time and place; just as Joyce's work is relentlessly grounded, so must our own be. In *Ulysses,* Joyce wrote a novel so insistent in its specificity that he imagined Dublin's physical landscape might be reconstructed from the book's pages should the city ever be destroyed, but he has also made it possible for us to reconstruct far more of his native space than just its streets and its monuments. Joyce has been as careful to replicate turn-of-the-century behaviors, habits, and attitudes as he has been to re-create pubs and landmarks for his Dubliners; as we examine the detail that he proffers, we must remember that modernism itself is characterized by a cultural context as much as by an aesthetic: the interior landscapes of modernism are at once cultural and psychological. Historicizing Joyce enables us not just to plumb psychological depths but also to explore the connections of these depths to the cultural and social forces that produce and continually shape them. In its fuller context, Bloom's voyeurism—to take just one example—thus becomes not just an amusing, individual quirk indicative of the sexual frustration within his marriage but part of the cultural fabric itself; Bloom's incessant looking allows Joyce to suggest the intrusive gaze of the social reformer as well as the en-gendered contests for the public space that were features of the fin de siècle landscape. Joyce's detail ultimately surpasses both realism and symbolism; it allowed him to read, interpret, and critique his own culture as he tried to reveal to his readers the hazards it contained.

Joyce's work is conventionally presented as the pinnacle of high modernism, and stylistically this claim is irrefutable. But it has been my argument here that Joyce's characters are confined within late Victorian/Edwardian sensibilities and that while they might expose the fragility of the constructs that shut them in, they never escape their boxes. Simply crying "the Emperor has no clothes" will not dismantle the structures that maintain institutional authority and supplant their control with the authority of the individual; Joyce's characters have internalized the forms that repress them and never exert thought that is free from such influence. As Stephen recognizes, "All thinking must be bound by its own laws" (*P* 187).

Ultimately the benefactors of Joyce's exposure of the hidden, discursive mechanisms of social control are his readers, not his characters. By showcasing discourse as constructed and socially produced rather than as natural or essential, Joyce highlights the fissures it contains within itself as it assimilates subjectivity. The question remains, however, whether Joyce's readers, unlike his characters, might actually free themselves from the influence of these structures once they gain awareness of their presence and their power. If Joyce's characters continue, like the Daedalus of Greek myth, to perpetuate the structures that detain them, then so might our own thoughts be the unwitting agents of our own confinement; finally, perhaps, the cultural labyrinth may only be perceived but never fully escaped. Like Icarus and Joyce's own Dedalus, we may dream of continuing flight, only to find ourselves sinking once again beneath the powerful currents of discourse.

Notes

Introduction: Dilemmas of Discourse

1. See Norris, *The Decentered Universe of Finnegans Wake: A Structural Analysis*; see also Leonard's recent book, *Reading Dubliners Again: A Lacanian Perspective,* in which he argues that Joyce's fiction manifests an "antiessentialism" of the self and begins to undermine "the mythic ideology of unified consciousness" as early as *Dubliners* (4).

2. In just one example, Richard Ellmann reports that as Joyce constructed the "Nausicaa" episode of *Ulysses,* he "asked his aunt to check 'whether there are trees (and of what kind) behind the Star of the Sea church in Sandymount visible from the shore and also whether there are steps leading down at the side of it from Leahy's terrace'" (*James Joyce* 473).

3. In his important study, *Surface and Symbol: The Consistency of James Joyce's Ulysses,* Robert Adams observed the ways in which Joyce manipulated many such cultural artifacts in order to imbue them with symbolic resonance and layers of meaning far beyond the literal; Cheryl Herr has expanded Adams's scope and premise by demonstrating that "the most inert detail of Irish life can be—indeed, must be—recognized as bearing a relation to one or another social institution" and is therefore ideologically charged and potentially symbolic (*Joyce's Anatomy of Culture* 283).

4. In *Course in General Linguistics,* Saussure's emphasis on the fundamental distinction between signifier and signified as well as his articulation of the "synchronous" aspects of language (the idea that signification derives from a system of contextual relationships that exist between signs rather than from the connection of a sign to an external reality) led poststructuralists to appropriate his theories but to dismiss his conclusions. While Saussure held that the "linguistic sign is arbitrary" (meaning it has "no natural connection with the signified"), he also believed that it was relatively stable within the system it occupied: "the individual does not have the power to change a sign in any way once it has become established in the linguistic community" (79). Poststructuralists rejected this supposed fixity and focused instead on the indeterminate core implied by Saussure's linguistic theory, concluding that the system of signs from which meaning derives is constantly shifting; therefore, poststructuralists argue, language is an inherently unstable phenomenon. In "The Agency of the Letter," Lacan held that the unconscious, the locus of the self, is structured like a language and is therefore subject to the same decentered propensities and instabilities that characterize language.

5. Fairy tales, like any other narratives, are ideologically charged, and the one

Simon Dedalus spins is no exception: it not only invokes an idyllic Dedalus household ("a very good time it was"), it also reinforces the desired behavior on the part of the child: he was "a nicens little boy" (*P* 7).

6. Robert Spoo argues that Joyce "rehabilitates Stephen as the novel's hero by showing that the persistent historiographic concerns of *Ulysses* are ultimately his concerns" (8). James Fairhall makes a similar point, that "Stephen's desire in *A Portrait* to escape the nets of family, country, and religion, whose effects on his growing mind are precisely delineated, is replaced in the second half of *Ulysses* and in the *Wake* by a generalized desire to escape the authority of the word and the imprisonment of narrative" (9–10).

7. For more, see chapter 6, as well as Devlin, "The Romance Heroine Exposed: 'Nausicaa' and *The Lamplighter*," and Leonard, "The Virgin Mary and the Urge in Gerty: The Packaging of Desire in the 'Nausicaa' Chapter of *Ulysses*."

8. See, for instance, James Van Dyck Card, "'Contradicting': The Word for Joyce's 'Penelope.'"

1. Colonial Pathology and the Ideology of Irishness in Victorian and Edwardian Dublin

1. In *Joyce, Bakhtin, and Popular Literature: Chronicles of Disorder,* Kershner argues that Stephen derives his "romantic and heroic" self-image from Dantes and vicariously enacts through Melnotte (who rises from gardener to colonel) a desire to let his own class difference "fall away" (198, 227).

2. These include the lectures "Ireland, Island of Saints and Sages" and "James Clarence Mangan," both delivered in 1907, and the articles "Fenianism," "Home Rule Comes of Age," and "Ireland at the Bar," all published in 1907. Two later pieces, "The Home Rule Comet" and "The Shade of Parnell," were published in 1910 and 1912.

3. Katharine Simms, in "The Norman Invasion and the Gaelic Recovery," provides a concise explanation of the twelfth-century struggles for omnipotence among the various Irish kings, including MacMurrough, who was also known as king of Dublin: "Dubliners," Simms notes, "apparently preferred the prestige and comparative independence of association with a distant national ruler to the domination of a local tyrant" (47).

4. Broader treatments of Irish cultural nationalism that touch on Joyce's views include Declan Kiberd's *Inventing Ireland: The Literature of the Modern Nation* and David Lloyd's *Anomalous States: Irish Writing and the Post-Colonial Moment.*

5. Under the leadership of Paul Cullen, archbishop of Dublin, 1852–78 (who became Ireland's first cardinal in 1866), the earlier comradeship that had grown up between priests and rebels was rescinded as the Church began to avoid "overt commitment to political movements not under its own patronage [and] issued maledictions against Fenianism" (Fitzpatrick 182). In his autobiographical account, "O'Donovan Rossa's Prison Life" (1874), Jeremiah O'Donovan Rossa de-

scribes the change in climate from the Fenian perspective: O'Donovan Rossa observes that during the prosecutions of the Protestant Reformation, "Catholic Irishmen came to feel that, in fighting against Protestantism, they were fighting against England, and, in fighting for Catholicity, they were fighting for Ireland. The priest was the person most sought after, most persecuted by the English, and the most loved, most looked to, and most protected by the Irish" (261). But England, in the interests of maintaining its dominion, had changed its policy of Catholic prosecution, O'Donovan Rossa argues, and in the late nineteenth century had begun to patronize the Church, relying on its influence to dissuade the people from rebellion. "There was no diocese in Ireland where the men who were organizing means to fight England, were not denounced from the altars and sent away from the confessionals unshriven," O'Donovan Rossa writes. "The tongues and hands of [supportive] clergymen 'were tied' as they themselves would say, by the higher ecclesiastics, while the 'bad priests,' as we called them, were allowed full scope to denounce us and brand us as infidels" (261). Cullen is mentioned scornfully by Simon Dedalus in *Portrait* (38).

6. Unlike Joyce, Davitt blamed Parnell for the divide and saw Parnell's act as a betrayal of the nationalist cause: "The Irish party was split in two, and with it the entire league movement throughout the world. The Irish Samson had pulled the pillars from beneath the temple of a great cause in his own downfall" (642). Michael Patrick Gillespie has cataloged this volume among those resident in Joyce's Trieste library (81).

7. Moran's essay, "The Battle of Two Civilizations," appeared in *Ideals in Ireland* in 1901.

8. "If the Irish programme did not insist on the Irish language I suppose I could call myself a nationalist," Joyce wrote to Stanislaus in 1906 (*Letters II* 187).

9. For instance, Joyce does in fact appear to espouse many sentiments of Revivalist rhetoric in his essays: his sense that denunciations of "the English despoiler" were wastes of time parallels the argument made by Hyde ("The Necessity of De-Anglicising Ireland") and Moran ("The Battle of Two Civilizations") that Ireland itself was at least partly responsible for its own malaise (*CW* 173). Joyce also appears to echo Hyde's 1892 language about the assimilative nature of the Irish race, which becomes in Joyce's rendering, "More Irish than the Irish themselves" (*CW* 161). Though Joyce may have shared some of the assessments made by these nationalists, however, he also dismissed their proposed linguistic solutions, their appeals to Ireland's past glory, and their desire to purge the culture of foreign influence: he noted that "ancient Ireland is dead just as ancient Egypt is dead" (*CW* 173) and objected to Arthur Griffith's paper *Sinn Fein* because it "educat[ed] the people of Ireland on the old pap of racial hatred" (*Letters II* 167).

10. I use Benedict Anderson's term "nation-ness" to imply that "imagined political community" that may be infused by, but is ultimately distinct from, nationalism(s) (4).

11. Joyce himself owned the fourth edition of this work, published in 1905 (Gillespie 124).

12. Three articles by Oliver Gogarty appeared in *Sinn Fein* in late 1906 decrying the immorality and hypocrisy of the English "common man"; Joyce mentioned Gogarty's September 15 piece to Stanislaus. Ellmann quotes an excerpt of the "full flavour" Joyce noted; Gogarty wrote: "In his righteousness he [the Englishman] has called out with holy horror against the immorality of the French nation, rejoicing meanwhile like the publican that his own house is clean. When the facts of the case are only too clear to anyone who has the unblended eye to see them, that it is this English monster that demands and supports whatever indecencies Paris can produce" (Ellmann, *Selected Letters,* 108n). In *Ideals in Ireland,* both Moran and Yeats also railed against the infiltration of Ireland by cheap and "vulgar" English periodicals (Moran, "The Battle of Two Civilizations" 33, and Yeats, "The Literary Movement in Ireland" 90). For more on ways this perceived cultural degradation fueled social reform movements in both England and Ireland, see my chapter 5.

13. Casey's opposition to being called a Protestant perhaps is rooted in the changed conventions described by O'Donovan Rossa: "The tradition that my boyhood received of fighting for my religion in fighting for my country, and in fighting for my country I was fighting for my religion, was broken; for here I had sworn to fight for Ireland, and I was set upon as an enemy of Catholicity" (261). Casey's final proclamation, "No God for Ireland! . . . We have had too much God in Ireland. Away with God!" (*P* 39) also recalls O'Donovan Rossa's statement: "I don't put my country before my God; but I put it before religious ascendancy of any denomination" (262).

14. Innumerable representations in Irish revolutionary ballads depict Ireland as an embattled woman whose virginity has been vanquished by a vicious colonizer: Simms reports that as early as 1364, the inauguration ode for one native Irish ruler, Niall Mor O'Neill, began:

> Ireland is a woman risen again
> from the horrors of reproach . . .
> she was owned for a while by foreigners,
> she belongs to Irishmen after that. (76)

More contemporary to Joyce's era, *The Rising of the Moon* (a play by Augusta Gregory, produced by the Abbey Theatre in 1907) turns on an Irish ballad that employs the suffering, assaulted female to symbolize Irish oppression. "The Song of Granuaile" introduces a "matron fair" who sings of the wrongs done to Granuaile/Ireland/herself:

> Her head was bare, her hands and feet with iron bands were bound,
> Her pensive strain and plaintive wail mingles with the evening gale,
> And the song she sang with mournful air, I am old Granuaile. (58)

15. Spoo argues that Stephen's mother, appearing as she does in the ghoulish dream he recollects early in *Ulysses'* "Telemachus" episode, also personifies the "nightmare" of history that Stephen attempts to contest throughout the novel. According to Spoo, "For Joyce and for Stephen history is the uncanny maternal body returning to menace the surviving son, a compulsive ghost that represents a meaningless, horrific repetition of the same" (18).

16. Adams's *Surface and Symbol* provides an early analysis of the errors in Deasy's discourse; Don Gifford's and Robert Seidman's *Ulysses Annotated* is similarly helpful in sorting out verity from falsehood. In his discussion of "Nestor," Spoo also supplies important analysis of Deasy's inconsistencies.

17. In "Nationality and Imperialism," the essay that leads *Ideals in Ireland,* Russell writes, "It is not merely Gaelic which is being suppressed [by colonialism], but the spiritual life of our race" (19).

18. For accounts of this schism, see Kain and O'Brien (32); for additional background, see Kelly and Schuchard (3.715–18).

19. Qtd. in Eglinton's *Irish Literary Portraits* (9). First published in 1935, Eglinton's book records his impressions of (and his distaste for) "the Irish Literary Movement" and its principal figures: Yeats, Russell, Moore, and Joyce. "For me," Eglinton writes, "Ireland has always been a country rather than a 'nation.' . . . I was brought up to an inherited dislike for the green flags and reedy orchestration of nationalist demonstrations, and this remained at the back of my mind even when Yeats, A.E. and Arthur Griffith got hold of me and tried to turn me into a nationalist. . . . The actual program of Irish nationalism, the escapade of having a separate language, the apotheosis of Wolfe Tone and Parnell, the jubilation over everything that embarrassed England . . . were entirely distasteful to me. Ireland will always appear to me to have been more interesting, both to itself and to the world at large, under the old conditions: a country which has rejected its natural spiritual destiny, and whose poets all made the mistake of going into politics" (10–11).

20. Among them:

• *February 8, 1903:* "Words cannot measure my contempt for AE at present . . . and his spiritual friends. . . . And so help me devil I will write only the things that approve themselves to me and I will write them the best way I can. . . . So damn Russell, damn Yeats, damn Skeffington, damn Darlington, damn editors, damn free-thinkers, damn vegetable verse and double damn vegetable philosophy!" (*Letters II* 28).

• *November 6, 1906:* "I would call such people as Gogarty and Yeats and Colm [a Russell protégé] the blacklegs of literature. Because they have tried to substitute us, to serve the old idols at a lower rate when we refused to do so for a higher" (*Letters II* 187).

• *February 1907, after the Abbey Theatre riots over Synge's Playboy of the Western World:* "I am sure that many of the hermetists don't know which to choose. . . . And as for pore [*sic*] old A.E. I suppose he is nibbling cabbages up in Rathgar in quite an excited frame of mind at the amount of heresy which is rife in Dublin" (*Letters II* 208–9).

21. In August 1922, Joyce wrote to Augusta Gregory to petition for the exclusion of "all letters of mine and all mention of me" from a history of the Irish literary movement that she was preparing: "In doing so you will be acting strictly in accordance with the spirit of that movement, inasmuch as since the date of my letter, twenty years ago, no mention of me or of my struggles or of my writings has been made publicly by any person connected with it" (*Selected Letters* 290).

22. Joyce also professed his admiration for *The Countess Cathleen* in a 1916 letter to the elder poet (*Selected Letters* 220–21).

23. Although Yeats certainly comes in for his share of criticism in *Ulysses,* it does not emanate from Stephen. It is Mulligan who accuses Yeats of hypocrisy in praising his patron, Augusta Gregory, while Stephen has "slate[d] her drivel to Jaysus" (*U* 9.1160).

24. Wilde was not the only Irish writer to swap allegiances, as Stephen sees it; he is the rule rather than the exception. In "Nestor," Stephen reflects: "Why had they chosen all that part? Not wholly for the smooth caress. For them too history was a tale like any other too often heard, their land a pawnshop" (*U* 2.45–47).

2. "Religions of Unbelief": Spiritual Orthodoxies and Romantic Dissent

1. Peter Dorsey has expanded Cranly's observation, suggesting that Stephen embodies a "paradoxical dependence" on the faith he disdains (509), and Alan Shepard has implied, with Mulligan, that the Church's influence on Stephen is more pervasive still. Stephen remains always a product of steadfast doctrinal values that prize authority and obedience, Shepard contends; Dedalus ridicules the Church only "to protect himself from the guilt that he still occasionally feels for his defection from the community of believers" (109).

2. Joyce appears to have personally identified with Stephen's sentiment, writing to Augusta Gregory in 1902, "though I seem to have been driven out of my country here as a misbeliever, I have found no man yet with a faith like mine" (*Letters I* 53).

3. For more, see Rene Wellek's "The Concept of 'Romanticism' in Literary History."

4. Gifford and Seidman note the term originated with English theologian and philosopher Anthony Collins in his 1713 treatise, *Discourse of Freethinking* (24).

5. In his own eccentric way, Blake attempts to explain Milton's "mistake": "Note: The reason Milton wrote in fetters when he wrote of Angels & God, and at liberty when of Devils & Hell, is because he was a true Poet and of the Devil's party without knowing it" (*The Marriage of Heaven and Hell* 70).

6. See Joyce's 1901 essay, "The Day of the Rabblement," which begins: "No man, said the Nolan, can be a lover of the true or the good unless he abhors the multitude; and the artist, though he may employ the crowd, is very careful to isolate himself" (*CW* 69).

7. My identification of the passage as a reference to Blake is indebted to Gifford (247).

8. Lady Caroline Lamb, one of his mistresses, called him in her diary "mad, bad and dangerous to know" (qtd. in David Perkins 779); Byron perpetuated this image of himself in his letters to friends. While in Italy, he wrote enthusiastically to Augusta Leigh (presumably after the close of their own affair, which evidently produced his child) of his "liaison" with the twenty-year-old married Countess Guiccioli, who "miscarried in May, and sent for me here [in Ravenna]" (*Letters and Journals* 6.185).

9. For further discussion of Stephen's appropriation of the Byronic hero, see Kershner (209–15).

10. Joyce shared Stephen's admiration. In a letter to Harriet Shaw Weaver, Joyce opined: "Nobody has ever written English prose that can be compared with that of a tiresome footling little Anglican parson who afterward became a prince of the only true church" (*Letters I* 366).

11. Ellmann reports that the incident in question actually happened to Joyce, who remarked that his choice of Newman in the face of confrontation "sounded goody-goody but was really stylistic" (*James Joyce* 40).

12. Muller's primary source, which she paraphrases here, is Newman's *The Idea of a University Defined and Illustrated*. University College, Dublin (formerly the Catholic University of Ireland), was founded in 1851 by Newman "as a site for the practical application of the educational theories set out" in his treatise (Muller 593).

13. For more on Shelley's utopian visions, see Kenneth Neill Cameron's essay, "The Social Philosophy of Shelley."

14. See, for instance, "The Chimney Sweeper" in *Songs of Experience*, in which it is "God & his Priest & King / Who make up a heaven of our misery," or "Merlin's Prophecy": "The King & the Priest must be tied in a tether / Before two virginities can meet together."

15. According to Nethercot, Annie Besant had several ties to Ireland. Though born in London, she claimed to be three-quarters Irish: her father had been born in Galway and took a medical degree at Trinity College (3). She also attended the 1867 London trial of the "Manchester Martyrs," Fenians whose accidental killing of a British constable sparked race riots in Manchester and earned three of them speedy hangings. The experience marked Besant; she would write in 1924 that "the love of liberty first awoke in her" when she heard the condemned men shout as their sentence was pronounced, "God Save Ireland" (27). Joyce owned two books by Besant, including *Une introduction à la théosophie,* published in 1907, and *The Path of Discipleship: Four Lectures Delivered at the Twentieth Anniversary of the Theosophical Society, at Adyar, Madras, December 27, 28, 29, and 30, 1895,* published in 1904 (Gillespie 47).

16. Russell became a pivotal member of the Second Dublin Lodge (Gifford and Seidman 146); he changed the name of his group to the Hermetic Society and

endeavored to "keep the study of HPB and WQJ [W. Q. Judge, one of Blavatsky's organizers] initiated" (Cranston 473).

17. The passage Herr cites is this one: "His lips lipped and mouthed fleshless lips of air: mouth to her moomb. Oomb, allwombing tomb. His mouth moulded issuing breath, unspeeched: ooeeehah: roar of cataractic planets, globed, blazing, roaring wayawayawayawayawayaway" (*U* 3.401–4). Herr notes the similarity between Stephen's "oomb" and suggests its relationship to Blavatsky's "aum,"—both the higher self and "an efficacious syllable of mystic and Oriental religious thought" ("Theosophy" 49–50). For more, see Gilbert, *James Joyce's Ulysses,* pp. 191–92.

18. Cousins's wife, Margaret, served as his medium; her trances often produced material from ancient Celtic literature that her husband, in turn, used as the basis for much of his poetry (Dumbleton 18).

19. In "Scylla and Charybdis," Stephen recalls that A.E. has mentioned the conversation to "some yankee interviewer" (*U* 9.54), who may have been radio reporter W. R. Rodgers, whose interviews with Russell, Yeats, Eglinton, and others are recounted in his book, *Irish Literary Portraits.* Because of dissension among the Revival's key figures, Rodgers interviewed each one separately and spliced their answers together to create the illusion of a radio "discussion." The anecdote about the aspiring writer who visited Russell is recounted in Rodgers's book, though Joyce is not mentioned by name as the young man.

20. Gifford and Seidman helpfully translate the theosophical term "elemental" as "essentially the 'lower' or 'mortal' nature of man, one-fourth of which is visible as the physical body, three-fourths invisible as the astral . . . body, the life principle, and the principle of desire. The joke involves Blavatsky's disciples' claim that she would appear to them after her death; it also involves the non-Theosophical pun on genitals" (198).

21. Gregory Castle has astutely observed Stephen's unsuccessful attempts, especially within the context of "Proteus," to appropriate Nietzsche's "will to power" —that is, to "will himself into being" by imposing his own perspective on all that surrounds him (293).

3. "Do you call that a man?":The Discourse of Anxious Masculinity in *Ulysses*

1. See Suzette Henke, "Gerty MacDowell: Joyce's Sentimental Heroine"; Kimberly Devlin, "The Romance Heroine Exposed: 'Nausicaa' and *The Lamplighter*"; and Garry Leonard, "The Virgin Mary and the Urge in Gerty: The Packaging of Desire in the 'Nausicaa' Chapter of *Ulysses.*"

2. See Kimberly Devlin, "Pretending in 'Penelope': Masquerade, Mimicry, and Molly Bloom," and Cheryl Herr, "'Penelope' as Period Piece."

3. The Irish Republican Brotherhood was born in the late 1850s; Michael Davitt's Irish National Land League helped to liberalize tenancy restrictions during the "land war" of 1879–82; the Home Rule movement gained momentum under Parnell's leadership in the 1880s. For more, see R. F. Foster, "Ascendancy and Union," and David Fitzpatrick, "Ireland since 1870."

4. For more on Carlyle, see *On Heroes, Hero-Worship and the Heroic in History,* as well as Norma Clarke's analysis, "Strenuous Idleness: Thomas Carlyle and the Man of Letters as Hero." In *Boys Will Be Girls: The Feminine Ethic and British Children's Fiction, 1857–1917,* Claudia Nelson has demonstrated that the term "manliness" itself—connoting a "blend of compassion and courage, gentleness and strength, self-control and native purity"—was in fact applied androgynously to both men and women during the early years of the nineteenth century (37).

5. Devlin has examined the role of the gender masquerade in Joyce's work: see "Castration and Its Discontents: A Lacanian Approach to *Ulysses*" and "Pretending in 'Penelope.'"

6. For more on the discourse of colonialism and its construction of the native presence, see Homi K. Bhabha's "The Other Question: Difference, Discrimination and the Discourse of Colonialism." It should also be noted that simianized images of the Gaels were not unique to Kingsley; they saturated the popular press, appearing in publications such as *Punch* and *Harper's Weekly.* For an excellent discussion and reproductions of these images, see L. Perry Curtis, *Apes and Angels: The Irishman in Victorian Caricature,* as well as Vincent J. Cheng's chapter "Catching the Conscience of a Race" in *Joyce, Race, and Empire.*

7. For more on these convergences, see Maurizia Boscagli's excellent study, *Eye on the Flesh: Fashions of Masculinity in the Early Twentieth Century.*

8. Allen Warren notes that the founder of the Boy Scouts, Robert Baden Powell, addressed the issue of physical purity on a variety of levels; he assailed "self-abuse" in the 1908 handbook, *Scouting for Boys,* and extolled the virtues of "clean blood" and "regular bowel movements" (202).

9. I am indebted here to the work of Richard Dellamora, who, though he does not discuss its relation to Charles Kingsley, advances this argument in his book *Masculine Desire: The Sexual Politics of Victorian Aestheticism.* James Eli Adams ("Pater's Muscular Aestheticism" and *Dandies and Desert Saints*) and Thais E. Morgan ("Reimagining Masculinity in Victorian Criticism: Swinburne and Pater") also have done useful work in this area.

10. Alan Sinfield offers the conversation between Wilde and Frank Harris, *Fortnightly Review* editor, during the second of Wilde's three trials as typical of the general view of the allegations against the playwright; in their exchange, Wilde exclaimed to Harris: "'You talk with passion and conviction, as if I were innocent.' 'But you are innocent,' cried Harris in amazement, 'aren't you?' 'No,' said Wilde. 'I thought you knew that all along.' 'No,' Harris replied. 'I did not know. I did not believe the accusation. I did not believe it for a moment'" (*The Wilde Century* 1).

11. Among the examples Condren cites, for instance, is the rhetoric of Patrick Pearse, which equated nationalistic violence with manly virility: "Bloodshed is a cleansing and sanctifying thing, and the nation which regards it as the final horror has lost its manhood" ("Sacrifice" 160–61). Joseph Valente has helpfully detailed some of the feminized images of Ireland that permeated British colonial discourse and has observed the gendered nature of colonial rule there, noting that "gender

hierarchy and male control were naturalized as the ultimate referents of the colonial mission" ("The Myth of Sovereignty" 189).

12. For more on the sociohistorical context of this figure, especially its sources in Richard von Krafft-Ebing's *Psychopathia Sexualis* and Otto Weininger's *Sex and Character,* see Robert Byrnes, "Bloom's Sexual Tropes: Stigmata of the 'Degenerate' Jew." For more recent analysis, see Marilyn Reizbaum, "Weininger and the Bloom of Jewish Self-Hatred in Joyce's *Ulysses,*" and Natania Rosenfeld, "James Joyce's Womanly Wandering Jew."

13. See Devlin, "Castration and Its Discontents"; Suzette Henke, *James Joyce and the Politics of Desire,* especially chapter 4; Colleen Lamos, "Joyce and Gender Justice in Ulysses"; and Cheryl Herr, *Joyce's Anatomy of Culture,* especially chapters 4 and 5.

14. Note that Molly Bloom also associates the "bull neck" with male potency; the priest she suspects of deriving prurient pleasure from her confession has a "bullneck in his horsecollar" (*U* 18.115).

15. In his essay on Shelley, Matthew Arnold reports both female and male perspectives on Shelley's physical appearance; the "feminine enthusiasm" of a "Miss Rose" is confirmed by a "Captain Kennedy," who, though expected by Arnold to "Keep his head," reported Shelley's beauty in terms even more effusive than the ones Rose selected ("Shelley" 379–80).

16. The 1958 film *Indiscreet,* starring Cary Grant as a diplomat-playboy who pretends to be married so as to only date, rather than marry, the wealthy actress played by Ingrid Bergman, showcases the dangers to masculine identity that Bloom has imagined (*U* 13.1058) and that I believe occur here. When Bergman's character discovers Grant's secret, she withdraws her validating gaze, though the hero assumes it is still present. In a wonderfully underplayed scene, Grant's performance before Bergman and her friends suddenly becomes ridiculous rather than debonair.

17. Garry Leonard's "'A Little Trouble about Those White Corpuscles': Mockery, Heresy, and the Transubstantiation of Masculinity in 'Telemachus'" suggests that Mulligan's every act in "Telemachus" draws attention to the fact that he is preparing to venture forth "as a man" (10).

18. Dellamora observes that the name "Whitman" itself came to "signify desire between men" to some Victorians, as well as to indicate an associated Hellenism (86).

19. Erwin R. Steinberg has verified Bloom's claim of Jewish persecution in Morocco; see "Persecuted, Sold in Morocco Like Slaves."

20. The event alluded to is Dermot MacMurrough's request of Henry II in 1166 for assistance in securing his throne against Rory O'Connor, the new high king of Ireland. While MacMurrough had carried off the wife of another rival, the Citizen's unfounded charge suggests that the Norman invasion was instigated by this woman (Simms 47–48).

21. For discussions of these images, see Valente, "The Myth of Sovereignty,"

and Declan Kiberd, "Irish Literature and Irish History." For revivalist representations of Cathleen ni Houlihan, see Yeats, *Cathleen ni Houlihan* and *The Countess Cathleen;* for revivalist representations of Granuaile, see Augusta Gregory, *The Rising of the Moon.*

4. Urban Spectatorship, Victorian Vice, and the Discourse of Social Reform

1. Designed to eradicate the rampant venereal disease that plagued the British military forces, the 1864 act applied only to eleven garrison and dock towns in southern England and Ireland and compelled the compulsory gynecological examination of any woman suspected to be a prostitute. Women found to be afflicted were confined to "lock" hospitals for a mandatory stay of up to three months. The 1866 act expanded both the affected territory and the powers of the local police forces, now requiring a "system of periodic fortnightly inspection . . . of all known prostitutes." The 1869 act added five more districts, expanded jurisdiction to a ten-mile radius outside these districts, and set a nine-month maximum hospital detention. Women could be picked up without any hard evidence that they were engaged in prostitution; "suspicious" dress or behavior, such as simply talking with a man in public, was enough to justify both the accusation and examination. For more, see Judith Walkowitz's excellent study, *Prostitution and Victorian Society: Women Class, and the State.*

2. See Walkowitz (*City* 16) and Jane Flax, "Postmodernism and Gender Relations in Feminist Theory" (624).

3. This figure is necessarily male because feminine perambulations within the public space of the metropolis were always encoded with messages of sexual jeopardy: as Walkowitz notes, "in public, women were presumed to be both endangered and a source of danger to those men who congregated in the streets" (*City* 21). By the late nineteenth century, women were taking an active role in social reform movements, but they did not shed their relationship to sexual danger. Female reformers were often advised not to enter brothels or, if they did, to be sure "never to eat or smell anything, to stand near the door and above all not to look scared" (Bristow 70).

4. The laundry was founded in 1856 and was labeled "Female Penitentiary" on the 1909 Ordnance Survey Map of Dublin. Florence Walzl has located its prospectus in a 1902 publication known as *Dublin Charities: A Handbook of Dublin Philanthropic Organisations and Charities* ("Joyce's 'Clay'" 127–28).

5. Ellmann briefly notes the connection between Francis Sheehy-Skeffington and McCann (*James Joyce* 62).

6. In "Beef to the Heel: Harlotry with Josephine Butler, William T. Stead, and James Joyce," Eckley argues that Bloom is an incarnation of Stead until she encounters Bloom's support for the medical inspection of prostitutes (a stance antithetical to Stead's agitation for the repeal of the Contagious Diseases Acts), at which point she problematically modifies her position to assert that Stead's abolitionist torch is passed on to Stephen Dedalus (75). Eckley has argued at length that

Stead's influence on Joyce's work, especially *Finnegans Wake,* was much more direct and pervasive than I find tenable. Eckley claims, for instance, that Stead is the "epic hero" of *Finnegans Wake* and the model for HCE; she also maintains that the Stead "source" subsumes all others (*The Steadfast Finnegans Wake* 46). For more, see Eckley's "The Entertaining *Nights* of Burton, Stead, and Joyce's Earwicker."

7. For more on the vice societies of the period and their agendas, see Bristow; for more on the Salvation Army, see Bailey. Luddy's *Women and Philanthropy in Nineteenth-Century Ireland* is an excellent source of information about the Dublin-area movements of the era.

8. It should be noted here that Leopold Bloom observes a similarly prurient—and avaricious—interest in reports of the divorce trial of Capt. William Henry O'Shea and his wife, Katherine, which identified Charles Stewart Parnell as her lover. When it was revealed that Parnell "had shared her bedroom," Bloom recalls, a "thrill went through the packed court literally electrifying everybody." Bloom knows, too, that witnesses testified to having seen Parnell, in his nightclothes, "scrambling out of an upstairs apartment with the assistance of a ladder . . . having gained admittance in the same fashion." The whole escapade, he notes, was a "fact the weeklies . . . simply coined shoals of money out of" (*U* 16.1373–79).

9. The book was originally known as *Ruby. A Novel. Founded on the Life of a Circus Girl* before Joyce modified its title. As Mary Power has noted, Bloom's assumptions about the picture are incorrect. It is not Ruby who lies at the feet of the cruel circus master but another character, Victoria Melton (118).

10. Engels perhaps would have been dismayed at the appropriation of his philosophy by the social reformers; he objected to the class characterizations of vice: "the Salvation Army, . . . revives the propaganda of early Christianity, appeals to the poor as the elect, fights capitalism in a religious way, and thus fosters an element of early Christian class antagonism, which one day may become troublesome to the well-to-do people who now find the ready money for it" (qtd. in Bailey 133).

11. Jacques Lacan carefully has distinguished the voyeuristic "eye" or "look" —produced by the individual and situated firmly within the realm of desire—from the Otherness of the societal "gaze," which remains outside desire and outside the voyeuristic act, producing sensations of shame and embarrassment within the subject it surprises. Kaja Silverman argues that feminist film theory has wrongly equated the male voyeur with the gaze, that Lacan's *Four Fundamental Concepts* "suggests, on the contrary, that it is at precisely that moment when the eye is placed at the keyhole that it is most likely to find itself subordinated to the gaze" (130). I believe that *Ulysses* in fact enacts Silverman's application of Lacan. Each of Bloom's looks discussed in this chapter—his libidinous "girl-watching" and his philanthropic, social regard—is emphatically underwritten by desire, defined by Lacan as that gap that exists between "demand" and "need" (*Ecrits* 311). Most obvious among Bloom's lacks is his "want" of sexual relations with his wife; less

overt—until it is exposed in "Circe"—is Bloom's desire for social approbation and recognition by the Other. These two insufficiencies are connected, both in Circean sequencing and in Lacan's observation that "the recognition of desire is bound up with the desire for recognition" (*Ecrits* 172).

12. Gifford and Seidman note that the ruby ring is also the "coronation ring of Scotland" (474).

13. For more on the historical context of this phenomenon, see Storch. Dilke was an English liberal politician whose career, like Parnell's, was ruined when, during a divorce trial, the accused wife admitted to having committed adultery with him. Of course, Parnell's political demise following the O'Shea divorce trial also was related in no small way to Ireland's staunch Catholicism, as Joyce makes clear in the virulent Christmas dinner argument that takes place around the Dedalus table in *Portrait* (32–39). But it is worth noting that Dante Riordan's first stated objection to Parnell is phrased in terms of public morality: "He was no longer worthy to lead. . . . He was a public sinner" (32).

14. His pathology, however, does underscore his sexual Otherness, which owes it source principally to his Judaic heritage. Sander Gilman has traced nineteenth-century constructions of the Jew's body to "the underlying ideology of anti-Semitism, to the view that the Jew is inherently different" (38), especially sexually. Consequently, Bloom's hereditary epilepsy is the "consequence of unbridled lust" (*U* 15.1778); the elephantiasis that he may yet inherit is characterized by an enlargement of the legs and scrotum; his hypospadia will undoubtedly produce a malformation of the genitourinary tract (Gifford and Seidman 481).

15. For more on Joyce, surveillance, and the State, see "Joyce and the Police: A Special Issue."

16. For a thorough investigation of the fiduciary aspects of "Eumaeus" in particular and of *Ulysses* in general, see Mark Osteen's *The Economy of Ulysses*.

17. Stuart Gilbert asserts in *James Joyce's Ulysses* that Bloom in "Eumaeus" "is too exhausted to achieve a logical ending to most of his periods" (360); in *Ulysses on the Liffey*, Ellmann calls the style "tired" (151). Kenner, however, provides a corrective to such readings; as he notes, "Joyce invites close critical attention to the thousands of absurd locutions he employs" (*Dublin's Joyce* 260).

18. Karen Lawrence has perceptively noted the comedy in Bloom's "bourgeois-ification of socialist concepts" ("Beggaring Description" 361): Bloom argues for revolution "on the due instalments plan" (*U* 16.1101) and misquotes Marx, converting the famous axiom "From each according to his abilities, to each according to his needs" into what Lawrence calls "a jumbled mix of socialism and capitalism": "Everyone according to his needs or everyone according to his deeds" (*U* 16.247).

5. Deconstructing the Discourse of Domesticity

1. Joyce indicated that he had chosen to marry at this time for "testamentary reasons" and made a will shortly thereafter to secure his royalties first to Nora Barnacle and then to his children and their heirs (Maddox 269, 272).

2. Mary Jane (Murray) Joyce died of liver cancer on August 13, 1903. She was forty-four.

3. Gilbert and Gubar have noted the "clear line of literary descent from divine Virgin to domestic angel" (*Madwomen* 20); other studies have also engaged the synthesis of these icons, among them Nina Auerbach's *Woman and the Demon: The Life of a Victorian Myth,* which explores the authority implicit in the figure of the angel as well as the sensuality that subtends her, and Mary Condren's *The Serpent and the Goddess: Women, Religion, and Power in Celtic Ireland,* which provides a thorough, historical analysis of the cult of the Virgin as it evolved in Ireland.

4. The motherless Ruth is seduced; Hardy's Tess is either raped or seduced; Herminia's "New Woman" rejects Alan Merrick's invitation of marriage in order to live freely with him. The attempted subversion of the texts is evident: reading Ruth's tale of surrender, we believe with the old man in the street that "such a one as her has never been a great sinner" (Gaskell 425); we agree with Hardy's titular insistence, *"Tess of the D'Urbervilles: A Pure Woman"*; we admire Herminia's New Woman vitality and idealism as she pursues love outside the shackles of marriage. The deaths of these women constitute final, forced orderings within the nineteenth-century novel and showcase the era's deeply conflicted beliefs about the nature of woman. It is as if the writers of these books could not quite manage, after all, to pick the locks of feminine ideological confinement. Joyce's specific mention in *Ulysses* of other Victorian texts that depict domestically trapped or resisting women—Wilkie Collins's *The Moonstone* and *The Woman in White,* Margaret Wolfe Hungerford's *Molly Bawn,* and Mrs. Henry (Ellen) Wood's *East Lynne* and *The Shadow of Ashlydyat*—suggests a wider familiarity with engendered narratives than even his extensive library reveals.

5. For more, see Mary Hederman's "Irish Women and Irish Law." Also of interest is Donncha O'Corrain's excellent "Women in Early Irish Society," in which he explains the status and extensive rights of women (even within marriage) as they had evolved under Brehon law by the late seventh century.

6. In England, an unmarried woman could own property, vote in municipal elections if she paid taxes (under the 1869 Municipal Corporations Act), be a member of the school board (under the 1870 Elementary Education Act), and vote for, as well as serve as, a Poor Law guardian under the same property qualifications as men. Similar rights were also extended to Irish women in the nineteenth century, though not always simultaneously. For example, although Irish women could vote for Poor Law guardians in the 1880s, they were not able to stand for election until the Women Poor Law Guardian Act was passed in 1896. In 1898 the Local Government (Ireland) Act gave Irish women the right to vote in and stand for election in all rural and municipal contests on the same property qualification as men, although women were not permitted to serve as county councilors until 1911. For more, see Blackburn (268–70); various biographical essays of Irish women activists in Cullen and Luddy (especially Cullen's essay, "Anna Maria Halsam"); and Walkowitz, *City of Dreadful Delight* (65–68).

7. The Reform Act of 1832, which extended the vote to previously disenfranchised middle-class workers and realigned parliamentary representation, also legislated the exclusion of married women from both the franchise and public office, codifying the opinion expressed by James Mill (father of John Stuart Mill) in his "Essay on Government": "One thing is pretty clear, that all those individuals whose interests are indisputably included in those of other individuals may be struck off from political rights without inconvenience. In this light may be viewed all children up to a certain age, whose interests are involved with those of their parents; in this light also women may be regarded, the interest of almost all of whom is involved either in that of their fathers or that of their husbands" (qtd. in Blackburn 12).

8. A husband was legally entitled to collect any income from his wife's landed property, although he was not permitted to sell it, in England or in Ireland, without her consent (Cullen 169).

9. Under the 1883 Married Women's Property Act (enacted almost three years after Joyce's parents were married and one year after Joyce was born), wives in England and Ireland were empowered to enter into contracts, to sue and be sued, to make a will without their husband's consent, and to "hold as [their] own, without settlement of any kind, not only property coming to [them] subsequent to marriage, but also property belonging to [them] previous to marriage" (Cox 428). But even as late as 1905, although a wife could now act as executor of trust property and be sued as an individual in cases involving "stocks, funds, debentures, etc.," she was still constrained, due to an omission in the law, to act without her husband's consent and signature in the case of landed property (Ignota 516). In 1886 the passage of the woefully inadequate Maintenance of Wives Act for the first time required husbands to support their wives and children financially; it applied only to abusive husbands, however, and required a wife to first win her spouse's conviction on an aggravated assault charge and obtain a separation order before any payments would be made. In 1895 the Summary Jurisdiction Act deleted the requirement for conviction and enabled a woman whose husband had been "guilty of such persistent cruelty to her, or of such wilful [sic] neglect to provide reasonable maintenance for her, or her infant children whom he is legally liable to maintain, as to cause her to leave and live apart from him" to apply to a court for an order that would legitimize her separation from her husband, give her custody of any children under age sixteen, and require maintenance payments (not to exceed two £ per week) by her husband for their support. Of course, such relief was granted only at the discretion of the (male) magistrates and required the woman to have left home (Ignota 521). None of these laws, however, provided any recourse to a woman still living with a spendthrift husband.

10. Caroline Norton's battles to regain access to her children and to secure her finances in the wake of her abusive husband's duplicity (which I will discuss later in the chapter) led to the passage of the 1839 Infant Custody Act, which gave women separated from their husbands some limited rights with regard to their

children, as well as the 1857 Divorce Act, which established divorce courts in England and removed the need for a special Act of Parliament to dissolve the matrimonial contract. It would not be until the passage of the first Married Women's Property Act in 1870, however, that a married woman would be entitled to keep and spend her own wages; up until this point, any money she earned also belonged to her husband, who could demand that her employer pay her wages directly to him. For more, see Joan Perkins (114–17). For more information on the activist agitation in Ireland surrounding the Married Women's Property Acts, see Maria Luddy's "Isabella M. S. Todd."

11. Although this may in fact be another self-deception on Maria's part—she is not nearly as worldly and independent as she would like others to believe—the presence in the story of such a statement still attests to the relative autonomy of single women when compared to married women.

12. Judith Walkowitz originated this argument; for more, see *Prostitution and Victorian Society: Women, Class, and the State.*

13. The prohibition on divorce in Ireland would be incorporated into the 1937 Constitution (Article 41.3.3) and would not be rescinded until 1995, although the state was willing to recognize divorces obtained outside the country (Hederman 57).

14. As Richard Brown has written, "Joyce's writing presses towards . . . this sexual heart of things . . . in persons, phenomena, and institutions that are normally supposed to be chaste" (127).

15. Stone argues that Scott's story elides Mary's sexuality (350), but Kershner notes otherwise (48).

16. In his 1990 book, *The Commodity Culture of Victorian England: Advertising and Spectacle, 1851–1914,* Richards traces Gerty's very appearance on the beach to the sexually charged figure of the "seaside girl" in Victorian advertising, suggesting that it was Joyce's intent to link Gerty to "the seaside resort [that] not only promoted the diversification of sexual practices such as nude bathing, but it also refined the forms that sexual desire and gratification took" (227). Leonard asserts that Gerty is a "self-conscious image manipulator who views herself as a commodity that must be carefully packaged and advertised, in accordance with a media representation of what is 'feminine,' in order to attract a male consumer" ("Virgin Mary" 4).

17. Isabel Vane weds Carlyle because of financial and emotional indebtedness; Laura Fairlie belongs with Walter Hartright, not Percival Glyde. Even Vaughan has misallied himself and realizes it: "He began to meditate upon those fireside and domestic joys which had always figured in his dreams of married life. But his wife did not share these fond aspirations, and the child [Mabel] . . . was soon abandoned to the care of strangers, save as the father strove at intervals, by fond and injudicious indulgence to atone for the mother's neglect" (Cummins, *Mabel Vaughn* 1.13).

18. See chapter 6.

6. Female Complaints: "Mad" women, Malady, and Resistance in Joyce's Dublin

1. The driver's sense of the institution's amplitude, however, is borne out by statistics gathered from the annual reports of the Inspectors of Lunatics and the census of Ireland, which indicate an increase of 158 percent in the first-admission residency rate for the Mullingar District Asylum between 1871 and 1901, from 394 to 623 inmates per 10,000 population (Finnane 135 table). The driver's pleasure in the burgeoning number of commitments in this area of Ireland might also be traced to the infectiousness of an English attitude, which—in an attempt to explain why England led the world in the number of insanity cases diagnosed—held madness to be a disease affecting only highly "civilized" and "intellectually advanced" populations (Halliday 80). According to this logic, the driver's pride could be attributed to a belief that the asylum's fullsomeness is indicative of Ireland's cultural advancement.

2. Florence Walzl borrows both Mrs. Mooney of "The Boarding House" and Mrs. Kearney of "A Mother" to support her claim that Joyce makes the "dominant female a central figure in his picture of Irish society" in *Dubliners* (46); Margot Norris includes Molly Ivors among women in "The Dead" who offer "back answers" to subvert the masculine authority of Gabriel Conroy (*Joyce's Web* 97–108); Bonnie Scott offers a feminist reading of *Stephen Hero*'s Emma Clery and Stephen Dedalus's response to her (*Joyce and Feminism* 133–55); Carol Shloss argues that Molly Bloom's speech at the end of *Ulysses* is a voluble act of resistance and self-assertion against both marriage and colonialism.

3. Taken together, these account for 16.2 percent of all female admissions to asylums in England and Wales between 1878 and 1887, more than any other individual cause besides "previous attacks" (18.9 percent) and "hereditary influence" (22.1 percent). The hereditary cause was also seemingly activated by femaleness, being precipitated by "some period of physiological activity, [such as] puberty, childbirth, [or] climacteric [menopause]" (Tuke 2.696).

4. "Ordinary" confinements in Ireland's public asylums originally required an application to the manager of the asylum by a relative or friend of the affected person, affirmation by a magistrate or clergyman that the person was poor enough to qualify for public care, and a medical certificate indicating the person's insanity; admission was recommended by the institution's manager and its physician and approved by the asylum board. By the 1870s, however, admission no longer required the board's authorization and could be made on the authority of the asylum superintendent. Private asylums required application by a relative or friend of the affected person as well as medical certificates from two physicians, rather than one, to guard against wrongful confinement. Under an 1837 law, "dangerous" lunatics, for example, those persons even suspected of harboring the potential for committing violent crime, could be committed to the jails by any two justices of the peace without any medical evidence at all.

5. Literary constructions of the period also conceptualize reason and unreason

in terms of gender. Charlotte Brontë's *Jane Eyre,* Wilkie Collins's *The Woman in White,* Mary Elizabeth Braddon's *Lady Audley's Secret,* and Sir Walter Scott's *The Bride of Lammermoor* all harbor a "mad" woman—and a "reasonable" man—at their core. An annotated copy of *Jane Eyre* was present in Joyce's Trieste library, and *The Woman in White,* a tale of two wrongfully confined women (one in marriage, the other in a madhouse), is mentioned by name in *Ulysses.* Molly Bloom is a reader of both Collins and Braddon (she has read *The Moonstone* and indicates it is the "first" of Collins's work she has perused; she also mentions Braddon's *Henry Dunbar,* though not *Lady Audley's Secret*) (U 18.653–54), and Leopold Bloom recalls scenes from the popular operatic adaptations of Scott's work, *Lucia di Lammermoor* (U 6.852–53).

6. Until the mid-nineteenth century, asylum statistics show that men were far more likely than women to be institutionalized. By the 1850s, however, women had outpaced men in this dubious honor, and in 1851, Charles Dickens, a visitor at St. Luke's Hospital in England, observed: "The experience of this asylum did not differ, I found, from that of similar establishments, in proving that insanity is more prevalent among women than among men. Of [18,759] inmates St. Luke's Hospital has received in the century of its existence, [11,162] have been women" (qtd. in Showalter 51). The increase in women inmates continued in both public and private establishments, and by the 1890s, Showalter notes, "the only remaining institutions with a majority of male patients were asylums for the criminally insane, military hospitals, and idiot schools" (52). In Ireland, male and female commitment rates increased at approximately equal rates between 1881 and 1901, but the percentage of asylum residents who were married women always remained above the percentage of married men (Finnane 131 tables).

7. Wrongful confinements of women were notoriously common throughout the period; as early as 1728, Daniel Defoe lamented the ease with which women could be committed:

> This leads me to exclaim against the vile Practice now so much in vogue among the better Sort . . . . the sending their Wives to Mad-Houses at every Whim or Dislike, that they may be more secure and undisturb'd in their Debaucheries. . . . If they are not mad when they go into these cursed Houses, they are soon made so by the barbarous Usage they there suffer. . . . Is it not enough to make any one mad to be suddenly clap'd up, stripp'd, whipp'd, ill fed, and worse us'd? To have no Reason assign'd . . . , no Crime alleg'd, or accusers to confront? And what is worse, no Soul to appeal to. . . . ("Demand for Public Control of Madhouses," rpt. in Szasz 7–8)

Even after laws were tightened to prevent wrongful commitments, the possibility still loomed large in literary imaginations: Mary Wollstonecraft's unfinished novel, *Maria; or The Wrongs of Woman* (1797), deals with the subject, as do two of the nineteenth-century works I have already mentioned, Collins's *The Woman in White* and Braddon's *Lady Audley's Secret.*

8. By the latter years of the nineteenth century, asylums were staffed predominantly by men as the medical profession came to dominate the management of public institutions; in 1859 the Commissioners in Lunacy announced that, while women would not be completely barred from obtaining licenses to operate private asylums, the commissioners would look most favorably on applications from medical men.

9. Neurasthenia and anorexia were the other two major nervous disorders. Sufferers of neurasthenia shared with hysterics many common symptoms (among them headaches, insomnia, and depression), but the former were considered to be less rebellious and more well bred than hysterics and thus received the approbation of their doctors, who often prescribed the notorious "rest cure" devised by S. Weir Mitchell, a harrowing account of which appears in Charlotte Perkins Gilman's short story "The Yellow Wallpaper." For her part, the anorexic woman seemed to suffer not because she rebelled against her domestic role but because she observed it far too well. In therapy, these women were perceived to have internalized the "womanly" ideals of self-sacrifice, often continuing "a hectic round of feminine duties" in the face of near-starvation. Astoundingly, their doctors frequently praised them for their "unselfish" efforts.

10. Records show that a twenty-four-year-old domestic servant from Cork, Marian Slater, was committed to Carlow asylum in 1869 for "hysteria"—a condition "to which almost any female is liable" remarked an inspector—after being jilted by an unscrupulous fiancé (Finnane 160).

11. Affixing influence in Joyce is always a troublesome task, but it is made even more difficult in this case by Joyce's insistent disdain for what Stephen calls "the new Viennese school" (U 9.780). Ellmann observes that Joyce's interest in the unconscious mind, particularly in regard to dream theory, predates Freud, whose Interpretation of Dreams appeared in 1900 (James Joyce 85n, 126, 340, 436–38). Yet as Sheldon Brivic (Joyce Between Freud and Jung), John Bishop (Joyce's Book of the Dark), and Kimberly Devlin (Wandering and Return in Finnegans Wake) have demonstrated, Joyce's work manifests Freudian influence in ever-increasing ways, culminating, of course, in the dream text and night language of Finnegans Wake. Joyce certainly intuited a sympathetic connection between body and mind when writing Ulysses; he explained to Frank Budgen that part of the technique of the novel was to record these links (Ellmann, James Joyce 436). In spite of his protests against Freud's theories, Joyce's Trieste library included Eine Kindheitserinnerung des Leonardo da Vinci (A childhood memory of Leonardo da Vinci), published in 1910 and Zur Psychopathologie des Alltaglebens (On the psychopathology of everyday life), published in 1917 (Ellmann, The Consciousness of Joyce 109). After his daughter Lucia was diagnosed in 1932 as suffering from "hebephrenic" psychosis, Joyce consented to psychoanalysis, among various other treatments, for his daughter. Carl Jung was her twentieth physician (Ellmann, James Joyce 676).

12. In "Molly's Resistance to the Union," Carol Shloss argues that "the act of speaking," for Molly Bloom as much as for Stephen Dedalus, "is itself a political

act, an act of assertion, a search for definition in the face of a domineering Other" (113). Molly's last words, Shloss observes, are concerned with "issues of authority, privilege, and financial dependence in her relationships with men" and, as such, set up an intriguing two-way mirror between gender and colonial relations in *Ulysses* (107).

13. Freud's case study "Fragment of an Analysis of a Case of Hysteria," which introduces "Dora," the most famous of Freud's hysterical patients, provides an excellent example of the multiple kinds of authority that the psychoanalyst wielded over his patient. Freud interprets Dora's symptoms, especially her loss of voice, according to his own paradigm and insists on his reading even in the face of her protestations; as he does so, he becomes both the author of her treatment and the literal author of her narrative. Dora, of course, attempts to resist Freud's authority, challenging his conclusions about the cause of her symptoms and ultimately denying him the closure to the case that he so desperately desired by walking out on their sessions. Her subsequent history, however, illustrates that this gesture signaled only a fleeting moment of empowerment on Dora's part: Showalter reports that she spent the rest of her life "going from doctor to doctor in search of a remedy for various psychosomatic complaints" (161).

14. We know that Eveline's father "used to go for Harry and Ernest" and that in their absence, Eveline "sometimes felt herself in danger of her father's violence," though we are never told directly that Mr. Hill abused Eveline's mother. However, Eveline does suggest obliquely that her mother was victimized in some way during her lifetime; as she ponders marrying Frank, the daughter thinks, "She would not be treated as her mother had been" ("Eveline" 37). Gerty MacDowell is somewhat more explicit in that she notes having witnessed "deeds of violence caused by intemperance" in her home, acts perpetrated by an alcoholic father against female members of the household, presumably her mother if not Gerty herself. Gerty thinks: "the man who lifts his hand to a woman save in the way of kindness, deserves to be branded as the lowest of the low" (*U* 13.298–302).

15. Norris asserts that "The Dead" subversively dismantles the cultural fictions of paternalistic authority and willing subservience; she observes that the "lie" the narration tells us at the story's opening (that Julia is still the leading soprano at Adam and Eve's), along with the idyllic vision of domesticity the narrative attempts to spin, is soon exposed by the text as the falsehood it is (*Joyce's Web* 116–17).

16. Donald Torchiana fixes the date for the Morkan gathering as Wednesday, January 6, 1904 (225); on June 16, 1904, Leopold Bloom reflects that a now deceased Julia Morkan "kept her voice up to the very last" (*U* 8.417–18).

17. Because her breakup with Duffy actually took place four years since, I would suggest that Emily Sinico's decline might in fact have begun earlier than her inattentive husband reports. His report is somewhat suspect on other time-related fronts as well; he indicates he wasn't in town at the time of the accident (10 p.m.) because he had arrived "only that *morning*" from Rotterdam.

18. Finnane reports that the medical certificate of Patrick Britt, a seventeen-year-old laborer committed at Clonmel asylum, diagnosed his symptoms as "maniacal" because "he can't be kept at home—but wanders about" (110).

19. See Michael West and William Hendricks, "The Genesis and Significance of Joyce's Irony in 'A Painful Case.'"

7. New Women, Male Pests, and Gender in the Public Eye

1. In her valuable essay, *"Dubliners:* Women in Irish Society," Walzl describes the positions promoted by the Irish Central Bureau for the Employment of Women in 1904. The bureau's *Open Doors for Irishwomen: A Guide to the Professions Open to Educated Women in Ireland* lists twenty-five main occupations for middle-class women (along with the domestic service jobs they had historically performed), including nurse, teacher, secretary, typist, apothecary, institution matron, and Civil Service clerk. Although qualifications were high—two foreign languages were required of secretaries, for instance—and the number of candidates often exceeded the number of positions available, Walzl reports that *Thom's Official Directory* for 1904 indicates: "Women monopolized dressmaking, millinery, and sewing enterprises; owned 30 percent of the bakeries, fruit stores, and dairies and over 10 percent of the butcher shops and groceries; operated all the boarding houses listed, 75 percent of the lodging houses, and 20 percent of the hotels; were approximately a third of the teachers of dancing, elocution, and languages; made up a majority of all professional musicians; and finally, were directors or owners of all the 'Seminaries for Young Ladies' in Dublin" (*"Dubliners"* 38–41).

2. Anne Jellicoe founded Alexandra College, Dublin, in 1866 to provide women with opportunities in higher education; Jellicoe's vision was to "prepare girls for the degrees of the Royal University of Ireland" and the success of the college, along with the agitation of Jellicoe and other activists, was instrumental in getting the legislation passed (O'Connor 139). Professors at the Protestant-run Trinity College often lectured at Alexandra and allowed women to take degrees from Trinity in 1904 (O'Connor 145).

3. For fascinating accounts of such figures in Ireland, see the biographical collection edited by Mary Cullen and Mary Luddy, *Women, Power and Consciousness in 19th Century Ireland: Eight Biographical Studies.* Also of interest is C. L. Innes's *Woman and Nation in Irish Literature and Society, 1880–1935,* especially the section "A Voice in Directing the Affairs of Ireland."

4. Among them Penrose, the peeping-Tom student who "nearly caught [Molly] washing through the window" (*U* 18.574); John Henry Menton, the solicitor whose pass Molly once deflected; Valentine Blake Dillon (Lord Mayor of Dublin), who ogled her "with his dirty eyes" the night of the Glencree dinner (*U* 18.428); Lenehan, who in the return carriage the same evening "was tucking the rug under her and settling her boa all the time" in order to sexually excite himself—"the lad stood to attention anyhow" (*U* 10.562–65); Christopher Callinan, who observed

this mauling; "an unknown gentleman in the Gaiety Theatre," who stared discomfitingly at Molly during a performance of *The Wife of Scarli* (*U* 17.2138); and Joseph Cuffee, Bloom's former boss to whom Molly applied for his reinstatement, who "gave me a great mirada once or twice" and spent most of their conversation "looking very hard at my chest" (*U* 18.512, 529). Cases could undoubtedly be made for other men as well; the entire list may be found at *U* 17.2133–42.

5. Leonard claims that this episode before Miss Delacour actually boosts Farrington's self-esteem before he heads out for the evening (*Reading* 15), but Leonard overlooks the psychological impact of the exacted apology. As Farrington awaits the cashier and contemplates both the apology and his position in the office, Joyce tells us Farrington "felt savage and thirsty and revengeful, annoyed with himself and with everyone else" (*D* 92).

6. My analysis in this section is indebted to Leonard's *Reading Dubliners Again*, in which he argues that the Phallic Order and the masculine subject that aspires to unite with it are repeatedly exposed by Joyce as extraordinarily fragile, illusory charades.

7. As late as 1909, all political and cultural nationalist organizations in Ireland, with the exception of Sinn Fein and the Gaelic League, continued to exclude women from their memberships. Innes records the complaints of Constance Markievicz in an editorial that appeared in *Bean na h-Eireann*, a feminist-nationalist newspaper in February 1909: "Women are denied a place in some of the most important political organizations in Ireland. The United Irish League (with the exception of one branch, we believe), the Loyal Orange Association, the Liberal Home Rule Association are exclusively masculine bodies. The Gaelic League and the Sinn Fein Organization are the only ones in existence at present where women are on an equal footing with men" (qtd. in Innes 138–39).

8. If Gifford is correct that "the promise was that the contracted fee would be paid if the concert was a financial success; if not the performers would share in whatever proceeds there were after expenses had been paid" (98–99), then why has the baritone already received his money?

9. Noting that "readers of the 'Penelope' episode usually refer to it as Molly's monologue or stream-of-consciousness," Susan Bazargan has recharacterized Molly's narrative as "dialogic not only because it seems directed toward an interlocutor and informed by a variety of rhetorical stances, but also because it is characterized by those features essential to dialogism: her narrative is the site of interaction of a multiplicity of competing voices" (128).

10. Molly is acutely conscious of the impact male appropriations of phallic power have on women; fears of male violence—inflicted not only at the hands of the "hardened criminal[s]" she reads about in *Lloyd's Weekly News* (*U* 18.992) but also by lovers and husbands—punctuate her ruminations, as do intense sensations of confinement. The "determined vicious look" in Boylan's eyes during their lovemaking makes her "halfshut" her own (*U* 18.153–54); Molly also imagines that an eccentric man like Josie Breen's husband, Denis, "might murder you any

moment" (*U* 18.224). Even Bloom, Molly thinks, has injured her and might again: he once tried to bite her nipple, leaving a mark and making her scream ("arent they fearful trying to hurt you" [*U* 18.570]); his upside-down recumbence in bed not only irritates but also frightens her ("its well he doesnt kick or he might knock out all my teeth" [*U* 18.1200]).

11. Renditions of the first position include Bonnie Kime Scott's claim that Molly intends her "unpolitic" selection of music for the St. Theresa's concert to be more a tribute to Gardner than a statement of her own political beliefs, a sign that "love outweighs career" (*Joyce and Feminism* 164). Susan Bazargan and Enda Duffy set out the terms of the second argument, though Duffy still persists in labeling Molly's antinationalist position "apolitical" (185–86).

12. For a more detailed discussion of this phenomenon, see chapter 3.

13. Nationalist support for the Boer forces as striking a blow against British imperialism was highly ironic, however, as the Boers were not an indigenous population attempting to throw off the colonial yoke but were, in fact, colonizers themselves.

14. This is not the first time in the text that Molly's Irishness is called into question; in the "Sirens" episode, Simon Dedalus is queried about her heritage, which he ambiguously affirms: "O, she is . . . My Irish Molly, O. . . . From the rock of Gibraltar . . . all the way" (*U* 11.512–14).

15. See, for instance, James Van Dyck Card's "'Contradicting': The Word for Joyce's 'Penelope.'"

16. Bhabha writes: "Pastness . . . is not necessarily a faithful sign of historical memory but a strategy of representing authority" ("The Commitment to Theory" 35).

Bibliography

Acton, William. *The Functions and Disorders of the Reproductive Organs in Childhood, Youth, Adult Age, and Advanced Life Considered in Their Physiological, Social, and Moral Relations.* 3rd ed. London: John Churchill 1862.

Adams, James Eli. *Dandies and Desert Saints: Styles of Victorian Masculinity.* Ithaca, N.Y., and London: Cornell University Press, 1995.

———. "Pater's Muscular Aestheticism." In Hall, *Muscular Christianity.* 214–38.

Adams, Robert. *Surface and Symbol: The Consistency of James Joyce's Ulysses.* New York: Oxford University Press, 1962.

Allen, Grant. *The Woman Who Did.* Boston: Roberts Bros., 1895.

Althusser, Louis. "Ideology and Ideological State Apparatuses." In *Lenin and Philosophy,* trans. Ben Brewster. New York: Monthly Review Press, 1971. 127–86.

Anderson, Benedict. *Imagined Communities: Reflections on the Origin and Spread of Nationalism.* Rev. ed. London: Verso, 1991.

Armstrong, Nancy. *Desire and Domestic Fiction: A Political History of the Novel.* New York: Oxford University Press, 1987.

Arnold, Matthew. *Culture and Anarchy.* "Hebraism and Hellenism." In Culler, *Poetry and Criticism of Matthew Arnold.* 465–75.

———. "Shelley." In Culler, *Poetry and Criticism of Matthew Arnold.* 363–80.

Auerbach, Nina. *Woman and the Demon: The Life of a Victorian Myth.* Cambridge: Harvard University Press, 1982.

Bailey, Victor. "'In Darkest England and the Way Out': The Salvation Army, Social Reform, and the Labor Movement, 1885–1910." *International Review of Social History* 29 (1984): 133–71.

Bazargan, Susan. "Mapping Gibraltar: Colonialism, Time and Narrative in 'Penelope.'" In Pearce, *Molly Blooms.* 119–38.

Besant, Annie. *The Ancient Wisdom: An Outline of Theosophical Teachings.* 1897. Reprint, Adyar, Madras, India: Theosophical Publishing House, 1992.

Bhabha, Homi K. "The Commitment to Theory." In *The Location of Culture.* London and New York: Routledge, 1994. 19–39.

———. "DissemiNation: Time, Narrative, and the Margins of the Modern Nation." In *Nation and Narration.* London: Routledge, 1990. 291–322.

———. "Of Mimicry and Man: The Ambivalence of Colonial Discourse." *October* (1984): 125–33.

———. "The Other Question: Difference, Discrimination and the Discourse of Colonialism." In *Literature, Politics and Theory: Papers from the Essex Conference 1976–84,* ed. Francis Barker, Peter Hulme, Margaret Iversen, and Diana Loxley. London: Methuen, 1986. 148–72.

Bishop, John. *Joyce's Book of the Dark: Finnegans Wake.* Madison: University of Wisconsin Press, 1986.

Blackburn, Helen. *Women's Suffrage: A Record of the Women's Suffrage Movement in the British Isles.* London: Williams and Norgate, 1902.

Blake, William. "Auguries of Innocence." In Perkins, *English Romantic Writers.* 113–14.

———. *The Book of Urizen.* In Perkins, *English Romantic Writers.* 82–92

———. *The Marriage of Heaven and Hell.* In Perkins, *English Romantic Writers.* 68–75.

———. "Merlins Prophecy." In *Blake's Poetry and Designs,* ed. Mary Lynn Johnson and John E. Grant. Norton Critical Edition. New York: W. W. Norton, 1979. 185.

———. *Milton.* In Perkins, *English Romantic Writers.* 114–56.

———. *Songs of Experience.* In Perkins, *English Romantic Writers.* 56–65.

———. "There is no Natural Religion." In Perkins, *English Romantic Writers.* 49.

———. *A Vision of the Last Judgment.* In Perkins, *English Romantic Writers.* 161–63.

Blavatsky, Helena Petrovna. *The Complete Works of H. P. Blavatsky.* Ed. A. Trevor Barker. Vol. 1, 1874–79. London: Rider, 1933.

———. *The Key to Theosophy: An Abridgement.* Ed. Joy Mills. Wheaton, Ill.: Theosophical Publishing House, 1972.

Booth, Charles. *Life and Labour of the People in London.* London and New York: Macmillan, 1892–97.

Booth, William. *In Darkest England and the Way Out.* New York: Funk & Wagnalls, 1890.

Boscagli, Maurizia. *Eye on the Flesh: Fashions of Masculinity in the Early Twentieth Century.* Boulder, Colo.: Westview Press–HarperCollins, 1996.

Bourke, Joanna. *Husbandry to Housewifery: Women, Economic Change, and Housework in Ireland, 1890–1914.* Oxford: Clarendon Press, 1993.

Boyle, Robert S. J. "Penelope." In *James Joyce's Ulysses: Critical Essays,* ed. Clive Hart and David Hayman. Berkeley: University of California Press, 1974. 407–33.

Braddon, M. E. *Lady Audley's Secret.* 1861–62. Reprint, Oxford: Oxford University Press, 1992.

Breuer, Josef, and Sigmund Freud. *Studies on Hysteria.* 1895. Reprint, New York: Avon Books, 1966.

Bristow, Edward J. *Vice and Vigilance:. Purity Movements in Britain since 1700.* Dublin: Gill and Macmillan, 1977.

Brivic, Sheldon. *Joyce Between Freud and Jung.* Port Washington, N.Y.: Kennikat Press, 1980.

Brontë, Charlotte. *Jane Eyre.* 1847. Reprint, Toronto: Bantam-Doubleday, 1988.

Brown, Richard. *James Joyce and Sexuality.* Cambridge: Cambridge University Press, 1985.

Bulwer-Lytton, Edward. *The Lady of Lyons.* In *Dramatic Works.* Freeport, N.Y.: Books for Libraries Press, 1972. 103–76.

Byrnes, Robert. "Bloom's Sexual Tropes: Stigmata of the 'Degenerate' Jew." *James Joyce Quarterly* 27 (1990): 303–23.

Byron, Lord. [George Gordon]. *Byron's Letters and Journals.* Vols. 2 and 6. Ed. Leslie A. Marchand. Cambridge: Harvard-Belknap Press, 1972, 1976.

———. *Childe Harold's Pilgrimage.* In *The Poetical Works of Byron.* 2–83.

———. *Don Juan.* In *The Poetical Works of Byron.* 744–998.

———. *Hours of Idleness.* In *The Poetical Works of Byron.* 84–138.

———. *Manfred.* In *The Poetical Works of Byron.* 478–97.

———. *The Poetical Works of Byron.* Cambridge Edition. Boston: Houghton Mifflin, 1975.

———. "Prometheus." In *The Poetical Works of Byron.* 191.

Cairns, David, and Shaun Richards. *Writing Ireland: Colonialism, Nationalism, and Culture.* New York: Manchester University Press, 1988.

Cameron, Kenneth Neill. "The Social Philosophy of Shelley." In *Shelley's Poetry and Prose,* ed. Donald H. Reiman and Sharon B. Powers. Norton Critical Edition. New York: W. W. Norton, 1977. 511–19.

Card, James Van Dyck. "'Contradicting': The Word for Joyce's 'Penelope.'" *James Joyce Quarterly* 11 (1974): 17–26.

Carlyle, Thomas. *On Heroes, Hero-Worship and the Heroic in History.* London: Chapman and Hall, 1894.

———. *Past and Present.* Ed. Richard D. Altick. 1842. Reprint, New York: New York University Press, 1965.

———. *Sartor Resartus.* Oxford: Oxford University Press, 1987.

Castle, Gregory. "'I am almosting it': History, Nature, and the Will to Power in 'Proteus.'" *James Joyce Quarterly* 29 (1992): 281–96.

Chatterjee, Partha. *The Nation and Its Fragments: Colonial and Postcolonial Histories.* Princeton, N.J.: Princeton University Press, 1993.

Cheng, Vincent J. *Joyce, Race, and Empire.* Cambridge: Cambridge University Press, 1995.

Chitty, Susan. *The Beast and the Monk: A Life of Charles Kingsley.* London: Hodder and Stoughton, 1974.

Cixous, Hélène, and Catherine Clement. *The Newly Born Woman.* Trans. Betsy Wing. Minneapolis: University of Minnesota Press, 1988.

Clarke, Norma. "Strenuous Idleness: Thomas Carlyle and the Man of Letters as Hero." In Roper and Tosh, *Manful Assertions.* 25–43.

Collins, Wilkie. *The Moonstone.* 1868. Reprint, New York: Signet-Penguin, 1984.

———. *The Woman in White.* 1860. Reprint, New York: Signet- Penguin, 1985.

Condren, Mary. "Sacrifice and Political Legitimation: The Production of a Gendered Social Order." *Journal of Women's History* 6.4 (1995): 160–89.

———. *The Serpent and the Goddess: Women, Religion, and Power in Celtic Ireland.* New York: HarperCollins, 1989.

Conrad, Joseph. *Heart of Darkness.* New York: Penguin, 1973.

Cote, Jane, and Dana Hearne. "Anna Parnell." In Cullen and Luddy, *Women, Power and Consciousness in 19th Century Ireland.* 263–93.

Cowper, Katie. "The Decline of Reserve among Women." *Nineteenth Century* 27 (1890): 65–71.

Cox, John George. "The Changed Position of Married Women." *Dublin Review* 9 (1883): 417–42.

Cranston, Sylvia. *H.P.B.: The Extraordinary Life and Influence of Helena Blavatsky, Founder of the Modern Theosophical Movement.* New York: Putnam's, 1993.

Cullen, Mary. "Anna Maria Haslam." In Cullen and Luddy, *Women, Power and Consciousness in 19th Century Ireland.* 161–96.

Cullen, Mary, and Maria Luddy, eds. *Women, Power and Consciousness in 19th Century Ireland: Eight Biographical Studies.* Dublin: Attic Press, 1995.

Culler, Dwight A. *Poetry and Criticism of Matthew Arnold.* Boston: Houghton Mifflin, 1961.

Cummins, Maria Susanna. *The Lamplighter.* 1854. Ed. and Introd. Nina Baym. Reprint, New Brunswick, N.J.: Rutgers University Press, 1988.

———. *Mabel Vaughan.* Boston: John P. Jewett, 1857.

Curran, Constantine. *James Joyce Remembered.* Oxford: Oxford University Press, 1968.

Curtis, L. Perry. *Apes and Angels: The Irishman in Victorian Caricature.* Rev. ed. Washington, D.C.: Smithsonian Institution Press, 1997.

Darwin, Charles. *The Descent of Man and Selection in Relation to Sex.* 1871. Reprint, New York: J. A. Hill, 1904.

David, Diedre. *Intellectual Women and Victorian Patriarchy: Harriet Martineau, Elizabeth Barrett Browning, and George Eliot.* Houndmills, England: Macmillan, 1987.

Davitt, Michael. *The Fall of Feudalism in Ireland or The Story of the Land League Revolution.* London and New York: Harper and Brothers, 1904.

Deane, Seamus, gen. ed. *The Field Day Anthology of Irish Writing.* Vol. 2. Derry: Field Day/W. W. Norton, 1991.

Dellamora, Richard. *Masculine Desire: The Sexual Politics of Victorian Aestheticism.* Chapel Hill: University of North Carolina Press, 1990.

Devlin, Kimberly J. "Castration and Its Discontents: A Lacanian Approach to *Ulysses.*" *James Joyce Quarterly* 29 (1991): 117–44.

———. "Pretending in 'Penelope': Masquerade, Mimicry, and Molly Bloom." In Pearce, *Molly Blooms.* 80–102.

———. "The Romance Heroine Exposed: 'Nausicaa' and *The Lamplighter.*" *James Joyce Quarterly* 22 (1985): 383–96.

———. *Wandering and Return in Finnegans Wake: An Integrative Approach to Joyce's Fictions.* Princeton, N.J.: Princeton University Press, 1991.

Dickens, Charles. *Bleak House*. Ed. George Ford and Sylvere Monod. Norton Critical Edition. New York: W. W. Norton, 1977.

Dorsey, Peter. "From Hero to Portrait: The De-Christification of Stephen Dedalus." *James Joyce Quarterly* 26 (1989): 505–13.

Duffy, Enda. *The Subaltern Ulysses*. Minneapolis: University of Minnesota Press, 1994.

Dumas, Alexandre. *The Count of Monte Cristo*. Garden City, N.Y.: International Collectors Library, n.d.

Dumbleton, William A. *James Cousins*. Boston: Twayne Publishers, 1980.

Eckley, Grace. "Beef to the Heel: Harlotry with Josephine Butler, William T. Stead, and James Joyce." *Studies in the Novel* 20.1 (1988): 64–77.

———. "The Entertaining *Nights* of Burton, Stead, and Joyce's Earwicker." *Journal of Modern Literature* 13.2 (1986): 339–44.

———. *The Steadfast Finnegans Wake: A Textbook*. Lanham, Md.: University Press of America, 1994.

Eglinton, John. *Irish Literary Portraits*. 1935. Reprint, Freeport, N.Y.: Books for Libraries Press, 1967.

Ellmann, Richard. *The Consciousness of Joyce*. Toronto: Oxford University Press, 1977.

———. *James Joyce*. Oxford: Oxford University Press, 1982.

———. *Ulysses on the Liffey*. New York: Oxford University Press, 1972.

Engels, Friedrich. *The Condition of the Working Class in England*. Trans. and ed. W. O. Henderson and W. H. Chaloner. New York: Macmillan, 1958.

Fairhall, James. *James Joyce and the Question of History*. Cambridge: Cambridge University Press, 1993.

Fanon, Frantz. *The Wretched of the Earth*. Preface by Jean Paul Sartre. New York: Grove Press, 1963.

Felman, Shoshana. *What Does a Woman Want? Reading and Sexual Difference*. Baltimore: Johns Hopkins University Press, 1993.

Finnane, Mark. *Insanity and the Insane in Post-Famine Ireland*. London: Croom Helm, 1981.

Finneran, Richard J., ed. *The Poems of W. B. Yeats*. New York: Macmillan, 1983.

Fitzpatrick, David. "Ireland since 1870." In Foster, *The Oxford History of Ireland*. 174–229.

Flax, Jane. "Postmodernism and Gender Relations in Feminist Theory." *Signs: Journal of Women in Culture and Society* 12 (1987): 621–43.

Foster, R. F. "Ascendancy and Union." In *The Oxford History of Ireland*. 134–73.

———. *The Oxford History of Ireland*. Oxford: Oxford University Press, 1992.

Foucault, Michel. *Discipline and Punish: The Birth of the Prison*. Trans. Alan Sheridan. New York: Pantheon, 1977.

———. *Madness and Civilization: A History of Insanity in the Age of Reason*. Trans. Richard Howard. New York: Random House, 1965.

Freud, Sigmund. "Fragment of an Analysis of a Case of Hysteria." In *The Freud Reader,* ed. Peter Gay. New York: W. W. Norton, 1989. 172–239.

Gaskell, Elizabeth. *Ruth.* 1853. Reprint, London: J. M. Dent & Sons, 1967.

Gifford, Don. *Joyce Annotated: Notes for Dubliners and A Portrait of the Artist as a Young Man.* 2nd ed. Berkeley: University of California Press, 1982.

Gifford, Don, and Robert Seidman. *Ulysses Annotated: Notes for James Joyce's Ulysses.* 2nd ed. Berkeley: University of California Press, 1988.

Gilbert, Sandra M., and Susan Gubar. *The Madwoman in the Attic: The Woman Writer and the Nineteenth-Century Literary Imagination.* New Haven, Conn.: Yale University Press, 1984.

Gilbert, Stuart. *James Joyce's Ulysses.* New York: Vintage-Random, 1955.

Gillespie, Michael Patrick. *James Joyce's Trieste Library: A Catalogue of Materials at the Harry Ransom Humanities Research Center the University of Texas at Austin.* Austin, Tex.: Harry Ransom Humanities Research Center, 1986.

Gilman, Charlotte. "The Yellow Wallpaper." In *The Yellow Wallpaper and Other Writings.* Introduction by Lynne Sharon Schwartz. New York: Bantam, 1989. 1–20.

Gilman, Sander. *The Jew's Body.* New York: Routledge, 1991.

Gladstone, William E. *The Gladstone Diaries.* Ed. M. R. D. Foot and H. C. G. Matthew. Vols. 4 and 11. Oxford: Clarendon Press, 1974, 1990.

Gregory, Lady Augusta. "Our Irish Theatre." In Harrington, *Modern Irish Drama.* 377–84.

———. *The Rising of the Moon.* In Harrington, *Modern Irish Drama.* 54–62.

———, ed. *Ideals in Ireland.* Edinburgh: Morrison & Gibb, 1901.

Haley, Bruce. *The Healthy Body and Victorian Culture.* Cambridge: Harvard University Press, 1978.

Hall, Donald E. *Muscular Christianity: Embodying the Victorian Age.* Cambridge: Cambridge University Press, 1994.

Halliday, Sir Andrew. *A General View of the Present State of Lunatics and Lunatic Asylums in Great Britain and Ireland, and in Some Other Kingdoms.* London: Thomas & George Underwood, 1828.

Hardy, Thomas. *Tess of the D'Urbervilles: A Pure Woman.* 1891. Afterword by Donald Hall. Reprint, New York: Penguin Books, n.d.

Harrington, John P., ed. *Modern Irish Drama.* Norton Critical Edition. New York: W. W. Norton, 1991.

Harrowitz, Nancy A., and Barbara Hyams, eds. *Jews and Gender: Responses to Otto Weininger.* Philadelphia: Temple University Press, 1995.

Hederman, Mary. "Irish Women and Irish Law." *The Crane Bag* 4.1 (1980): 55–59.

Henke, Suzette. "Gerty MacDowell: Joyce's Sentimental Heroine." In Henke and Unkeless, *Women in Joyce.* 132–49.

———. *James Joyce and the Politics of Desire.* New York: Routledge, 1990.

Henke, Suzette, and Elaine Unkeless. *Women in Joyce.* Urbana: University of Illinois Press, 1982

Herr, Cheryl. *For the Land That They Loved: Irish Political Melodramas, 1890–1925.* Syracuse, N.Y.: Syracuse University Press, 1991.

———. *Joyce's Anatomy of Culture.* Urbana: University of Illinois Press, 1986.

———. "'Penelope' as Period Piece." In Pearce, *Molly Blooms.* 63–79.

———. "Theosophy, Guilt, and 'That Word Known to All Men' in Joyce's *Ulysses.*" *James Joyce Quarterly* 18 (1980): 45–54.

Hirsch, Edward. "The Imaginary Irish Peasant." *PMLA* 106 (1991): 1116–33.

Hogarth, Janet E. "The Monstrous Regiment of Women." *Fortnightly Review* 68 (1897): 926–36.

Houghton, Walter E. *The Victorian Frame of Mind, 1830–1870.* New Haven, Conn.: Yale University Press, 1985.

"How Ladies Are Annoyed in London Streets." *Pall Mall Gazette,* July 19, 1887, 1–2.

"How Ladies Fare in London Streets." *Pall Mall Gazette,* July 22, 1887, 3.

Hughes, Thomas. *Tom Brown's School Days.* New York: Cornwall Press, 1911.

Hungerford, Margaret Wolfe. *Molly Bawn.* 3 vols. London: Smith, Elder, 1878.

Hutchinson, John. *The Dynamics of Cultural Nationalism: The Gaelic Revival and the Creation of the Irish Nation State.* London: Allen and Unwin, 1987.

Hyde, Douglas. "The Necessity for De-Anglicising Ireland." In Deane, *The Field Day Anthology of Irish Writing.* 527–33.

Ibsen, Henrik. *A Doll's House.* In *Eight Plays by Henrik Ibsen.* New York: Modern Library–Random House, 1982. 3–77.

———. *Hedda Gabler.* In *Eight Plays by Henrik Ibsen.* New York: Modern Library–Random House, 1982. 509–89.

Ignota. "The Present Legal Position of Women in the United Kingdom." *Westminster Review* 163 (1905): 513–20.

Indiscreet. Dir. Stanley Donen. Republic Studios, 1958.

Innes, C. L. *Woman and Nation in Irish Literature and Society, 1880–1935.* Athens: University of Georgia Press, 1993.

"Intrusive Woman." *Pall Mall Gazette,* October, 11–12, 1883, 2.

Irigaray, Luce. *This Sex Which Is Not One.* Trans. Catherine Porter. Ithaca, N.Y.: Cornell University Press, 1985.

Jackson, John Wyse, and Bernard McGinley. *James Joyce's Dubliners: An Illustrated Edition.* New York: St. Martin's, 1993.

Jameson, Fredric. *The Political Unconscious: Narrative As a Socially Symbolic Act.* Ithaca, N.Y.: Cornell University Press, 1981.

Jeffreys, Sheila. "Free From All Uninvited Touch." *Women's Studies International Forum* 5.6 (1982): 629–45.

———. "Women and Sexuality." In *Women's History: Britain, 1850–1945: An Introduction,* ed. June Purvis. New York: St. Martin's, 1995. 193–216.

Joyce, James. *The Critical Writings of James Joyce.* Ed. Ellsworth Mason and Richard Ellmann. New York: Viking, 1959. Reprint, Ithaca, N.Y.: Cornell University Press, 1989.

————. *Dubliners.* Ed. Robert Scholes in consultation with Richard Ellmann. New York: Penguin, 1967.

————. *Finnegans Wake.* New York: Viking-Penguin, 1939.

————. *Letters of James Joyce.* Vol. 1. Ed. Stuart Gilbert. New York: Viking, 1957.

————. *A Portrait of the Artist as a Young Man.* Middlesex, England: Viking-Penguin, 1985.

————. *Selected Letters of James Joyce.* Ed. Richard Ellmann. New York: Viking Press, 1975.

————. *Stephen Hero.* New York: New Directions, 1963.

————. *Ulysses.* Ed. Hans Walter Gabler, with Wolfhard Steppe and Claus Melchior. New York and London: Vintage-Random House, 1984.

"Joyce and the Police: A Special Issue." *Novel: A Forum on Fiction* 29.1 (1995).

"The Jubilee." *The Times,* June 20, 1887, 9.

Kain, Richard M., and James H. O'Brien. *George Russell (A.E.).* Cranbury, N.J., and London: Association of University Presses, 1976.

Kelly, John, and Ronald Schuchard, eds. *Biographical and Historical Appendix to The Collected Letters of W. B. Yeats.* Gen. Ed. John Kelly. Vol. 3. 1901–4. Ed. John Kelly and Ronald Schuchard. Oxford: Clarendon Press, 1994. 694–733.

Kenner, Hugh. *Dublin's Joyce.* 1956. Reprint, New York: Columbia University Press, 1987.

————. *Joyce's Voices.* Berkeley: University of California Press, 1978.

————. "Molly's Masterstroke." *James Joyce Quarterly* 10 (1972): 19–28.

Kershner, R. B. *Joyce, Bakhtin, and Popular Literature: Chronicles of Disorder.* Chapel Hill: University of North Carolina Press, 1989.

Kiberd, Declan. *Inventing Ireland: The Literature of the Modern Nation.* Cambridge: Harvard University Press, 1995.

————. "Irish Literature and Irish History." In Foster, *The Oxford History of Ireland.* 235–40.

Kingsley, Charles. *Charles Kingsley: His Letters and Memories of His Life.* Ed. Frances Eliza Grenfell Kingsley. London: Kegan Paul, Trench, 1888.

Lacan, Jacques. "The Agency of the Letter." In *Ecrits: A Selection.* 146–78.

————. *Ecrits:. A Selection.* Trans. Alan Sheridan. New York: W. W. Norton, 1977.

————. *The Four Fundamental Concepts of Psycho-Analysis.* Trans. Alan Sheridan. New York: Norton, 1978.

Lamos, Colleen. "Joyce and Gender Justice in Ulysses." *In Joyce in Context,* ed. Vincent J. Cheng and Timothy Martin. Cambridge: Cambridge University Press, 1992. 91–99.

Lawrence, Karen. "'Beggaring Description': Politics and Style in Joyce's 'Eumaeus.'" *Modern Fiction Studies* 38.3 (1992): 355–76.

————. "Joyce and Feminism." In *The Cambridge Companion to James Joyce,* ed. Derek Attridge. Cambridge: Cambridge University Press, 1996. 237–58.

Lee, Joseph J. "Women and the Church Since the Famine." In Mac Curtain and O'Corrain, *Women in Irish Society.* 37–45.

Leonard, Garry. "'A Little Trouble about Those White Corpuscles': Mockery, Heresy, and the Transubstantiation of Masculinity in 'Telemachus.'" In *Ulysses —En-gendered Perspectives: Eighteen New Essays on the Episodes,* ed. Kimberly J. Devlin and Marilyn Reizbaum. Columbia: University of South Carolina Press, 1999. 1–19.

———. *Reading Dubliners Again: A Lacanian Perspective.* Syracuse, N.Y.: Syracuse University Press, 1993.

———. "The Virgin Mary and the Urge in Gerty: The Packaging of Desire in the 'Nausicaa' Chapter of *Ulysses.*" *University of Hartford Studies in Literature* 23.1 (1991): 3–23.

Levin, Harry. *James Joyce: A Critical Introduction.* New York: New Directions, 1960.

Lloyd, David. *Anomalous States: Irish Writing and the Post-Colonial Moment.* Durham, N.C.: Duke University Press, 1993.

Lotman, Yury M. "The Text within the Text." *PMLA* 109 (1994): 377–84.

Luddy, Maria. "Isabella M. S. Todd." In Cullen and Luddy, *Women, Power and Consciousness in 19th Century Ireland.* 197–230.

———. *Women and Philanthropy in Nineteenth-Century Ireland.* Cambridge: Cambridge University Press, 1995.

Macaulay, Thomas Babington, Lord. In *The History of England: 1848–61,* ed. Hugh Trevor-Roper. Reprint, London: Penguin, 1968.

Mac Curtain, Margaret. "Women, the Vote and Revolution." In Mac Curtain and O'Corrain, *Women in Irish Society.* 46–57.

Mac Curtain, Margaret, and Donncha O'Corrain, eds. *Women in Irish Society: The Historical Dimension.* Westport, Conn.: Greenwood Press, 1979.

Maddox, Brenda. *Nora: The Real Life of Molly Bloom.* Boston: Houghton Mifflin, 1988.

"The Maiden Tribute of Modern Babylon." *Pall Mall Gazette,* July 6, 1885.

"The Male Pest of the Streets." *Pall Mall Gazette,* July 27, 1887, 1–2.

Mangan, J. A. "Social Darwinism and Upper-class Education in Late Victorian and Edwardian England." In Mangan and Walvin, *Manliness and Morality.* 135–59.

Mangan, J. A., and James Walvin, eds. *Manliness and Morality: Middle-class Masculinity in Britain and America 1800–1940.* New York: St. Martin's, 1987.

Mayhew, Henry. *London Labour and the London Poor.* Introduction by Victor Neuburg. New York: Viking-Penguin, 1985.

Mikhail, E. H., ed. *The Abbey Theatre: Interviews and Recollections.* Totowa, N.J.: Barnes and Noble, 1988.

Montrose, Louis. "Professing the Renaissance: The Poetics and Politics of Culture." In *The New Historicism,* ed. Harold Veeser. New York: Routledge, 1989. 15–36.

Moran, D. P. "The Battle of Two Civilizations." In Gregory, *Ideals in Ireland.* 23–41.

Morgan, Thais E. "Reimagining Masculinity in Victorian Criticism: Swinburne and Pater." *Victorian Studies* 36.3 (1993): 315–33.

Muller, Jill. "John Henry Newman and the Education of Stephen Dedalus." *James Joyce Quarterly* 33 (1996): 593–603.

Mulvey, Laura. *Visual and Other Pleasures.* Bloomington: Indiana University Press, 1989.

Nelson, Claudia. *Boys Will Be Girls: The Feminine Ethic and British Children's Fiction, 1857–1917.* New Brunswick, N.J.: Rutgers University Press, 1991.

Nethercot, Arthur H. *The First Five Lives of Annie Besant.* Chicago: University of Chicago Press, 1960.

Newman, John Henry. *Apologia pro vita sua: Being a History of His Religious Opinions.* 1864. With an introduction by Basil Willey. Reprint, London: Oxford University Press, 1964.

———. *The Idea of a University Defined and Illustrated.* Westminster, Md.: Christian Classics. 1982.

———. *Loss and Gain.* 1848. Reprint, New York: Garland, 1975.

———. "Secular Knowledge not a Principle of Action." *The Oxford Book of Essays.* Ed. John Gross. Oxford: Oxford University Press, 1991. 166–70.

News-Stead: A Journal of History and Literature. Ed. Grace Eckley. Insert with biographical sketch. n.d.

Nietzsche, Friedrich. *Thus Spoke Zarathustra.* In *The Portable Nietzsche,* ed. Walter Kaufmann. New York: Viking-Penguin, 1982. 112–440.

Nolan, Emer. *James Joyce and Nationalism.* London and New York: Routledge, 1995.

Nord, Deborah Epstein. *Walking the Victorian Streets: Women, Representation, and the City.* Ithaca, N.Y., and London: Cornell University Press, 1995.

Norris, Margot. *The Decentered Universe of Finnegans Wake: A Structuralist Analysis.* Baltimore: Johns Hopkins University Press, 1974.

———. *Joyce's Web: The Social Unraveling of Modernism.* Austin: University of Texas Press, 1992.

O'Connor, Anne V. "Anne Jellicoe." In Cullen and Luddy, *Women, Power and Consciousness in 19th Century Ireland.* 125–60.

O'Corrain, Donncha. "Women in Early Irish Society." In Mac Curtain and O'Corrain, *Women in Irish Society.* 1–13.

O'Donovan Rossa, Jeremiah. "O'Donovan Rossa's Prison Life." In Deane, *The Field Day Anthology of Irish Writing.* 260–63.

Oppenheim, Janet. *The Other World: Spiritualism and Psychic Research in England, 1850–1914.* Cambridge: Cambridge University Press, 1985.

Osteen, Mark. *The Economy of Ulysses: Making Both Ends Meet.* Syracuse, N.Y.: Syracuse University Press, 1995.

The Oxford English Dictionary. 2nd ed. Vol. 18. Oxford: Clarendon Press, 1989.

Parnell, Charles Stewart. "To the People of Ireland." In Deane, *The Field Day Anthology of Irish Writing*. 312–15.

Patmore, Coventry. *The Angel in the House*. In *Victorian Women: A Documentary Account of Women's Lives in Nineteenth Century England, France, and the United States*, ed. Erna Olafson Hellerstein, et al. Stanford, Calif.: Stanford University Press, 1981. 134–40.

Pearce, Richard. "How Does Molly Bloom Look Through the Male Gaze?" In *Molly Blooms*. 40–62.

———, ed. *Molly Blooms: A Polylogue on "Penelope" and Cultural Studies*. Madison: University of Wisconsin Press, 1994.

Perkins, David. "George Gordon, Lord Byron." In *English Romantic Writers*. 779–87.

———, ed. *English Romantic Writers*. Fort Worth, Tex.: Harcourt Brace Jovanovich, 1967.

Perkins, Joan. *Victorian Women*. New York: New York University Press, 1993.

Platt, L. H. "Joyce and the Anglo-Irish Revival: The Triestine Lectures." *James Joyce Quarterly* 29 (1992): 259–66.

Poovey, Mary. *Uneven Developments: The Ideological Work of Gender in Mid-Victorian England*. Chicago: University of Chicago Press, 1988.

Power, Arthur. *Conversations with James Joyce*. Ed. Clive Hart. New York: Harper and Row, 1974.

Power, Mary. "The Discovery of *Ruby*." *James Joyce Quarterly* 18 (1981): 115–21.

"Public School Education." *Dublin Review* 5 (1865): 1–43.

"A Queen of Bluestockings." *Dublin Review* 140 (1907): 418–22.

Reizbaum, Marilyn. "Weininger and the Bloom of Jewish Self-Hatred in Joyce's *Ulysses*." In Harrowitz and Hyams, *Jews and Gender*. 207–14.

"Resident and Stipendiary Magistrates." In *The Oxford Companion to Irish History*, ed. S. J. Connolly. Oxford: Oxford University Press, 1998.

Richards, Thomas. *The Commodity Culture of Victorian England: Advertising and Spectacle, 1851–1914*. Stanford, Calif.: Stanford University Press, 1990.

Rodgers, W. R., ed. *Irish Literary Portraits. W. B. Yeats: James Joyce: George Moore: J. M. Synge: George Bernard Shaw: Oliver St. John Gogarty: F. R. Higgins: AE (George Russell)*. New York: Taplinger, 1973.

Roper, Michael, and John Tosh. "Historians and the Politics of Masculinity." In *Manful Assertions*, 1–24.

———, ed. *Manful Assertions: Masculinities in Britain since 1800*. London and New York: Routledge, 1991.

Rosen, David. "The Volcano and the Cathedral: Muscular Christianity and the Origins of Primal Manliness." In Hall, *Muscular Christianity*. 215–38.

Rosenfeld, Natania. "James Joyce's Womanly Wandering Jew." In Harrowitz and Hyams, *Jews and Gender*. 215–26.

Ruskin, John. "Nature of Gothic." In *Unto the Last and Other Writings*, ed. Clive Wilmer. New York: Viking-Penguin, 1985. 77–110.

Russell, George [A.E.]. "A Letter to W. B. Yeats." In Deane, *The Field Day Anthology of Irish Writing*. 541.

———. "Nationality and Imperialism." In Gregory, *Ideals in Ireland*. 13–22.

Said, Edward. *Culture and Imperialism*. New York: Knopf, 1993.

Saussure, Ferdinand de. *Course in General Linguistics*. In *Literary Theory: An Anthology*, ed. Julie Rivkin and Michael Ryan. Malden, Mass., and Oxford: Blackwell, 1998. 76–90.

Schults, Raymond L. *Crusader in Babylon: W. T. Stead and the Pall Mall Gazette*. Lincoln: University of Nebraska Press, 1972.

Scott, Bonnie Kime. "Hanna and Francis Sheehy-Skeffington: Reformers in the Company of Joyce." In *James Joyce and His Contemporaries*. New York: Greenwood Press, 1989. 77–85.

———. *Joyce and Feminism*. Bloomington: Indiana University Press, 1984.

Scott, Sir Walter. *The Abbot*. London: Adam and Charles Black, 1913.

———. *The Bride of Lammermore*. London: J. M. Dent & Sons, 1991.

Shakespeare, William. *The Tragedy of Hamlet Prince of Denmark*. *The Complete Works of William Shakespeare*. The Cambridge Text. Ed. John Dover Wilson. London: Octopus Books, 1980. 883–919.

Shelley, Percy Bysshe. *A Defence of Poetry*. In Perkins, *English Romantic Writers*. 1072–87.

———. "Hymn to Intellectual Beauty." In Perkins, *English Romantic Writers*. 970–71.

———. *Julian and Maddalo: A Conversation*. In Perkins, *English Romantic Writers*. 976–69.

———. *The Necessity of Atheism*. In *Shelley and Zastrozzi: Self-Revelation of a Neurotic,* by Dr. Eustace Chesser. London: Gregg Press, 1965. 161–65.

———. "The Sensitive Plant." In Perkins, *English Romantic Writers*. 1028–32.

Shepard, Alan. "From Aristotle to Keats: Stephen's Search for 'The Good Life' in *A Portrait of the Artist As a Young Man*." *English Studies* 74.1 (1993): 105–12.

Shloss, Carol. "Molly's Resistance to the Union: Marriage and Colonialism in Dublin, 1904." In Pearce, *Molly Blooms*. 105–18.

Showalter, Elaine. *The Female Malady: Women, Madness and English Culture, 1830–1980*. New York: Pantheon–Random House, 1985.

Silverman, Kaja. *Male Subjectivity at the Margins*. New York: Routledge, 1992.

Simms, Katharine. "The Norman Invasion and the Gaelic Recovery." In Foster, *The Oxford History of Ireland*. 44–87.

Sinfield, Alan. *Faultlines: Cultural Materialism and the Politics of Dissident Reading*. Berkeley: University of California Press, 1992.

———. *The Wilde Century: Effeminacy, Oscar Wilde and the Queer Movement*. New York: Columbia University Press, 1994.

Spivak, Gayatri Chakravorty. "Subaltern Studies: Deconstructing Historiography." In *In Other Worlds: Essays in Cultural Politics*. New York: Routledge, 1987. 197–222.

Spoo, Robert. *James Joyce and the Language of History: Dedalus's Nightmare.* New York: Oxford University Press, 1994.

Springhall, John. "Building Character in the British Boy: The Attempt to Extend Christian Manliness to Working-Class Adolescents, 1880–1914." In Mangan and Walvin, *Manliness and Morality.* 52–74.

Steinberg, Erwin R. "Persecuted, Sold in Morocco Like Slaves." *James Joyce Quarterly* 29 (1992): 615–22.

Stone, Harry. "'Araby' and the Writings of James Joyce." In *Dubliners: Text, Criticism, and Notes,* ed. Robert Scholes and A. Walton Litz. New York: Viking, 1969. 344–67.

Storch, Robert D. "Police Control of Street Prostitution in Victorian London." In *Police and Society,* ed. David H. Bayley. Beverly Hills, Calif.: Sage, 1977. 49–72.

Svaglic, Martin J., ed. *Apologia pro vita sua: Being a History of His Religious Opinions.* By John Henry Newman. Oxford: Clarendon Press, 1967.

Synge, John M. *In the Shadow of the Glen.* In *The Complete Plays of John M. Synge.* New York: Vintage-Random, 1935. 99–118.

Szasz, Thomas, ed. *The Age of Madness: The History of Involuntary Mental Hospitalization Presented in Selected Texts.* New York: Anchor-Doubleday, 1973.

T. F. W. "Notes on Higher Education of Women." *Dublin Review* 129 (1901): 148–54, 408–11.

Tennyson, Alfred, Lord. *Idylls of the King and a Selection of Poems.* New York: Signet-Penguin, 1961. 13–255.

———. *In Memoriam A. H. H.* In *Tennyson: Poems and Plays.* London: Oxford University Press, 1967. 230–66.

Thackeray, William Makepeace. *The History of Pendennis: His Fortunes and Misfortunes and His Greatest Enemy.* 1850. Ed. Donald Hawes. Introduction by J. I. M. Stewart. Reprint, New York: Viking-Penguin, 1986.

Tindall, William York. *James Joyce: His Way of Interpreting the Modern World.* New York: Charles Scribner's Sons, 1950.

Torchiana, Donald. *Backgrounds for Joyce's Dubliners.* Boston: Allen & Unwin, 1986.

Tuke, Daniel Hack, ed. *A Dictionary of Psychological Medicine Giving the Definition, Etymology, and Synonyms of the Terms Used in Medical Psychology with the Symptoms, Treatment and Pathology of Insanity and the Law of Lunacy in Great Britain and Ireland.* 2 vols. London: J. & A. Churchill, 1892.

"Two Years Ago." Review. *Saturday Review,* February 21, 1857, 176–77.

Valente, Joseph. "Beyond Truth and Freedom: The New Faith of Joyce and Nietzsche." *James Joyce Quarterly* 25 (1987): 87–103.

———. "The Myth of Sovereignty: Gender in the Literature of Irish Nationalism." *English Literary History* 61 (1994): 189–210.

Walkowitz, Judith R. *City of Dreadful Delight: Narratives of Sexual Danger in Late-Victorian London.* Chicago: University of Chicago Press, 1992.

———. *Prostitution and Victorian Society: Women, Class, and the State.* Cambridge: Cambridge University Press, 1980.

Walzl, Florence L. "*Dubliners:* Women in Irish Society." In Henke and Unkeless, *Women in Joyce.* 31–56.

———. "Joyce's 'Clay': Fact and Fiction." *Renascence: Essays on Values in Literature* 35 (1983): 119–37.

Warren, Allen. "Popular Manliness: Baden Powell, Scouting and the Development of Manly Character." In Mangan and Walvin, *Manliness and Morality,* 199–219.

Webster's New Universal Unabridged Dictionary. 2nd ed. New York: Simon and Schuster, 1983.

Wellek, Rene. "The Concept of 'Romanticism' in Literary History." *Comparative Literature* 1.1 (1949): 147–72.

West, Michael, and William Hendricks. "The Genesis and Significance of Joyce's Irony in 'A Painful Case.'" *ELH* 44 (1977): 701–27.

"What the 'Male Pests' Have to Say for Themselves." *Pall Mall Gazette,* July 30, 1887, 2.

Whitman, Walt. "Song of Myself." In *Leaves of Grass.* The First (1855) Edition. Ed. Malcolm Cowley. New York: Viking-Penguin, 1959. 25–86.

Wilde, Oscar. "The Critic as Artist." In *The Prose of Oscar Wilde.* n.p.: Boni-books-Cornwall Press, 1935. 89–200.

———. "The Decay of Lying." In *De Profundis and Other Writings.* London: Viking-Penguin, 1986. 55–87.

Wilson, Elizabeth. "The Invisible *Flâneur.*" *New Left Review* 191 (1992): 90–110.

Wolff, Janet. "The Invisible *Flâneuse:* Women and the Literature of Modernity." In *The Problems of Modernity: Adorno and Benjamin,* ed. Andrew Benjamin. London: Routledge, 1989. 141–56.

"Women and Work." *Dublin University Magazine* 80 (1872): 670–82.

Wood, Mrs. Henry. *East Lynne.* 1861. Reprint, London: Everyman Library, 1994.

———. *The Shadow of Ashlydyat.* 1863. Reprint, London: Macmillan, 1900.

Yeats, William Butler. *Cathleen ni Houlihan.* In *Eleven Plays of William Butler Yeats,* ed. A. Norman Jeffares. New York: Collier-Macmillan, 1964. 221–31.

———. *The Collected Letters of W. B. Yeats.* Gen. ed. John Kelly. Vol. 3. 1901–4. Ed. John Kelly and Ronald Schuchard. Oxford: Clarendon Press, 1994.

———. *The Countess Cathleen.* London: T. Fisher Unwin, 1912.

———. "An Irish National Theatre." In Harrington, *Modern Irish Drama.* 388–91.

———. "The Literary Movement in Ireland." In Gregory, *Ideals in Ireland.* 87–102.

———. "PostScript." In Gregory, *Ideals in Ireland.* 105–7.

———. "The Song of Wandering Aengus." In Finneran, *The Poems of W. B. Yeats.* 59–60.

———. "The Trembling of the Veil." In *Autobiographies: Memories and Reflections*. London: Bracken Books, 1995. 107–381.

———. *Uncollected Prose by W. B. Yeats*. Ed. J. P. Frayne. 2 vols. New York: Columbia University Press, 1970.

———. "Who Goes with Fergus?" In Finneran, *The Poems of W. B. Yeats*. 43.

Young, G. M. *Portrait of an Age: Victorian England*. London: Oxford University Press, 1977.

Index

Act of Union (1800), 18

Acton, William, 118

Adams, James Eli, 84

Adams, Robert, 197n. 3, 201n. 16

A.E. *See* Russell, George W.

Aestheticism: and Hellenism as style of masculinity, 72, 80, 87–89, 206n. 18; and homosexuality, 76–77; and Shelley, 57–58, 80

Allen, Grant: *The Woman Who Did,* 119, 201n. 4

Althusser, Louis, 3

Angel of the house: deconstruction of, by Joyce, 136; destabilization of, 11; endangered by domestic discourse, 123. *See also* Cult of the Virgin; Domestic angel; Patmore, Coventry

Anorexia, 215n. 9

Antinomianism, 50

Antivice organizations (England/Ireland), 98–100, 208n. 7; Dublin White Cross Vigilance Association, 99; National Vigilance Association, 99, 164; Society for the Reformation of Public Manners, 99; Society for the Suppression of Vice (Vice Society), 99; White Cross Society, 99

"The Arab's Farewell to His Steed," 127–28

Arnold, Matthew: *Culture and Anarchy,* 87–89; "Shelley," 206n. 15

Asylums, 194; admissions requirements of, 213n. 4; as agent of social control, 144–45; commitment statistics of, by gender, 213n. 3, 214n. 6; Dickens's observations of, 214n. 6; domestication of (England), 146–47; expansion of (England/Ireland), 146; history of, 144–46; in *Portrait* and *Stephen Hero,* 142–43; melancholia/mania admissions to, in Ireland (1901), 158;

Mullingar statistics, 213n. 1; operation and staffing of, 215n. 8; reform of, in England, 145–46; wrongful confinements to, 214n. 7; York West Riding Lunatic Asylum, 146. *See also* Madness

Barnacle, Nora, 4, 117–18, 209n. 1

Bazargan, Susan, 185, 218n. 9, 219n. 11

Bergman, Ingrid, 206n. 16

Besant, Annie, 61–62, 203n. 15

Bhabha, Homi, 30–32, 183, 219n. 16

Bishop, John, 215n. 11

Blake, William: as model for romantic dissent of Stephen D(a)edalus, 47–49, 59–60; spiritual rebellion of, 46–47

—*Works:* "Auguries of Innocence," 60; *The Book of Urizen,* 49; *The Marriage of Heaven and Hell,* 34, 46–47, 59, 202n. 5; *Milton,* 45, 47; *Songs of Experience,* 47, 203n. 14; "There Is No Natural Religion," 46–47; *A Vision of the Last Judgment,* 59–60

Blavatsky, Helena P., 44, 61–63, 64, 204n. 20. *See also* Theosophy

Blessed Virgin mythology, 11, 118–19; influence of, on Joyce's female characters, 124, 132–36; and Virgin-mother paradox, 124. *See also* Cult of the Virgin

Bloom, Leopold: confrontation of hypermasculine nationalism by, 89–92; and cultural discourse, 10–11; as male pest, 164, 167; as muscular Christian, 79–84; and racial/sexual Otherness, 78–79, 90–91, 109, 209n. 14; as reformer, 106–12, 208–9n. 11; as romantic aesthete, 80; and W. T. Stead, 207–8nn. 6, 8; voyeurism of, 106–12, 181–82, 208–9n. 11

Bloom, Molly: collective unconscious fractured by, 11–12; on empire and nationalism, 186–87, 219nn. 11, 14; Feminine Ideal exploded by, 182–83; and gender indeterminacy, 183, 188; harassment of, by male pests, 184–85, 217n. 4; investment of, in phallic dominance, 185–86; on madhouses and marriage, 148–49; male gaze deflected by, 182; male violence feared by, 218–19n. 10; as New Woman, 163, 167; order of discourse disrupted by, 11–12, 13–14, 163, 182, 188, 213n. 2, 215–16n. 12; and public space, 183–85; reading madness, 214n. 5; and self-contradiction, 187–88

Blue Books, 93. *See also* Social reform

Boer War, 187, 219n. 13

Booth, Charles: *Life and Labour of the People in London*, 93

Booth, William: *In Darkest England and the Way Out*, 93

Boscagli, Maurizia, 81

Boys' Brigade, 76

Boy Scouts, 76, 205n. 8

Braddon, Mary Elizabeth: *Lady Audley's Secret*, 213–14n. 5, 214n. 7

Breuer, Joseph: "Anna O." in *Studies on Hysteria*, 148

British imperialism, 24; confrontation of, by Stephen Dedalus, 40–41; Joyce's attitudes toward, 4, 5, 19, 43; and masculinity, 75–76; Molly Bloom's support for, 186–87

Brivic, Sheldon, 215n. 11

Brontë, Charlotte: *Jane Eyre*, 213–14n. 5

Brown, Richard, 212n. 14

Butler, Josephine, 99, 109, 111

Bulwer-Lytton, Edward: *The Lady of Lyons*, 7, 17, 198n. 1

Byron, George Gordon, Lord, 54, 56; imitation of, by Leopold Bloom, 80; influence of, on apostasy of Stephen Dedalus, 50–51, 59; and masculinity, 206n. 14; ostracism of, perceived by Stephen, 45, 50–51; sexual impropriety of, 51, 203n. 8

—Works: *Childe Harold's Pilgrimage*, 50; *Don Juan*, 50; *Manfred*, 50, 51; *Prometheus*, 51

Byronic hero, 50–51, 59

Carlyle, Thomas: on the dandy, 84; on masculinity and national character, 73

Castle, Gregory, 68, 204n. 21

Catholic Church, 193; artistic imagination stifled by, 45, 49–50, 59–60; authority of, contested, 13, 49–51; and empire, 43; and Fenianism, 198–99n. 5; influence of, on Stephen D(a)edalus, 13, 43–44, 202n. 1; influence of, on Joyce, 4, 5–6; role of, in Parnell's demise, 209n. 13

Catholicism. *See* Catholic Church

Chatterjee, Partha, 29

Cheng, Vincent J., 19, 25, 98

Christian manliness. *See* Muscular Christianity

Clement, Catherine, 148, 150

Collective unconscious, 11–12

Collins, Wilkie: *The Moonstone*, 105; *The Woman in White*, 137, 201n. 4, 212n. 17, 213–14n. 5, 214n. 7

Colonialism: discourse of, 75–76, 90, 205–6n. 11; and nationalist self-betrayal in "Circe," 40–42; and oppression, 39–40

Colonial mimesis, 29, 30–32

Colonial politics. *See* Colonialism; Irish nationalism

Condition of England debates, 73

Condren, Mary, 91, 205n. 11

Contagious Diseases Acts (1864, 1868, 1869), 94, 109, 113, 121–22, 207n. 1; agitation for repeal of, 99, 207n. 6; Leopold Bloom's support for, 112

Coote, William, 99

Cousins, James and Margaret, 63, 204n. 18

Criminal conversation, 122

Criminal Law Amendment Act (1885), 76, 100, 102, 112, 165

Crisis of faith, 13, 44, 52–53

Critical Writings, 2, 18, 19, 22, 202n. 6

Cullen, Paul (Archbishop of Dublin), 198n. 5

Cult of domesticity, 117–19, 136–37, 193–94; in "Araby," 123; deconstructed by the Blooms, 139–40; impact of, on Gerty MacDowell, 123, 131, 137–39; in Victorian fiction, 131–32, 135, 137, 138–40

Cult of the Virgin, 118, 210n. 2; in "Araby," 126; contradictions within, 132–36; and Irish nationalism, 29; in "Nausicaa," 130, 132–33; subverted by "fallen" women, 11, 119. See also Blessed Virgin mythology; Domestic angel

Cultural discourse, 193; and culture as text, 2–3; disruption of, by Molly Bloom, 11–14, 163, 182, 188, 213n. 2, 215–16n. 12; inability of Joyce's characters to escape, 12; perception of, by Stephen Dedalus, 3; subversion of, by Leopold Bloom, 10–12

Cultural nationalism. See Irish nationalism

Cummins, Maria Susannah, 72; *The Lamplighter*, 131; *Mabel Vaughan*, 131–32, 137, 212n. 17

Curran, Constantine, 62

Dandies, 84–87

Darwin, Charles: *The Descent of Man*, 147

Davitt, Michael, 27, 198n. 6, 204n. 3; *The Fall of Feudalism in Ireland*, 20

Dedalus, Stephen: and British imperialism, 40–41; and Catholicism, 43–44, 47–49; confrontation by, of colonial self-oppression, 33–35; and failure of romantic imagination, 60; and opposition to Irish Revivalism, 25–27, 37–40, 63–66; voyeurism of, 181–82

Defoe, Daniel, 214n. 7

Dellamora, Richard, 87, 206n. 18

Devlin, Kimberly J., 11, 71, 84, 132, 133, 135, 183, 215n. 11

Dickens, Charles, 93; and asylum visits, 214n. 6; *Bleak House* and social reform, 97–98, 105

Divorce (England/Ireland), 122, 212n. 13

Divorce Act (1857), 122, 212n. 10

Domestic angel, 14, 118–19, 161, 193, 210n. 2; in "Araby," 124–30; and elision of female desire, 118–19; law's treatment of, 211nn. 9, 10; in Victorian fiction, 119. See also Angel of the house; Blessed Virgin mythology; Cult of domesticity; Cult of the Virgin; Patmore, Coventry

Domestic discourse. See Cult of domesticity

Domestic violence: depicted in Joyce's work, 121, 170; enabled by cult of domesticity, 123, 138; legality of, 120–21; in *Ulysses*, 138, 140–41, 216n. 14

Dorsey, Peter, 202n. 1

Dublin by Lamplight Laundry, 96, 100, 124, 207n. 4

Dubliners: and controlling force as male, 170–71; cult of domesticity in, 124–30; cult of the Virgin in, 123; destabilized phallic order in, 170–74; ideological constraint in, 6; madness in, 143, 150–60; presence of unruly women in, 170–78; social reform in, 96–97; "Araby," 6, 124–30, 168; "The Boarding House," 121, 143, 168, 213n. 2; "Clay," 96–97, 121; "Counterparts," 121, 168–70, 218n. 5; "The Dead," 143, 152–53, 156, 174–78, 213n. 2, 216n. 15; "Eveline," 138, 150–51, 153–56, 216n. 14; "Grace," 121, 143, 151–52, 170–77; "Ivy Day in the Committee Room," 20, 170–71; "A Mother," 6, 170–74, 186, 213n. 2, 218n. 8; "A Painful Case," 143, 156–60, 216n. 17, 219n. 11

Dublin Review, 119, 162, 172
Duffy, Enda, 19, 25
Dumas, Alexandre: *The Count of Monte Cristo*, 7, 17, 198n. 1

Eckley, Grace, 98, 207–8n. 6
Education reform (Ireland): Intermediate Education Act (1878), 162; Royal University of Ireland Act (1879), 162
Eglinton, John, 35, 201n. 19
Elementary Education Act (1870), 210n. 6
Ellmann, Richard, 10, 17, 111, 197n. 2, 207n. 5, 209n. 17, 215n. 11
Engels, Friedrich, 104, 108, 208n. 10; *The Condition of the Working Class in England in 1844*, 93
English Common Law, 120
Englishness: and immorality, 28–29; and madness, 213n. 1

Fairhall, James, 12, 198n. 6
Faith. *See* Crisis of faith
"Fallen" women. *See* Cult of the Virgin
Fanon, Frantz, 22, 24
Felman, Shoshana, 149, 156
Female nervous disorder, 143–44, 147; and "Grace," 151–52. *See also* Hysteria; Madness
Feminine Ideal, 6, 191; aphasia of, 182; demystification of, in Joyce, 167; exploded by Molly Bloom, 182–83
Fenianism. *See* Irish nationalism
Finnane, Mark, 146, 158, 217n. 18
Finnegans Wake: and domestic fiction, 189–90; madness in, 149; marriage as entrapment in, 189–90; reconstitution of gender discourse in, 188–89; and selfhood as fictional construct, 1; and threat of eruption of female discourse, 189–90
Flâneur, 95, 163, 166
Fortnightly Review, 162
Foucault, Michel: and history of madness, 142, 144–45; and panopticism, 94, 109–10, 113
Freethinking, 46

Freud, Sigmund: "Dora," 216n. 13; *Studies on Hysteria*, 148

Gaelic League. *See* Irish nationalism
Gaelic Revival. *See* Irish nationalism
Gaskell, Elizabeth, 93; *Ruth*, 119, 201n. 4
Gender contests for public space, 161–63, 165–67, 191, 195; in British Museum Reading Room, 161; Joyce's representations of, 167–68 (in *Dubliners*, 168–74); and Molly Bloom, 184–85
Gender discourse. *See* Feminine Ideal, Masculine Ideal, Masculinism, Masculinity
Gilbert, Sandra, and Susan Gubar, 149, 210n. 2
Gilbert, Stuart, 111, 209n. 17
Gilman, Charlotte Perkins: "The Yellow Wallpaper," 215n. 9
Gilman, Sander, 209n. 14
Girl's Own Paper, 166
Gladstone, William E.: attempts by, to rescue prostitutes, 100–101, 102; demand of, for Parnell's resignation, 18
Grant, Cary, 206n. 16
Gregory, Augusta, 22, 26, 200n. 14, 202nn. 2, 21

Halliday, Sir Andrew, 146
Hardy, Thomas: *Tess of the D'Urbervilles*, 119, 201n. 4
Hebraism, 87–89
Hellenism. *See* Aestheticism
Henke, Suzette, 71
Henry II, 24
Herr, Cheryl, 12, 63, 71, 98, 106, 197n. 3, 204n. 17
Hirsch, Edward, 25–26
Hogarth, Janet, 161–62
Hopkins, Ellice, 99
Houghton, Walter, 44, 136–37
Hughes, Thomas: *Tom Brown's School Days*, 76, 82
Hungerford, Margaret Wolfe: *Molly Bawn*, 201n. 4

Hybridity: gendered, 191; linguistic, 31–33; racial, 21–23

Hyde, Douglas, 20–21, 26, 36, 199n. 9

Hypermasculinity. *See* Masculinity

Hysteria, 14, 147–49, 193, 215nn. 9–10; "Anna O.," 148; and domestic confinement, 148–51; in *Dubliners,* 150–51, 154–56, 157, 159–60; as impasse, 149–50; as rebellion, 150; rest cure for, 215n. 9; or shell-shock, 148; speaking through the body, 148, 150, 156, 157, 159–60. *See also* Female nervous disorder; Madness

Ibsen, Henrik, 56–57, 122–23, 167, 193

Ideals in Ireland, 26, 200n. 12, 201n. 17

Identity. *See* Modern consciousness; Subjectivity

Ideology, 193–94; effect of, on Joyce's characters, 6–7, 12; impact of, on Irish culture, 4. See also Catholic Church; Cult of domesticity; Cult of the Virgin; Irish nationalism; Masculinity; Muscular Christianity; Purity movements; Social reform

Infant Custody Act (1839), 211–12n. 10

Insanity. *See* Asylums; Madness

Intermediate Education Act (1878), 162

Ireland: colonial history of, 24, 34, 198n. 3; mythologized as woman, 78, 200n. 14; partition of, 24

Irigaray, Luce, 163, 173–74, 182–83, 187

Irish Literary Revival, 20–22, 78, 193; confrontation of, by Stephen Dedalus, 34–40; and peasant/pastoralism, 23, 25–27; and theosophy, 62–66; and Yeats/Russell split, 35–37. *See also* Irish nationalism

Irish nationalism, 4, 5, 193; artists' role in, 23–24; and Catholicism, 27–29; and chastity, 28–29, 200n. 12; and desire to de-Anglicize/purify Irish culture, 19–21, 22–24; and Gaelic Revival, 20–21; and impossibility of purifying language, 32–33; and Irish Literary Theatre, 21–22, 36; and

Joyce on language movement, 199n. 8; and masculinity, 77–78, 89–92, 205–6n. 11; and nativistic self-oppression, 29–32, 34–39; and political impotence in *Dubliners,* 20; role of women in, 218n. 7; and self-betrayal seen by Stephen Dedalus, 17–19, 22, 26–27; and theosophy, 62–66; and view of "Englishness" as immoral, 28–29, 200n. 12. *See also* Irish Literary Revival

Irishness: and chastity, 28–29, 200n. 12; as ideology, 13; 20–24, 25, 42, 194; and Molly Bloom, 187, 219n. 14; and peasant figure/pastoralism, 23, 25–27

Irish Parliamentary Party, 5, 18–19

Irish Revival. *See* Irish nationalism; Irish Literary Revival; Russell, George W.; Yeats, William Butler

Jameson, Fredric, 2, 3; 11

Jellicoe, Anne, 217n. 2

"The Jewel of Asia," 151–52

Joyce, James: on Catholicism, 5–6; concern of, with cultural context, 2; on domestic violence in *Dubliners,* 170; escape of, from Church/State, 5; on faith, 202n. 2; on Freud, 215n. 11; on gender constructs, 4–5, on Ireland, 6; on Irish character, 17; on Irishness, 2; on marriage, 4–5, 117–18, 209n. 1; on nationalism, 5, 199nn. 8, 9; ostracism of, from Literary Revival, 202n. 21; on Newman, 203n. 10; on purity, 28, 200n. 12; on Russell, 201–2n. 20; on social reform, 95–96; on Yeats, 36–37, 201–2nn. 20, 22. *See also* Bloom, Leopold; Bloom, Molly; Dedalus, Stephen; individual titles of works

Joyce, Mary Jane (Murray), 210n. 2

Kenner, Hugh, 129, 154, 209n. 17

Kershner, R. B., 12, 17, 44, 127, 154, 159, 198n. 1, 212n. 15

Kiberd, Declan, 22

Kingsley, Charles, 91–92; characterization of Irish race by, 75–76, 205n. 6; and Christian manliness, 13, 72, 74–79, 83; Mariolatry despised by, 75; on masculinity and national character, 73; on Newman's conversion to Catholicism, 54–55. *See also* Hebraism; Muscular Christianity

Lacan, Jacques, 2, 74, 178, 194, 197n. 4, 208n. 11

Lawrence, Karen, 181, 209n. 18

Leonard, Garry, 1, 71, 87–89, 125, 132, 136, 141, 152, 171, 197n. 1, 206n. 17, 212n. 16, 218nn. 5–6

Lloyd, David, 22

Local Government (Ireland) Act (1898), 210n. 6

Lotman, Yuri M., 2

Luddy, Maria, 100

Lunatics Act (1845), 146

Macaulay, Thomas Babington, Lord, 34

MacMurrough, Dermot, 18, 198n. 3, 206n. 20

Madhouses. *See* Asylums

Madness: causes/definitions of, 143, 147, 213n. 3; diagnosis statistics of, by gender, 146, 213n. 3, 214n. 6; in *Dubliners*, 144, 151–52, 153, 156–58; and Englishness, 213n. 1; and female reproductive systems, 143–44, 147, 213n. 3; feminization of, 146–48, 214n. 6; in *Finnegans Wake*, 149; history/treatment of, 142, 144–45; and illicit female sexuality, 152; as impasse, 156; Lunatics Act (1845), 146; and madwomen in Victorian literature, 149, 213–14n. 5; and moral insanity/moral management, 145–47; and patriarchal authority, 143–44, 156–60; suicide considered as, 158; in *Ulysses*, 148–49; wandering considered as, 158, 217n. 18. *See also* Asylums; Female nervous disorder; Hysteria

Magdalen asylums, 100, 194; in "Clay,"

96; Leopold Bloom poses as official of, 106–7. *See also Dublin by Lamplight Laundry*

"Maiden Tribute of Modern Babylon," 101–2, 103, 104, 105, 107

Maintenance of Wives Act (1886), 211n. 9

Male gaze, 163–64, 166–67, 181–84

Male pests, 85, 163–67, 180, 193; in "Counterparts," 168–70; harassment of Molly Bloom by, 184–85, 217n. 4; Leopold Bloom as, 164; Stephen D(a)edalus as, 164, 178–82. *See also* Gender contests for public space

Manliness, 205n. 4. *See also* Masculinity

Marriage: Joyce's attitude toward, 4–5, 117–18, 209n. 1; in nineteenth-century novel, 201n. 4; women's property rights within, 119–21

Married Women's Property Acts (1870, 1883), 121, 211n. 9, 212n. 10; feared to encourage adultery among women, 119–20; in "A Mother," 171–72

Masculine Ideal, 72, 74–75; demystification of, 167, and Gabriel Conroy, 178

Masculinism, 4, 95

Masculinity, 193–94; and ambivalence toward intellectualism, 81–82; and anxiety/Otherness, 71–79, 90–92, 174, 152; and authority, 73; and conception of male body, 74, 76, 77–78, 81–82; in "The Dead," 174–78; and female gaze, 75, 206n. 16, 174; and homosexuality, 76–77; and homosocial desire, 88; and hypermasculinity in *Ulysses*, 84–92; and Irish nationalism, 77–78, 89–92, 171, 205–6n. 11; and national character (British), 73, 75–76; as performance in *Ulysses*, 84–89; and Romantic poets, 80; and styles staged in *Ulysses*, 71–72. *See also* Aestheticism; Dandies; Male gaze; Male pests; Muscular Christianity

Matrimonial Causes Act (1878), 120

Maudsley, Henry, 147–48
Mayhew, Henry: *London Labour and the London Poor*, 93
Mill, James, 211n. 7
Modern consciousness: Joyce's attempt to liberate, 6, 14; represented in *Portrait* and *Stephen Hero*, 7–9; as social construct, 2–3. *See also* Subjectivity
Modernism, 195
"Monstrous regiment of women," 162
Montrose, Louis, 2
Moran, D. P., 21, 200n. 12
Muller, Jill, 52, 55, 203n. 12
Mulvey, Laura, 127
Municipal Corporations Act (1869), 210n. 6
Muscular Christianity, 13, 72, 79, 193; and education in Ireland, 77–78; influence of, on Boys' Brigade/Boy Scouts/Young Men's Christian Association, 76; Leopold Bloom as muscular Christian, 13, 78–84; and opposition to Mariolatry, 75; and Other-driven anxiety, 74–78; in *Tom Brown's School Days*, 76. *See also* Kingsley, Charles

Nelson, Claudia, 205n. 4
Neurasthenia, 215n. 9
Newman, John Henry, 44, 50; 55–56; dispossession of, 53–54; exchange of, with Kingsley upon conversion to Catholicism, 54–55; and faith versus reason, 52–53; influence of, on Stephen Dedalus, 45, 51–57; nonconformity of, 53–54; as prose stylist, 54–55, 203n. 10; romanticism of, 52–53; and Tractarianism, 54; views of, on Catholic education
—Works: *Apologia pro vita sua*, 53, 56; *The Idea of a University*, 55, 203n. 12; *Loss and Gain*, 53
New Woman, 14, 193, 201n. 4; blame on, for nervous breakdowns, 147; creation by, of male economic displacement, 162; defiance by, of patriarchal control, 161, 163–64, 167–68; destabilization by, of masculine ethos, 182; in *Dubliners*, 168–78; expression of desire by, 162–63; deflection of male gaze by, 163–64; Joyce's fascination with, 167–68; male pests react to, 166–67; Molly Bloom as, 163, 182; and platform women, 162–63; as public spectacle, 161–63; in *Stephen Hero* (Emma Clery), 178–81. *See also* Gender contests for public space
Nietzsche, Friedrich, 44, 60; appropriation of, by Buck Mulligan, 67–68; and influence of *Thus Spoke Zarathustra* on Stephen Dedalus, 66–68, 204n. 21
The Nineteenth Century, 162
Nolan, Emer, 19
Nord, Deborah Epstein, 166
Norris, Margot, 1, 10, 39, 97, 141, 152–53, 213n. 2, 216n. 15
Norton, Caroline, 127–28, 211–12n. 10

Obscene Publications Act (1857), 100
O'Donovan Rossa, Jeremiah, 198–99n. 5, 200n. 13
O'Shea, Katherine, 28–29, 208n. 8

Pall Mall Gazette, 101, 108, 161, 165–67, 180
Parnell, Charles Stewart, 5, 198n. 6, 204n. 3; betrayal of, 18–19; effect of purity crusades on, 109, 209n. 13; Leopold Bloom's interest in scandal of, 208n. 8; "To the People of Ireland," 18; scandal in *Portrait*, 27–29
Patmore, Coventry: *The Angel in the House*, 118–19, 135
Pearce, Richard, 182
Pearse, Patrick, 205n. 11
Peasant: Kingsley's impressions of, 75–76; as signifier of Irish purity, 20, 25–26
Pinel, Philippe, 145
Platt, L. H., 40

Political discourse. *See* Irish nationalism
Portrait of the Artist as a Young Man:
colonial self-betrayal in, 17–19, 27–
33; composition of, 9–10; cultural
discourse in, 3; madness in, 142–43;
modern consciousness restrained in,
3, 7–9; Nietzschean ethos in, 66–67;
Parnell scandal in, 27–29; romantic
dissent in, 44–46; romanticism in, 8,
44–45, 59; Stephen as male pest in,
164, 180; and Stephen's appropriations of romantic writers (Blake, 48–
49, Byron, 50–51, Newman, 51–57,
Shelley, 57–59)
Power, Arthur, 45, 190–91
Power, Mary, 103, 208n. 9
Prostitutes, 109. *See also* Contagious
Diseases Acts
Public morality. *See* Purity movements;
Social reform
Purity movements, 4, 93, 99, 194, 200n.
12, 205n. 8; cultural, 24–25, 32–33;
Joyce's attitude toward, 28, 95–96,
200n. 12; and muscular Christianity,
76–77; racial, 24–25; sexual, 28, 76–
77, 119. *See also* Social reform
Purity pledge, 99

Reform Act (1832), 211n. 7
Richards, Thomas, 131–32, 212n. 16
Rodgers, W. R., 204n. 19
Romanticism: as cultural constraint, 8;
effects of, on Stephen Dedalus, 45–
46; enacted in *Portrait*, 8, 44–45, 59;
limitation of, in *Ulysses*, 59; as mode
of religious dissent, 44; opposed to realism, 45, and theosophy, 60–64
Romantic poet(s)/writer(s), 44; artistic
imagination of, stifled by Church, 45,
49–50, 59–60; atheism of, 45; masquerade of Leopold Bloom as, 80; as
models of dissent for Stephen
Dedalus, 45–46; and styles of masculinity, 80. *See also* Blake, William;
Byron, George Gordon, Lord;
Newman, John Henry; Nietzsche,
Friedrich; Shelley, Percy Bysshe

Royal University of Ireland Act (1879),
162
Ruby: the Pride of the Ring, 62, 208n.
9; and social reform, 103, 108
Ruskin, John: on masculinity and national character, 73
Russell, George W. (A.E.), 204n. 19; and
cultural/literary revival, 21, 37–39,
201n. 17; Joyce's manuscripts in pos-
session of, 36; *New Songs* published
by, 36; opposition of Stephen Dedalus
to, in *Ulysses*, 37–39; and split with
Yeats, 35–36; and theosophy, 62–65,
203–4n. 16

Said, Edward, 22, 29, 32–33
Salvation Army, 99, 112, 208n. 10
Sandow, Eugen, 81
Saturday Review, 74, 79
Saussure, Ferdinand de, 2, 197n. 4
Scott, Bonnie, 11, 98, 123, 178, 213n.
2, 219n. 11
Scott, Sir Walter: *The Bride of
Lammermoor*, 213–14n. 5
Sepoy Resistance, 73–74
Sheehy-Skeffington: Francis, 95, 98,
207n. 5; Hanna, 98
Shelley, Percy Bysshe: aesthetics of
beauty of, 57–58; and Aquinas, 58;
art as religion of, 57–58; atheism of,
45; influence of, on Stephen Dedalus,
58–59; Leopold Bloom and Shelleyan
androgyny, 80; and masculinity,
206n. 15; and political independence
movements, 57; and role of poet, 58
—Works: *A Defence of Poetry*, 57–58;
"Hymn to Intellectual Beauty," 57–
58; *Julian and Maddalo*, 57; *The Ne-
cessity of Atheism*, 57
Shell-shock. *See* Hysteria
Shepard, Alan, 202n. 1
Shloss, Carol, 213n. 2, 215–16, n. 12
Showalter, Elaine, 142, 145, 149–50,
214n. 5, 216n. 13
Silverman, Kaja, 208n. 11
Simony, 129
Sinfield, Alan, 3–4, 10, 77, 205n. 10

Sinn Fein, 5, 199n. 9, 218n. 7

Social discourse. *See* Cultural discourse

Social purity movement. *See* Purity movements

Social reform, 193–95; activity of, in Ireland, 99; and Blue Book reports, 93–94; and class issues, 104–5, 208n. 10; in "Clay," 96–97; and "cleaning up the streets," 93, 114; Joyce sees hypocrisy in, 95–96; legislation supporting, 94, 99, 100, 102, 109; and Leopold Bloom as reformer, 13, 102–3, 106–12; and reformer's vulnerability to vice, 100–102; and regulatory gaze/surveillance in *Ulysses*, 94, 106–11, 113–14; and universal brotherhood, 98; urban conditions necessitating, 93–95; in Victorian literature, 93, 97–98, 105; and voyeuristic impulse, 94–95, 103–5, 108; women's involvement in, 207n. 3. *See also* Antivice organizations; Contagious Diseases Acts; "Maiden Tribute of Modern Babylon"; Purity movements; W. T. Stead

Spiritualism, 4. *See also* Theosophy

Spivak, Gayatri, 24–25

Spoo, Robert, 12, 33, 198n. 6, 200nn. 15, 16

Stead, W. T., 93, 98, 106, 111–12, 207–8n. 6; "The Maiden Tribute of Modern Babylon," 101–2, 104–5

Stephen Hero: betrayal in, 17; composition and destruction of, 9–10; madness in, 142; modern consciousness liberated in, 7–9, 43, 46; and Newman's influence on Stephen, 56–57; New Woman (Emma Clery) in, 143, 178–82, 213n. 2

Stone, Harry, 127

Street rescues, 99–101, 110–11

Subalternity. *See Ulysses*, subalternity in

Subjectivity, 193; and confinement within social discourse, 194; and possibilities for resisting social discourse, 3–4, 10–12, 14; shaped by social forces, 2–4; and language/indetermi-

nacy, 2; as text, 1. *See also* Modern consciousness

Suicide in Ireland: viewed as madness, 158

Summary Jurisdiction Act (1895), 211n. 9

Surveillance, social, 194. *See also* Foucault, Michel, panopticism; Social reform, regulatory gaze in *Ulysses*

Tennyson, Alfred, Lord, 34; "Charge of the Light Brigade," 162; *Idylls of the King*, 118; *In Memoriam*, 44

Theosophy, 4, 44, 193, 204nn. 17, 18; and Literary Revival, 62–66; as model of romantic dissent, 60–64; and nationalism, 62; Russell's involvement in, 62–65, 203–4n. 16; Yeats's practice of, 61, 63

Tuke, Daniel Hack, 143, 147

Ulysses: cult of domesticity/cult of the Virgin in, 123, 130–36; cultural discourse in, 3, 10–12, cultural essentialism in, 33–39; destabilization of racial authenticity in, 23, 90, 187; male pests in, 164–65, 167; masculinity in, 71–72, 78–92; Nietzschean ethos in, 67–68; regulatory gaze in, 94, 106–11, 113–14; repudiation of romanticism in, 44; social reform in, 95, 103–14; subalternity in, 23–25

Universal brotherhood, 98, 113

Universities Bill (1879), 55

Valente, Joseph, 66, 205–6n. 11

Vice Society. *See* Antivice organizations

Virgin, cult of. *See* Blessed Virgin mythology; Cult of the Virgin

Voyeurism, 195; and desire, 208–9n. 11; and patriarchal authority, 181–82; and social reform, 94–95, 105, 111–12

Walkowitz, Judith, 94–95, 109

Walzl, Florence, 162, 207n. 4, 213n. 2, 217n. 1

Warren, Alan, 205n. 8

Whitman, Walt, 89, 206n. 18

Wilde, Oscar, 59, 89, 205n. 10; and fracture of the Masculine Ideal, 72; relationship of, with Alfred Douglas, 77; as symbol of colonial oppression, 39–40, 202n. 24; trials of, 77

Wilson, Elizabeth, 166

Wolff, Janet, 166

Woman Question, 11

Women: contractual rights of, 172–73; custody rights of, 211–12n. 10; depicted in sentimental fiction, 131–32, 135; and disruption of patriarchal authority (in *Dubliners,* 170–78, in *Stephen Hero,* 178–81); and divorce (England/Ireland), 122, 212n. 10; and domestic violence, 120–21; and education (Ireland), 162, 217n. 2; iconic images of, 11, 14; legal rights of (England/Ireland), 210n. 6; and madness, 143–44; power/subjugation of, 118, 201n. 4; professions of (Ireland), 217n. 1; property rights of, 119–21, 211–12nn. 8, 9, 10; role of, in social reform, 207n. 3; as speaking subjects, 182; voting rights of (Ireland), 162; wage rights of, 212n. 10. *See also* Angel in the house; Cult of domesticity; Cult of the Virgin; Domestic angel; Female nervous disorder; Hysteria; Madness; Marriage; New Woman

Women Poor Law Guardian Act (1896), 210n. 6

Wood, Ellen (Mrs. Henry): *East Lynne,* 11, 137, 201n. 4, 212n. 17; *The Shadow of Ashlydyat,* 11, 201n. 4

Yeats, William Butler: and cultural/literary revival, 21–22; on English vulgarity, 200n. 12; "An Irish National Theatre," 35–36; Joyce's opinion of, 36–37; on peasantry, 26; and split from Russell, 35–36; Stephen Dedalus's opinion of, 202n. 23; and theosophy, 61, 63

—Works: *Cathleen ni Houlihan,* 26, 40; *The Countess Cathleen,* 202n. 22; "Who Goes with Fergus?" 4

York West Riding Lunatic Asylum, 146

Young Men's Christian Association, 76

Young, G. M., 44

Tracey Teets Schwarze is assistant professor of English at Christopher Newport University in Newport News, Virginia. She has published articles on Joyce and Victorian culture in *Twentieth Century Literature*, *Joyce Studies Annual*, and *European Joyce Studies*. This is her first book.

The Florida James Joyce Series
Edited by Zack Bowen

The Autobiographical Novel of Co-Consciousness: Goncharov, Woolf, and Joyce,
   by Galya Diment (1994)
Bloom's Old Sweet Song: Essays on Joyce and Music, by Zack Bowen (1995)
Joyce's Iritis and the Irritated Text: The Dis-lexic Ulysses, by Roy Gottfried (1995)
Joyce, Milton, and the Theory of Influence, by Patrick Colm Hogan (1995)
Reauthorizing Joyce, by Vicki Mahaffey (paperback edition, 1995)
Shaw and Joyce: "The Last Word in Stolentelling," by Martha Fodaski Black (1995)
Bely, Joyce, Döblin: Peripatetics in the City Novel, by Peter I. Barta (1996)
Jocoserious Joyce: The Fate of Folly in Ulysses, by Robert H. Bell (paperback edition, 1996)
Joyce and Popular Culture, edited by R. B. Kershner (1996)
Joyce and the Jews: Culture and Texts, by Ira B. Nadel (paperback edition, 1996)
Narrative Design in Finnegans Wake: *The Wake Lock Picked,* by Harry Burrell (1996)
Gender in Joyce, edited by Jolanta W. Wawrzycka and Marlena G. Corcoran (1997)
Latin and Roman Culture in Joyce, by R. J. Schork (1997)
Reading Joyce Politically, by Trevor L. Williams (1997)
Advertising and Commodity Culture in Joyce, by Garry Leonard (1998)
Greek and Hellenic Culture in Joyce, by R. J. Schork (1998)
Joyce, Joyceans, and the Rhetoric of Citation, by Eloise Knowlton (1998)
Joyce's Music and Noise: Theme and Variation in His Writings, by Jack W. Weaver (1998)
Reading Derrida Reading Joyce, by Alan Roughley (1999)
Joyce through the Ages: A Nonlinear View, edited by Michael Patrick Gillespie (1999)
Chaos Theory and James Joyce's Everyman, by Peter Francis Mackey (1999)
Joyce's Comic Portrait, by Roy Gottfried (2000)
Joyce and Hagiography: Saints Above!, by R. J. Schork (2000)
Voices and Values in Joyce's Ulysses, by Weldon Thornton (2000)
The Dublin Helix: The Life of Language in Joyce's Ulysses, by Sebastian D. G. Knowles
   (2001)
Joyce Beyond Marx: History and Desire in Ulysses *and* Finnegans Wake,
   by Patrick McGee (2001)
Joyce's Metamorphosis, by Stanley Sultan (2001)
Joycean Temporalities: Debts, Promises, and Countersignatures, by Tony Thwaites (2001)
Joyce and the Victorians, by Tracey Teets Schwarze (2002)